Public Faces, Private Voices

Public Faces, Private Voices

Community and Individuality in South India

Mattison Mines

UNIVERSITY OF CALIFORNIA PRESS
Berkeley · Los Angeles · London

University of California Press
Berkeley and Los Angeles, California

University of California Press, Ltd.
London, England

© 1994 by
The Regents of the University of California

Library of Congress Cataloging-in-Publication Data

Mines, Mattison, 1941–
   Public faces, private voices : community and individuality in
South India / Mattison Mines.
      p.   cm.
   Includes bibliographical references and index.
   ISBN 0-520-08478-0
   1. India, South—Social life and customs.   2. National
characteristics, East Indian.   I. Title.
DS484.4.M57   1994
954'.8—dc20   93-35609
                                                                      CIP

Printed in the United States of America
9 8 7 6 5 4 3 2 1

Contents

Figures and Maps

Acknowledgments

This book is the product of many years of work in India and incorporates the insights and assistance of many people. What little acknowledgment I can offer here for the time and efforts of those who have helped me is, therefore, but the smallest part of the gratitude I feel. Let me here thank but a few: P. Balasubramaniyam, V. R. Sondarajan, S. Sambandam, W. R. Jayraman, J. Gnanaprakasan, T. Ekambaram, A. Ramdas Chettiar, Pathatreya Sarma, Mohan Achari, and Rasappa Achari, all of whom were special friends in George Town; C. Gourishankar, who at my request took the photographs included in this book and helped me collect the data on temple procession routes, Vijayalakshmi Gourishankar, A. Meyyappan, Prakash Kumar, C. Natesan, Tara Cherian, all of whom helped me in ways too numerous to count; and my University of Madras colleagues, Professor N. Subba Reddy, Dr. Mohamed Kalam, and Professor D. Sundaram. Each was generous with his time, and with them I spent many hours talking about my research. Here, too, I would like to thank those who read this book in manuscript for their insights and suggestions: Elvin Hatch, A. F. Robertson, Donald E. Brown, Tom Harding, Diane Mines, and especially Bob Blaisdell, who helped me with editing, and Dirk Brandts, who composed the maps on his Macintosh. I also wish to thank warmly my anonymous reviewers for their suggestions and encouragement and Dr. Lynne Withey, my editor at the University of California Press, for her invaluable help. I owe a special debt to my wife, Gillian, who came to Madras to marry me, and to my children who have accompanied me to India on my various trips. Gillian's suggestions and perspective have greatly enriched this book; she has read every version. I warmly thank the American Institute of Indian Studies for funding the field research on which this book is based. Finally, to the Tamil people, what can I say to thank them? The richness of their lives and history have added greatly to mine; their hospitality and friendship have given me many experiences of pleasure. I am forever in their debt.

CHAPTER ONE

Introduction

Individuality in South India

The material available to a story writer in India is limitless.
Within a broad climate of inherited culture there are endless
variations: every individual differs from every other individual, not only economically, but in outlook, habits and day-
to-day philosophy. . . . Under such conditions the writer has
only to look out of the window to pick up a character (and
thereby a story).

R. K. Narayan, Malgudi Days

One of the things that has always impressed me about Indians is how
many people they keep tabs on. The news magazine *India Today* is written to appeal to this appetite for knowledge about people. The magazine, which is India's *Newsweek* or *Time*, can be purchased at nearly any
urban newsstand nationwide in India, a distinction that indicates its
place in national popular culture.

When my American students read the magazine, they tell me what im-
presses them is that coverage consists overwhelmingly of finely detailed
reporting about an amazing number of local-level public figures. In fact,
reporting is so highly personalized, it is hard for the outsider—anyone
unfamiliar with who these people are and what they do—to make sense
of the news. It seems Indians who read the magazine know something
about a large number of relatively minor public figures. This same fascination with specific individuals is also apparent when, as an outsider,
you listen to a political discussion among Indians. To me, this knowing
about large numbers of people—their names, what they do, how important and powerful they are, something about their leadership style—
is a defining feature of public life in India.

But knowing about large numbers of people is not restricted to the
political sphere. It is typical of public life generally. In the old, crowded
neighborhoods of Madras City, long-term residents know who lives in
their locality and can tell you detailed histories of the rise and fall of individuals and their families. The pattern is equally apparent among kin.

A middle-class, middle-aged merchant in Madras City, for example, can trace a genealogy that includes several hundred members, and he can describe who these people are (or were): what they do, where they live, when they were married, their level of education, which affines are related to whom, and so on. I believe this kind of detailed knowing about people reveals something important: individuality, in the sense of the aggregate of traits that distinguish who a person is, has great significance in Indian social life and is central to how Indians conceive of their society. Indians know their society in terms of who people are. This may seem an ordinary enough conclusion to draw from what for an American would be knowledge of an extraordinary number of people, but there is a problem.

A key tenet of Western social science lore about India is that individuality lacks importance in its social life. Indians are said to value collective identities, the identities of caste and family, *not* the identities of individuals (Dumont 1970a). And outside modern law (cf. Béteille 1986), it has been argued, Indians in ordinary life lack a ready abstract sense of the individual as an integrated whole (Marriott 1976; 1989).

I write this book to counter these commonplace views and to offer a theory of Tamil individuality. The Tamil people who are my concern live in the southern Indian state of Tamil Nadu. Although this book is particular to them, the role that individuality plays and its expressions in Tamil society call into question the validity of these commonplace views elsewhere in India as well. Specifically, I shall demonstrate that Tamils *do* recognize individuality as an essential feature of ordinary life; that individuality lies at the very crux of a Tamil's sense of self, as well as his or her sense of others; and that individuality plays a vital role in civic life. Nonetheless, Tamil individuality is distinct in several respects from Western notions of the individual.

Certainly the epigraph above, written by a contemporary south Indian writer, expresses a keen awareness of individuals. It suggests that no one meeting and knowing Indians would believe that they *weren't* individuals nor that they lacked awareness of their own or other's individuality. So how is it that there is a *position* in anthropology that contradicts experience and common sense? There are, I believe, two main reasons: The first is founded in the nature of Hindu culture itself; the second is the manner in which scholars have conceived of the person. Let us consider these reasons separately.

First, the Tamil Hindu does appear to conceive of the person differently from the way Westerners do. For example, the Western notion of individualism—the idea that the person has an identity separate from others and has a right, nay, an obligation to act as an autonomous person—is considered selfish by most Indians even today. Instead, in the Indian view, a person ought to comply with the collective interests of family and caste. An adult son should acquiesce to the interests of his father and mother. In south India, for example, out of deference, an adult son will avoid smoking in front of his father and many sons will remain their father's dependent until the day their father dies. Adult women are supposed to be dutiful wives and daughters-in-law. One of my former graduate students, a south Indian woman who lives with her husband in his parents' house as befits the south Indian ideal, would never think of going out without first asking her mother-in-law's permission. The individual lacks autonomy, therefore, and indeed, is perceived as sharing the collective identity of his or her family and caste. Given this perspective, it is easy to see why a person's actions reflect upon and represent such collective identities. An Indian's personal identity—who he or she is and how he or she is perceived to act—is commingled with and inseparable from these groups.

But there is much more to Indian inattention to an overarching notion of the individual than the above examples suggest. In the West, our fascination with individuality is elaborated in many ways: novels, biographies and autobiographies, personal diaries like that of Samuel Pepys, travelogues, which are a form of personal journal or diary, and the personal-interest stories of newspapers and magazines are examples taken from the media of the printed word. Portraiture, drama, even interior design are also strongly concerned with representations of individuals and are expressive of individuality. All of these various forms are also representations of self: expressions of idiosyncrasy and verbal or visual portraits of individuals that cause us to reflect on the interior person. Further, our interest in these many expressions stems from our own self-reflexive sense of who we are and how we act. Reflecting on others, each thinks about himself or herself.

Yet it is well known, if puzzling, that most of these expressions of individualism and individuality are missing from India's Hindu cultural assemblage prior to the nineteenth century and the advent of photography.[1] In fact, with the striking exception of photographic representations of individuals, many of these artifacts of individuality are still largely unrepresented in Hindu folk ideas and behavior. Take as an exception that proves the rule Kakar's characterization of Indian autobiographies (1982:7):

Even today, in the essentially Western-inspired genre of autobiography, Indian writings often tend to have a curiously flat quality as far as the scrutiny of the life in terms of a ruthless examination of motives and feelings are concerned. . . . With rare exceptions, Indian autobiographies are evocations of places and accounts of careers, records of events from which the self has been excised.

It would seem, then, these Indian autobiographies portray individuals who lack the introspection central to a Western understanding of the individual. In much the same manner, Kakar also contends that the characters portrayed in Indian novels and movies are created less to explore the individual than to "represent their societies in miniature" (Kakar 1989:4).

What is revealed by these examples is that, in comparison with the West, attention to individuality is noticeably understated in the Indian cultural assemblage that accompanies expressions of identity. If the Western artifacts of individualism mentioned above are understood as expressions of how persons are perceived and valued, then their near absence in India means Hindu conceptualizations of the person must be strikingly different. Awareness of this difference has colored scholarly attempts to define the ideology, behavior, and social patterns that surround Hindu Indian notions of personhood. This brings me to the second reason why the importance of individuality has gone unrecognized in Hindu society.

Stated simply, anthropologists have not been interested in the *empirical* encounter described in the epigraph because they see the "empirical" individual as a universal feature of being, and so have presumed it unproblematic—empty of interpretive meaning. The French anthropologist Louis Dumont (1970a) has led the way with this type of thinking.

Although Dumont's ideas about the Indian person build on those of others (e.g., Mauss 1985; Weber 1958),[2] it was his view that initiated the debate on individualism among South Asianists and has held center stage over the last twenty years (e.g., Dumont 1970a,b; Marriott 1969; Tambiah 1972; Barnett 1976; Shweder and Bourne 1984; Béteille 1986). Dumont distinguishes two meanings in the term "individual": first, "the empirical individual, present in every society," by which he means the self-conscious physical entity, and, second, the idea of the individual as a cultural value. In his view, anthropologists should use the term "individual" only when the idea of the individual is valued in a society. "One will thereby avoid inadvertently attributing the presence of the individual to societies in which he is not recognized, and also avoid making him a universal unit of comparison" (Dumont 1970a:9).

This understood, Dumont contends: "It is immediately obvious that there are two mutually opposed notions of the person: one is characteristic of traditional societies and the other of modern society." In modern society, the individual is valued, and the life of each person is its own end. In traditional societies, such as India, "the stress is placed on the society as a whole, as collective Man." Each "particular man in his place must contribute to the global order [of society]" (1970a:9). It is the order of society that is valued, *not* individual affairs. In other words, each lives for the interest of society, *not* for himself or herself.

According to Dumont, at the heart of Indian society is the hierarchical Hindu caste system, which represents a kind of caste-based division of labor that creates interdependence and ultimately India's collective solidarity as a society (1970a:105–8). The Indian's identity is that of groups, collectivities such as family, caste, village, and society itself. Actions are guided by what benefits and maintains these groups and their interdependence rather than by the person's own motivations and self-interests. If, in theory, Western society is based on the freedom and free will of the individual, then Indian society is based notionally on holistic identities and collective interests, just the opposite of the Western situation. In fact, Dumont goes so far as to argue that any approach to Indian society that focuses on the individual is misconceived (1970b).

The Dumontian view of the relationship between the person and society in India has been very influential and in fact continues to spread. But his view has also provoked disagreement among Indianists from the first (e.g., Marriott 1969; Tambiah 1972:835; Morris 1978; Béteille 1986, 1987; Jaer 1987; Dirks 1987; Raheja 1988a; Mines 1988; Mines and Gourishankar 1990, 1992). But here I am not interested in reviewing Dumont's many critics; much of what they have had to say is well-trodden ground. My aim is to explain briefly how it is that many scholars have come to think that individuality plays no role in Indian society and to indicate why this is a mistake.

For my purposes, let me simply point out that Dumont's conceptualization of the individual presumes that the idea of the individual can have only one valued manifestation—that of Western individualism. He implies that unless the idea of the individual is valued as it is in the West—Dumont refers to liberty, equality, and the pursuit of happiness as the values that support the idea of the individual—we should not use the term "individual." But what if Indians recognize individuality, but do not value individualism? I think no one would deny that Indians recognize personal uniqueness, value achievement, and assess personal motivation and reputation—all features of individuality—and regard these observations as crucial to the way they negotiate life. And what of other attributes of who a person is, of a distinctively Indian individuality? By denying the individuality of the Indian subject, Dumont has also denied agency to the Indian person and has created a myth of the Indian as Other, the radical antithesis of the Western individual (cf. Obeyesekere 1992:15–17).

Juxtaposed to Dumont's interpretation is that of McKim Marriott and Ronald Inden (Marriott and Inden 1977; Marriott 1976). They agree with Dumont that the Indian is misrepresented if depicted as an individual, but less because the person has a holistic-collectivist identity than because, according to Indian ways of thinking and explaining, each person is a composite of transferable particles that form his or her personal substance. A person is a "dividual" rather than an individual. According to Marriott's view, the Indian is unlike the American because, while the American conceives the individual as an independent, indivisible, skin-bound entity,[3] Indian "ethnosociology" explains the person as a dependent, divisible being with indefinite margins (Marriott 1989).[4] Thus, when an Indian cooks for another, some of the cook's personal substance is transferred into the food and so into the consumer. Giving and receiving, touching, eating—the Indian's very substance is transformed—sometimes adversely, sometimes beneficially—by these transactions. For example, a Tamil woman believes her blood gradually takes on the same qualities as her husband's, transformed as she absorbs his substance during sexual intercourse, when she eats the food of his house, sleeps with him, and engages in a myriad of other transactions with him. In the same fashion, she affects her husband's substance. Like Dumont, then, but for different reasons, Marriott and his followers contend that it is inappropriate to refer to Indians as individuals. To do so, they feel, is to be guilty of ethnocentrism because the very notion of the individual is alien to Indian senses of the person. So, like Dumont, Marriott and Inden too create a notion of the Indian subject that is the antithesis of the Western individual. Indian and Western subjects exhibit *no* similarities.

Marriott and Inden offer a theory of the Indian dividual, based largely on their interpretations of classical Hindu texts, but they offer no ethnographic defense of their arguments. Marriott has relied on his students to provide this (e.g., Barnett 1976; Raheja 1988a,b; cf. Marriott 1989). Among the efforts of these disciples, E. Valentine Daniel's book, *Fluid*

Signs: *Being a Person the Tamil Way* (1984), stands out as a crystalline semiotic analysis of Tamil beliefs supporting the dividualist idea. According to Daniel's depiction, the Tamil's central issue of being, given his or her dividual nature, is the search for an elusive state of equilibrium. Daniel states in the introduction (1984:2–3):

> My interest focuses on certain . . . properties of substances, namely, their ability to mix and separate, to transform and be transformed, to establish intersubstantial relationships of compatibility and incompatibility, to be in states of equilibrium and disequilibrium, and to possess variable degrees of fluidity and combinability.
>
> I intend to trace these properties of substances . . . by looking at certain phenomena in the cultural world of the Tamil villager, phenomena that are part of daily, ordinary, routine life. These phenomena are a Tamil's attempt to cope with the substance of his village . . . his house . . . his sexual partner, and his own body under conditions of sickness and health, and finally, to search for *the* substance from which all these various substances derive.

There is no question in my mind that Tamils are concerned with such things as Daniel describes. I have encountered just these concerns in my daily interactions with them when doing fieldwork in Tamil Nadu. Take the habit of one of my Tamil assistants. He would never eat foods that in Tamil thinking are classified as cool, because he himself had a cool body. He believed that should he eat cool foods—lime rice, for example, which although served hot is classified as cool—they would accentuate his own coolness, and he would catch a cold. But do Tamil conceptions of the person consist solely of these concerns and is personal motivation guided only by efforts to achieve the substance-mind balance Daniel describes as the Tamils' goal?

In his review of *Fluid Signs*, Arjun Appadurai (1986:757), who is sympathetic to Daniel's purposes, nonetheless indicates that "one finishes *Fluid Signs* with a nagging sense of unease. . . . [T]his is not an account that suggests that self-making is anything but a relatively harmonious process" (Appadurai 1986:756). He then goes on to wonder whether there are not other conflicting views and issues that when studied would fill in other dimensions of Tamil personhood. Clearly, Daniel's interest is not with inner voices, or with individuation, or even with the broad range of expressions that constitute the politics of identity in civil society. Daniel's semiotic view offers us important insights into how Tamils interpret themselves and understand their world, but it has not provided a full sense of Tamil individuality, of how Tamils think about themselves and the way their lives have gone, nor has it revealed anything about how the individual tries to project his or her identity in public life.

There is, however, one recent author, Margaret Trawick (see 1990; 1991), who offers a fuller, more person-centered sense of being Tamil. In her beautifully written book *Notes on Love in a Tamil Family* (1990), Trawick concentrates on the members of a single family. She describes how she returned to Tamil Nadu to see how the Tamil literary themes of love and ambiguity were expressed in an ordinary middle-class family, the family of her Tamil teacher. In her interpretation of her life with her teacher's family, the individual members come vividly to life. Her depictions of her subjects include an awareness of sex and gender, aspects of the person that are missing from Dumont's, Marriott's, and Inden's consideration and largely unexplored by Daniel as well. Her concern is particular persons in the flow of ordinary daily life, as subjects who describe their own feelings and motivations—their own inner sense of things. In many ways I feel that her book and this book of mine complement one another. Her concern is with Tamils in the context of the family—a slice in time; mine is with Tamil individuality in social history, in the public arena of business and civic life, but in domestic contexts, too, and in personal tellings about individuation, which are also histories, self-histories.

But in important ways I consider Trawick too to be a mystifier. In fact, mystification is her style (see Trawick 1991), and, while I agree with her intent, which I believe is to express the ambiguity and incompleteness of her subject's presentations and to represent the unbounded richness of Tamil culture and perspective, a richness that exceeds Western imagining and expectation, I disagree with the myth of the Other that she creates.[5] Here too, then, the Indian is depicted as the radical antithesis of the Western individual. Her subjects are presented intentionally as mysterious, unmaterialized, and sometimes bizarre (Trawick 1991; 1990:23, 42).

Ambiguity, incompleteness, love, desire, marriage, emotions, life as art, her own story, these are Trawick's interests. But these Tamils of her creation are not individuals; as she describes them, their consciousnesses lack boundaries and flow into one another. It's hard to tell where one person leaves off and another begins. This ambiguity is also represented forcefully in Trawick's compelling article, "Wandering Lost" (1991), which draws a parallel between a folk song and the life of its singer. Preserved as a recording on tape and removed from context, only part of what Trawick's disembodied informant sings and describes is intelligible.

Are Tamils really this insubstantial and confusing? What of a less artistic interpretation of aspects of social being that considers, for example, the individual in civic society, the person who is known to others, the politician of daily affairs, the striver for economic ends, the fool, the notorious, the enemy, the strong, the morally lax? These we barely glimpse if at all. The Tamil as an agent in the fullness of social life is still missing. Trawick, alas, is not an antidote to Dumont, Marriott, Inden, and Daniel. She too is a merchant of the exotic.

Despite their differences, therefore, it would appear, at least among these influential scholars, that there is agreement that the Indian person is ill conceived if depicted as an individual. The Indian is the antithesis of the Western subject. In fact, these scholars' views seem to fit well with Indian ideals that subordinate persons to groups—in Trawick's case, of women to men, children to adults, family members to the family, members of low castes to high. Yet, ideals and concepts aside, the reality of everyday Indian life and interaction in many of its features suggests that these views are overdrawn. I would argue, for example, that Marriott's view of the dividual overemphasizes physical notions of the Indian person, obscuring the importance Indians give to persons as unique social actors. Similarly, the Indian sociologist André Béteille criticizes Dumont's view precisely because he feels it exaggerates "the subordination of the individual to the collectivity" (Béteille 1987:191). After all, Béteille notes, for the greater part, the Indian Constitution is founded on the concept of the individual rather than groups. Then again, Trawick seems to me to exaggerate the strangeness of Tamil life, its shadowy and mysterious character, the insubstantiality of her Tamil subjects. I must ask again, are Tamils really so radically different from Western understandings?

Take perceptions of persons in daily life. Anyone familiar with Indian matrimonial ads is aware that individual achievements and attributes are central to descriptions of hopeful brides and grooms. These concerns about traits that distinguish individuals are readily understandable to the Western mind. This is true even while Indian matrimonial ads also seem impersonal to an American eye because they make no mention of personal likes and dislikes. Indians clearly conceptualize individuality differently from Americans, but in these ads Indians *do* conceptualize and value specific features of individuality.[6] In south India, a son with an engineering or other professional degree, for example, commands an extra dowry premium, in large part because his achievement of the degree implies individual ability and the high probability of a prestigious and successful future, independent of the achievements of other family members. It is my own awareness of this kind of valuing of the person separate from others that has led me elsewhere (Mines 1988, 1992; Mines and Gourishankar 1990) to criticize idealistic views of the Indian person that give little significance to individual achievement, self-interest, or responsibility, attributes of the self that distinguish persons as unique agents.[7] In fact, Marriott's collaborator in the development of the idea of the dividual, Ronald Inden (1986, 1990), has now himself disavowed aspects of his earlier interpretations of India, which gave primary emphasis to the caste basis of that society and little credence to the Indian person as the agent of history. Today, he prefers instead interpretations of Indian history that emphasize human agency (Inden 1990).

What I shall argue, then, stands in contrast to the views of Dumont, Marriott, Inden, Daniel, and Trawick—that in India persons conceive of neither themselves nor others as individuals. Instead, I shall argue that a sense of self and of individuality are absolutely central to how south Indian Tamils explain who they are, understand others, and conceive of their society. It behooves me, therefore, to explain here my sense of how Tamils understand their own individuality and recognize that of others. Doing so, my purpose is also to describe the framework of this book.

THE NATURE OF TAMIL INDIVIDUALITY

While residing as an anthropologist in Tamil Nadu State, south India, I found private and public expressions valuing individuality always close at hand. In houses, businesses, and community marriage halls, for example, portrait photographs are hung and honored with incense, flowers, sandalwood paste, and kumkum (red powder). Honored pictures of this sort commemorate specific kin, benefactors, political leaders, gurus, and deceased loved ones. These portraits and their uses reflect and symbolize the significance of a uniqueness defined by relationships: "This is *my* benefactor, mentor, wife, friend." Indeed, the individual always exists in relation to others and derives distinctiveness from these relationships. Although the Tamil word for "individuality," *tanittuvam*, connotes the individual separate from others, it also implies all that makes the person unique, including his or her relationships.[8]

These portraits also symbolize what a person has done. Tamils recognize individuals as responsible actors, whatever the forces that may ultimately impel their actions. People are individualized by their actions and acquire importance depending on the significance of what they have done. I once saw an unusually large photo portrait prominently displayed in a small handloom textile shop in Madras. The owner told me the miracu-

Figure 1.   The giver of Rs. 60,000 and his beneficiary's widow (center), daughter, and grandson. George Town, 1992.

lous story of how the old man of the photo had befriended him when he was young and years later had given him Rs. (rupees) 60,000 to start the shop (see fig. 1). The gift had rescued the shopkeeper from a lifetime of poverty and his gratitude was beyond simple expression.

Generosity (*vaḷḷaṇmai*) is an important feature of south Indian public life and acts of public philanthropy are common and widely evident. Generosity is an individual attribute that establishes and maintains relationships and is highly valued in politicians and leaders of all sorts. Just as photographs preserve identities, the inscribed names of donors and their donations on the walls of public buildings and temples preserve identities; donor names are engraved on the stairs leading to hilltop temples, on plaques attached to houses and buildings given as charity to temples, on public *choultries* (covered rest halls), schools, community libraries, production cooperatives, and occasionally on the wall of a medical dispensary. The ubiquitous leaflets and posters that announce political, social, and ritual events also list by name the sponsors, officers, and important guests of public functions. Why hang photos and list names but to announce who is responsible for what; to call attention to individuality; to give homage to particular persons?

But what kind of individuality is represented in these expressions and in the many others that I have observed over the years in south India? The main aim of this book is, of course, to explore at least a partial answer to this question. My informants are primarily urban Tamils, although many grew up in villages, and most are merchants and artisans, although many are not. My concern is with the nature of individuality as it emerges from daily lives: How have people explained themselves and their motivations to me, and how do they describe others around them? I am also concerned with the role that individuality plays in the organization of south Indian society and with the characteristics of its "civic" or public and sometimes corporate expressions.

Individuality, as Tamils conceive it, has both exterior and interior dimensions. In Tamil culture, this juxtaposed classifying of what is exterior (*puram*) with what is interior (*akam*) expresses a highly developed perception of societal and ultimately cosmic order (cf. Hart 1975). The exterior or public dimension of individuality involves what others "know" (experientially or by reputation) about an individual's appearance, achievements, roles, statuses, connections, and agency, and include the narrations of these others who participate in the construction of identity by telling stories about an individual's life. Others identify a person's individuality in part by what they know about his or her actions and by his or her reputation, which is an evaluation of the person's actions.

The Tamil's interior or private sense of individuality is revealed in the manner in which people represent themselves in personal narratives. These representations may express self-awareness, self-interest, contextualized motivations, agency, goals and choices, a sense of life-course, and a reflexive sense of both separation from and involvement with others, as well as a person's sense of mediating this polarity. Self-representations may also reveal personal struggles, contradictions, and strategies of presentation that reflect understandings of context and self that are dynamic and changing.

The book examines Indian individuality from these two main perspectives, exterior or public lives and interior or private lives, aspects of being that intertwine. To avoid confusion, let me here emphasize this point: public lives and private lives are intermixed. There is no clear separation of the two. Yet Tamils—like us—see some features of who they are as appropriately public, and these they present to others as their public face. Other aspects they reserve for their own inner thoughts and their closest associates. These constitute their private voice. Yet the dual dimensions of personhood, their public faces and their private voices, being inseparable, are often mixed together in peoples' interpretations of themselves and of others. What are private senses of success, failure, and shame but products of this public-private interaction? I have taken as my task the unraveling of these strands in order to understand better what Tamil individuality may be in its wholeness. My first concern in the book, then, shall be with expressions of individuality in public life, the exterior expression (chapters 2 through 6).

The central emphasis on individuality in public life is recognition of individual eminence within groups. This is true at all levels of organization from the family to the state. Preeminence defines the leader as a unique individual, and south Indians stress the leader's inequality of status when they value his or her individuality.

When I first meet older persons of accomplishment in Tamil Nadu—not persons who would be widely known, but those who have had some success in life—commonly they will begin describing themselves by listing the offices they hold in community institutions. Perhaps a man has played a role in a school building fund, or a woman is an officer in a small charitable organization, or a devotional society. Another more eminent person may list a more impressive series of offices, including, for example, that he is a trustee, or even the head trustee of a temple, that he is a sponsor of a major temple festival, that he is the president of the leather merchants' association, his caste association, and founder and head of a small local lending society—such offices are always occupied by men. What the person is describing is his or her "civic individuality." In effect, they are saying, "This is my public identity." When a Tamil thinks well of a successful acquaintance, he characterizes him with a similar list. If, however, he does not think much of the fellow, he might comment that the man's organizations are of no account, sarcastically adding that the man likes the look of his name on letterhead. What is being described is the individuality of leaders, defined by the eminence that men and, much more rarely, women achieve within groups. It is an individuality of inequality, but it is also a civic individuality that is associated with a tradition of service to constituents.

A number of Tamil leadership terms convey this sense of preeminence and prestige: headman (*talaivar*), village headman (*naaṭṭaanmaikaarar*), big-man (*periyar*), big-gift-giver (*periyadanakaarar*), the premier landlord or wealthiest person of a locale, eminent man among men (*nambi*). Many urban Indians also use the English terms "bigshot" and "boss" to express a similar sense of individuality defined by rank and responsibility, although men addressed by these latter terms are typically seen as being out for themselves rather than others. The ideal is to serve others altruistically; the reality is that the appearance of altruism often masks the self-interest of leaders.

Reflecting the civic importance of an individuality of inequality, at public functions leaders and their guests, both men and women, are often honored with speeches of appreciation and symbolic gifts that distinguish them as eminent and call attention to what they have done (see Caplan 1985:188–90). I myself have attended meetings where I have been singled out in this manner, being given flower garlands, a special piece of cloth, and other small gifts appreciating me as the ethnographer of the community. When gifts of this sort are given on important occasions and by important persons, they are highly prized, and because the presentations are public, they can suffuse identity with honor and prestige. The civic individual is made the center of attention.

Tamils generally believe that those who serve others will be rewarded; not only will people appreciate them generally, but they will fare well in life. The Tamil way for leaders to serve others is through institutions that they found or head, and each will have his or her own galaxy of institutions. This is another reason why a successful man, for example, will list the institutions in which he plays a leadership role. He is saying that the importance of his individuality is defined by his social responsibilities, and he is indicating who his constituents are. Each institution has its own constituency, although memberships overlap. Leadership in a locality, then, is composed of a field of leaders, their institutions, and their overlapping constituencies. In every urban community there are a myriad of institutions. Charities, temples, libraries, school building funds, scholarship funds, school hostel societies, school lunch programs, music societies, lending societies, marriage halls, medical dispensaries, caste associations, merchant associations, cooperatives, unions, and political parties are only several of the institutions in which leadership roles may be exercised. Important local leaders will head a number of these, while lesser leaders may participate in the management of only a few, their main role being primarily that of lieutenant to others. This institutional structure of leadership is a concomitant feature of civic individuality (Mines and Gourishankar 1990; Dickey 1993). Institutions and their constituents are important contexts of a leader's individuality.

Reflecting the preeminence of their leaders, institutions are highly personalized in India, much more so than in the West, where corporate bureaucracy mutes the roles of specific individuals. Individuality is actually more critical to the viability of Indian institutions than Western ones. People believe they should be able to approach the head of an institution directly because they see the head as a human being, open to appeals for assistance and able to circumvent bureaucratic red tape (Kakar 1981:40–41). I remember, for example, learning that one of south India's leading religious leaders, the Kanchi Sankaraacharya, is often approached by members of his following to assist them in obtaining private ends, such as gaining admission into a school or university for a child (Mines and Gourishankar 1990).

A good leader looks after his or her followers. It is no surprise, therefore, that an institution is epitomized by its head and that its popularity depends largely on the head's character and idiosyncratic style, features of charisma. Each leader also has a unique style of management that is well known to followers, and is yet another feature of the leader's civic individuality.

Women as well as men are leaders in Tamil society. Once early in my fieldwork career—this was back in 1968—I was asked by the head of Public Health in Tamil Nadu State, a woman by the name of Dr. Marakayar, why there seemed to be so few prominent leading women in the U.S., where women were supposed to be equal to men. By contrast, she felt, eminent women in Indian public life were numerous at both state and national levels, this despite the fact that Indian culture subordinates women to men.

There is more to Dr. Marakayar's paradox than her observation suggests. While women leaders are highly visible in India at state and national levels, there are very few eminent women at local levels, at the level of community and neighborhood. How is it that there are so few women leaders at grassroots levels?

I have found that a woman of local fame is known within her own neighborhood or community not because she is a leader, but more commonly because people say she is the first woman to have taken a university degree, or sometimes because she is believed to have special religious powers, or because she has chosen a religious life instead of marriage and family, or because as a childless widow she has endowed local temples or charitable institutions. Except within the field of social work and women's charitable organizations (Caplan 1985), women lack offices of local prominence.[9]

But why this disparity between local and state and national levels? My guess is that both gender and India's class structure play roles. At state and national levels, women leaders gain entree to positions of political leadership through men who are or were themselves leaders: these female politicians are the wives, daughters, widows, and—rarely—consorts of these men (Dickey 1993:347). Under the mentorship of their husbands, fathers, or lovers, these prominent women learned the skills of leadership, and often, even after they become leaders in their own right, they legitimate their role with their mentor's charisma, claiming to carry on in his name. At the local level, wives and daughters lack these opportunities of apprenticeship because, under the scrutiny of their families, husbands, in-laws, and neighbors, honor requires women to be good wives and dutiful daughters and daughters-in-law, roles that constrain the freedom that political and business aspirations require. Here at the local level, etiquette separates men and woman, so that it is difficult for women to mix outside their own gender. As a result, they are marginalized; they can lead among women but not among men.[10] A woman can transcend this limiting scrutiny only when, as a member of an elite family, her identity in politics, business, or similar activities extends beyond her neighborhood.

At these higher levels of organization, women leaders describe, organize, and display their public identities very much as men do (cf. Caplan 1985:190; Dickey 1993:348). When I interviewed her, Dr. Marakayar certainly did. This even though her personal life was in some ways different from that of most prominent men. For example, she never married because of the difficulty of finding a husband who would accept so accomplished a woman. A man with her education would have been considered a highly desirable mate. At a time when women doctors were rare, it was her father who had supported her in her ambition to become a doctor.

One finds, then, that both men and women are leaders in Tamil society and both sexes carry out their leadership in much the same personalized manner, but eminent women are rare at local levels of leadership. There were none in the business section of Madras City where I conducted the fieldwork on which the greater part of this book is based. Consequently, what I shall have to say about the individuality of inequality or eminence in public life has to do only with men. But do not think that men always achieve positions of leadership independently of women. Sometimes they too achieve access to power first through connections that are traced at least in part through wives or mothers. This is the case with one of the main characters of this book.

The second focus of the book is concerned with expressions of individuality in private lives (chapters 7, 8, and 9). When one examines civic individuality, which can only be done in the context of a community, one uncovers the community's social history. But when one examines the private self, one encounters the inner voice, which tells how that particular person has tried to mediate his or her relationship with society. Here we find tales of individuation, stories that describe the individual's struggles to take charge of the relationship between society and self.

Kakar (1981:34) writes that "the essential psychological theme of Hindu culture is the polarity of fusion and separation . . . a dynamic counterpoint between two opposite needs, to merge into and to be differentiated from the 'Other', where the 'Other' is all which is not the self." Kakar considers this polarity a psychological universal. Individuals in all societies must constantly mediate temporary resolutions in their relationships, seeking to balance their social need for relations with others (fusion) and their need for a sense of control in their lives (separation). Total fusion with others means loss of control over one's life, loss of individual identity, and despair, while complete separation spells loneliness and, ultimately, isolation. An individual who lives solely for others has no life of his or her own, but an individual who lives only for himself or herself has no enduring relationships. In south India, as in the United States, there is often talk about what the ideal balance is supposed to be. American talk tends to come down more on the side of autonomy over fusion; Indian discussions put more stress on the importance of fusion, giving group interests priority over personal interests.

But Indians, too, must meet their psychological needs for separation. These they express, for example, when they describe their private goals in life and explain what gives them their personal sense of meaning. As adult Indians grow older, they increasingly express a very strong sense of personal responsibility (*poruppu*) for how their lives have turned out. But not everyone begins adulthood with such a developed sense of self. Some of my older informants told me that they lacked this wisdom in their youth, a time when they believed that if they lived their lives according to the ideals of their society, things would naturally go well. For some of these, it was life's circumstances that compelled them to take charge and realize that they alone were responsible for their own lives. As Lakshmi, a fifty-two-year-old Tamil woman, who had tried to be a dutiful daughter-in-law and had suffered greatly during her younger adulthood due to lack of control in her life, exclaimed: "Don't blame others for your troubles. We're at fault for letting ourselves be cheated. We must stick up for ourselves." Responsibility, goals, and a sense of having some control over decisions affecting one's life are central to Tamil expressions of psychological individuality.[11]

Although in Tamil culture men and women share many understandings, sex and gender also prescribe different personal experiences for them. It is to be expected, therefore, that the private narratives of men and women express some concerns and issues that are different. Reflecting this, A. K. Ramanujan notes that the folktales men and women tell are different (Ramanujan 1991:52):

> While [men's] tales that feature princes who go off on a quest for the golden bird in the emerald tree invariably end in wedding bells, tales with women at the center of action never do so. The women meet their husbands and are married formally or informally in the first part of the tale, often at the very beginning, and then the real story, usually nothing but trouble, begins.

In a survey, I once asked informants to describe to me the happiest time of their lives and also the most difficult time of their lives. Men responded indicating that the happiest time for them was right after marriage, but before they had children. Women told me they were happiest before they married. As for difficult times, these were highly variable, but all my older informants—men and women—felt responsible for how they dealt with them.

In order to explore the nature of psychological individuality, I collected life histories of twenty-three Tamils selected from a wide range of locality, caste, and educational backgrounds. I have analyzed these life histories elsewhere (Mines 1988). In this book, my concern is to present in detail a few of these personal tellings, to reveal their themes. In relating my analyses of these, I have tried to maintain a sense of how interviewees explained themselves and how their view of their lives changed as they grew older and more experienced. Self-explanations reveal that culture as well as society is age-layered. As people age, their interpretation of themselves, their relationship with ideals, and how they fit in society changes. Self-explanations also reveal that a sense of control in life becomes increasingly important, while at the same time the cultural dictates limiting pursuit of personal interests diminishes. Tamil individuality is more freely expressed in older age than in younger, a reverse of what happens in the West, I believe (Mines 1988).

In addition to its psychological expressions, individuality in the private lives of Tamils involves a cultural sense of the valued and depreciated traits that characterize individuals as actors. These are traits deemed either under the control of individuals or idiosyncratic to them, and they assume individual responsibility for actions.[12] In Tamil culture some of the most important traits of individuality include generosity (*vallanmai*) versus stinginess (*karumitanam*); having dignity, honor (*maanam*) versus being a dishonorable person (*maanam ketta manidan*); being a trustworthy person (*nambagamana manidan*) versus being an untrustworthy person (*nambagamatra manidan*); being a prudent, intelligent person (*buttisaali*); being wise (*aringar*) or very wise (*peraringar*); and having modesty (*nan udaimai*). When persons exhibit these positive attributes, they are known as good persons (*nallavar*) who display good character (*nalla kunam*). When they are socially prominent, they may also be described as eminent persons (*nambi*) or as big-men and women (*periyar*), in the sense of important persons in contrast to ordinary (*saraasari manidan*) or bad persons (*kettavar*). Attributes such as these express the kind of person an individual is—a person's character (*kunam*)—and reflect the fact that definitions of character express a relationship between the private life of an individual and the greater society. It is through the cultural definition and valuing of character traits that individuality in private life intersects with individuality expressed in public life. Character defined in terms of public standards (e.g., honesty) demarcates a kind of "civic individuality," as opposed to an expressive or private form, defined by goals and responsibility for oneself. Individuals are ranked according to these standards and their social worth is judged greater or lesser in terms of them.

Here, let the reader pause for a moment to consider the two poles of Tamil individuality so far described, private expressions and civic or public lives. The reader, if used to thinking of individuality as at the heart of American individualism and as an expression of the person primarily in opposition to others, might find confusing the idea of public or civic forms of individuality that are defined and valued precisely in relationship to others. After all, where exactly is the individuality of a Tamil located? Is it located within the person—the locus of the physical and psychological self? Or is it located in the sense others have of the person, their perception (however conceived) of him or her as a distinct human being? The answer is, of course, both—that among Tamils expressions of individuality are located along a continuum that stretches between the private or interior self and the social or exterior self. Reflecting this, my Tamil informants tell me that their concept of individuality, *tanittuvam*, while it denotes separation, also conveys a sense of every distinguishing aspect of the person, including his or her relationships. Therefore Tamil individuality, while it is defined in part in terms of the private self, always is also in part defined in terms of social contexts, which distinguish the person in terms of his or her relationships with others.[13] Note again that what is private and what is public are intermixed aspects of individuality.

How then does a person achieve an identity as a civic individual? As Tamils clearly state, part of the answer is, by the person's social positions—for example, father or mother of sons, mother-in-law, textile merchant, head of household, head of an association, and friend. We have seen that the sum and character of a Tamil's social positions distinguish him or her. But the answer to our question is also that an individual's civic identity is achieved in part by behavior. One's actions, after all, determine one's reputation and direction in life. Individuals are distinguished by their actions precisely because they see themselves and are seen by others as responsible for them. It is this dual perception of responsibility, a person's own awareness of responsibility and society's judgment of the execution of these responsibilities, that joins private and civic expressions of individuality, the twin facets of a Tamil's sense of self.

Praneshacharya, the hero of a modern south Indian novel, *Samskara: A Rite for a Dead Man* (Murthy 1978:109–10), expresses his personal sense of individuation—that is, of becoming an individual—in exactly these terms. At one point the hero, who is a religious leader among his Brahman village fellows, is thrown into a quandary about what to do with himself because late one night in a thoughtless moment he succumbed to the wiles of a village concubine and slept with her. The act opens him to his selfish sexual appetites, which he now longs to fulfill (private self). But he is also painfully aware that, through his act of illicit lovemaking, he has forsaken the exemplary life of a Brahman religious leader and is now separated from the community of his fellow Brahmans (civic or public self). Having lost control of his life, he wanders the countryside (living neither for self nor society). Anxiously he ponders the issue of how to act and is acutely aware that his religious books have failed to guide him.

> Isn't this precisely why we have created the Books? Because there's this deep relation between our decisions and the whole community. In every act we involve our fore-fathers, our gurus, our gods, our fellow humans. Hence this

conflict. Did I feel such conflict when I lay with Chandri? Did I decide it after pouring and measuring and weighing? Now it's become dusky, unclear. That decision, that act gouged me out of my past world, the world of the brahmins, from my wife's existence, my very faith. . . .

Therefore the root of all my anxiety is because I slept with Chandri as in a dream. Hence the present ambiguity . . . I'll be free from it only through a free deliberate wide-awake fully-willed act. Otherwise, [I am] a piece of string in the wind, a cloud taking on shapes according to the wind. I've become a mere thing. By an act of will I'll become human again. I'll become responsible for myself. . . . I'll remake myself in full wakefulness.

Reflecting a sense of responsibility with which my older Tamil informants would be very comfortable,[14] Praneshacharya clearly sees that if he fails to take charge of himself, he will remain lost, buffeted by whatever he encounters. But there is a paradox in his solution. It is only if he takes separate responsibility for his actions, that is, if he is a self-willed agent, that he can regain his membership in society. The south Indian individual, therefore, must take responsibility and nurture individuality's dual aspects, the private self and the civic self. By not doing so, the person will either become isolated or, in exerting no will, lose his or her humanity and become "a string" blown in the wind.

We see, then, that individuality in the private and public lives of Tamils is expressed differently in different social contexts. There is no one way of characterizing south Indian individuality. For example, in private lives there is expressive psychological individuality, civic character, and the individuality of salvation, while in public life there is civic individuality defined by eminence and achieved public identity expressed as reputation, to mention two. The individual Tamil integrates these various selves—public and private—through a self-conscious acceptance of responsibility for his or her identity and actions.

By way of summation, let me list briefly here what I shall argue are distinguishing features of Tamil individuality. First and foremost, the Tamil is a *contextualized individual*, and it is by this term that Tamil individuality is best characterized. When I label the Tamil a contextualized individual I mean that the individuality of persons is recognized within the context of groups where they are known and within which they have a known set of statuses and roles. Contexts include the household, one's kin, and one's caste community, but they may also include neighborhood, political parties or other institutions, and in the case of important persons, the state or even the nation. These are contexts within which who a person is (e.g., one's character, behavior, caste, gender, name, locality identity, offices, roles) will be judged and valued.

Second, Tamil individuality is a *spatially defined individuality*: its dimension depends on the size and locality of the constituencies that form a person's social contexts. The individuality of important persons will be more widely known and their constituencies more widespread than will those of ordinary persons; but, more widely recognized, identity will also be more widely contested. And generally, the spatial dimension of a woman's individuality will be smaller and less contested than that of a man. Each person's identity is limited spatially to those among whom he or she is known.

Third, Tamil individuality is an *individuality of inequality*, and the more important and eminent a person is, the more his or her individuality is stressed. Rank is an important feature of a person's identity because it is closely associated with what a person can do—for example, whether a person has good connections or the autonomy to make decisions affecting a group. Consequently, Tamil individuality lacks an abstract sense of the individual wherein all persons are equal and equally valued. Tamil individuality is graded and particular to the social contexts in which one is known and has a role.

Fourth, individuality, as Tamils conceive it, has a *private* or *interior dimension*, as well as an *exterior* or *civic dimension*. The interior dimension is the self-reflecting person's private inner voice and includes feeling as well as other features of self-awareness (cf. Trawick 1990). The inner voice is the creative force behind agency, decision making, and direction taking. It evaluates and interprets experience. Personal narratives, which reveal these self-reflections, often describe private struggles and private conclusions about what the individual feels he or she has learned; they reveal understandings of context and self that are dynamic and changing. In private life, individuality is circumscribed by standards of civic character, which emphasize harmonious relationships and valued personal traits such as generosity. These moderate self-interest by acclaiming self-denial and service to others.

The Tamil's exterior sense of individuality involves what is known about an individual, particularly his reputation, which is an estimation of who he is: his character, his actions, his achievements, connections, statuses, and influence. What kind of person is he? What are his institutions, and what are the dimensions of his identity? As in private life, achievement of a valued civic identity is constrained by standards of civic character including the ideal in public life of altruistic service to the greater good of one's constituents. Such altruistic public figures play a major role maintaining social trust within their communities.

Eminence, civic individuality, reputation, social trust, the organization of groups, individual responsibility, goals, control, agency—all are features of the contextual individual, and all indicate that there remains much to explore regarding Indian notions and ways of valuing individuality. In the chapters that follow, I examine in detail these topics as they relate to the nature, varieties, and social importance of Tamil individuality. Men are my primary focus, although for this book some of my most important life stories are those of women. Young adults, established adults, and elderly adults, a few rich, many poor, some that are famous, but mostly what Tamils would consider ordinary people are my sources. What the book attempts to convey is a sense of the range of expression that individuality takes in the daily social lives of Tamils, as they themselves experience and describe it. In the face of the expectations of others, a few relate that they never felt strong enough to take full responsibility for themselves, even while they also describe turning points in their lives when they believe they could have done so. But when I reflect on my field interviews, the strongest memory is of how, the older my informants, the stronger and clearer their notion of individuality became, mirroring their own sense of how they had come to realize responsibility for themselves. Most describe how difficult it was to act on this awareness.

INTRODUCING TAMIL NADU AND MADRAS CITY

The people who are the subjects of my study live in Tamil Nadu, the southernmost state on India's eastern Coromandel Coast. I conducted the research on which this book is based primarily during two periods of fieldwork. The first was an eleven-month period in 1978–79, during which I worked partly in the dry central, Salem-Erode region of the state and partly in coastal Madras City, the state capital. The second period was a ten-month stint in 1985–86, when I worked again in Madras. Although my earlier field research, between 1967 and 1969, among Tamil-speaking Muslims does not play a direct role in this present book and my concern here is with Hindu views only, I mention it also because it was that research and the people I then came to know that led ultimately to my writing this book.

When I arrived in Madras City with my wife and eleven-month-old daughter on my first trip to India in 1967, my intention was to study spoken Tamil for three months before launching my fieldwork. I had studied Tamil in the U.S. but wanted to become more fluent. And so with

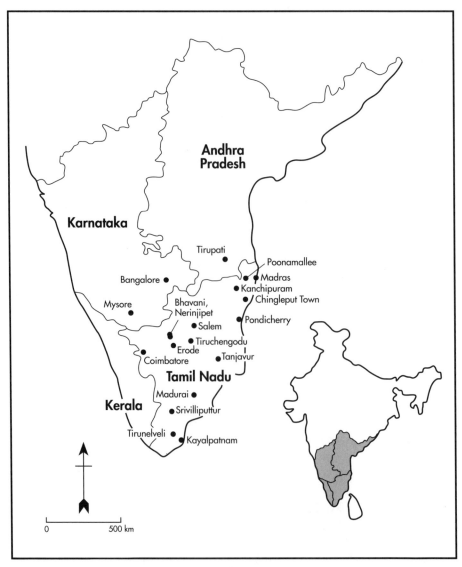

Map 1.   Selected towns in Tamil Nadu and nearby.

that purpose in mind, I went to the Tamil Department at the University
of Madras. The late Tiru M. Varadarajan was then professor and head
of the department. He told me of a recent graduate of his, C. Natesan,
who was living in a village near Salem City, some two hundred miles to
the southwest of Madras. Natesan had been his best student, and

Varadarajan thought he would make an excellent tutor. He would write, he said, and ask Natesan if he would like the job. A week later I met Natesan in Madras, employed him, and a week after that, the two of us traveled by bus to his village for a visit. It was my first trip into the Tamil countryside.

Bordered on the east by the Bay of Bengal, the Tamil Nadu landmass rises slowly toward the hills and ancient mountains that lie to its western side. "East" and "low," "west" and "up" are homonyms in the Tamil language. Lying west, Salem City is surrounded by mountain remnants. It is a beautiful countryside, a patchwork of villages, fields and broken rock, and high hills, one crowned by the ruins of a stone fort. Salem City and District are famous for handloom weaving. Not far to the south of Salem City is Erode Town, a major railway junction and the site of one of India's major handloom textile markets. The villages and towns that surround Erode weave for the town's master weavers and bazaar. Natesan's village, Akkamapet, is one of these. Remembering it now, I recall it as a village of whitewashed houses with roofs of thatch and red tile, adjacent to a small crescent-shaped reservoir or "tank," surrounded by fields of groundnut. At the center of the village stood the walled compound and mansion of the village landlord, the "zamindar." Behind the high walls, a flame tree was in full bloom.

I met Natesan's family in the small thatched house in which he and his mother lived. He was the youngest of his siblings, and his father had died some years before. They were weavers by caste, members of an ancient community in Tamil Nadu, the Kaikkoolars, who a thousand years before, they said, had been warriors in the royal armies of kings. There in the village, I met Natesan's elder brother, a village leader whose story plays a part later in this book. And several of the persons whose life stories and experiences I relate in the final chapters of this book come from the Salem-Erode axis.

Two years younger than I, Natesan was a thoughtful and astute observer of Tamil, Tamil society, and me. Over the course of the year and a half that formed my first stay, he taught me, and we became lifetime friends, although at first I think neither of us understood the other very well. I learned many years later from a long letter he wrote to me in Santa Barbara that he had kept a journal in which he had recorded his thoughts about our daily interactions and observations about me. In that letter, he shared some passages. It seems I, the studier, had been studied. Bound by our youthful experiences and subsequent times I spent with him and his family in later years, it was in fact because of Natesan that I did my second piece of fieldwork on the weavers, from 1978 to 1979, on which this present book is based in part.

I have another close friend from that earliest period of fieldwork, Abdul Wahab, a Tamil-speaking Muslim of my age who managed two shops, a textile shop and a general merchandise shop, which stood across the street from one another in Pallavaram, a suburb of Madras City. I was often the companion of these two men—Wahab and Natesan—and through them was introduced to Tamil society. Once all three of us traveled to Natesan's village and roamed the Salem countryside together.

When I lived in Salem City in 1978, I used to meet daily with Natesan, who by then had moved there, to talk about my fieldwork, study Tamil, and learn from his insights. Sometimes in the evening we would drive with our wives in my small, 1960 "Standard Super 10" to one of the foothills to enjoy the evening, look out over the valleys and nearby jungle preserve, and watch the sunset. I was told that wild elephants lived in the jungle.

The second piece of fieldwork on which I base this book—in sequence, my third field trip to India—I conducted in Madras City, in the old business center known today as George Town. I went there to study the traditional merchants of the city and its goldsmiths. Madras had been originally founded for purposes of trade in Indian manufactures, and I was interested in the traditions and organization of the centuries-old merchant neighborhoods and communities. On this trip, my research assistant was V. Gopalakrishna, an M.A. graduate in sociology from the University of Madras. "Gopal" was from a village near Pondicherry. He was quiet and thoughtful, and we worked well together. When we interviewed an informant, both of us would take notes. I told him that way both of us could write about what we learned. He was very relaxed in disposition and could cross a busy Madras street with a casual nonchalance that compared favorably to my fearful sprints, stops, and starts. I asked him how he did it. He replied that he wasn't nervous about crossing because he wasn't married. "I have no responsibilities," he said. Toward the end of my stay, however, he did marry, his elder sister's daughter—a desirable match in Tamil culture—and when I return to Madras, I look forward to seeing whether his street-crossing habits have changed. I once asked Gopal if he was learning anything new about Tamil society from the fieldwork we were conducting. "It's all new," he told me with animation. "I'm learning something every day." He was fascinated with how one line of inquiry would lead to another, building on what went before. Like detectives following leads, we were slowly unraveling the complexity of urban life in this Tamil city.

Named after their language, the Tamil people are the inheritors of an ancient culture, including, next to Chinese, the oldest continuous literary tradition in the world. Given today's popular Western images of India, which emphasize its poverty, its exotic cultures, and its distance and peripheral importance to European, East Asian, and American centers of trade, it is easy to forget that when the British founded a fort at Madras in 1639, India was then at the center of an economic and cultural "world system," with something like a quarter of the world's total manufacturing capacity located within its peninsular boundaries (Washbrook 1988:60).

It was to gain access to Indian manufactures that the British founded Fort St. George at Madraspatnam, which then was probably little more than a fishing village. The coastline runs straight where the city was founded, and the surf is usually high. The profits to be gained in trade were enormous and the city grew quickly. The British residents were few in number, and until the end of the eighteenth century, politics were often uncertain. The British had to fear the moods of European competitors and Indian rulers and chiefs alike. Just to the north of Madras, in Pulicut, the Dutch had a fort, and the French were in Pondicherry, ninety miles to the south. In the early years of English trade, the East India Company records, kept by the Company Council based at Fort St. George, reveal a highly competitive but personal society. Both Indians and Europeans are mentioned by name and sometimes the reader glimpses the personalities behind the names as well as a clear sense of motives, fears, animosities, and betrayals. At the end of the eighteenth century, the British became colonial rulers, and Madras City became the capital of what was to be Madras Presidency. After Independence in 1947, Madras was named the state capital, and subsequently the state was renamed Tamil Nadu.

Even today the architecture of the George Town area of Madras reveals a mixture of cultures. There is an Armenian church on Armenian Street, although after centuries of residence, only a few Armenians still live in Madras. There are the old British buildings, mosques and churches, the temples of Jains, Hindus, and one belonging to the Parsis. And lining the narrow streets are the houses of families who have lived in George Town for as long as anyone can remember. In one old temple in the heart of George Town, I saw a palanquin of the English style, a real museum piece. My informants told me the East India Company had donated it sometime in the misty past—"in those days," is what they said—for carrying the temple idol in processions. It is this area of Madras City and its people that are the primary focus of the first part of this book.

In the next five chapters, I explore civic individuality, examining its nature, how it is expressed and understood, and revealing the role it plays in Tamil society and culture. In later chapters, I present personal narratives and explore Tamil senses of the private self.

Public Faces

CHAPTER TWO

The Nature of Civic Individuality

The word *moka* (from the Sanskrit *mukha*) or face was heard
frequently in conversation. It stood for a person's image before others and for his self-respect. It was one of his most important possessions.

M. N. *Srinivas,* The Remembered Village

Before we can understand the community of George Town and examine why it is organized in the manner that it is, it is necessary to understand the nature of civic individuality and the highly personalized nature
of social relationships in south Indian society that make identity so important. Reputation, public trust, eminence, and the roles charismatic
community leaders play are all associated aspects of civic individuality.
What I am talking about is how relationships are formed and things accomplished, and the role that individuality plays in daily life.

Even today, when the growth of cities and the spread of bureaucracy
might lead one to expect that relationships would be increasingly depersonalized and that anonymity would be on the rise, south India remains a highly personalized society. By highly personalized, I mean that,
beyond the limits of kin and friends, personal relationships are important determinants of how one conducts one's life. A Tamil's success in
life vitally depends on maintaining good relationships and a good reputation within one's community.

To be successful in daily endeavors in Tamil Nadu society—say in
running a small business or in seeking employment—a person must be
trusted. This means either being well known to others, so that they know
personally what to expect of the person, or being known to the leading
men and women of the community, persons whose reputations are
known, so that they can vouch for the individual to those who seek to
estimate him or her. For example, lenders will give credit only to those

they know repay their loans, and employers hire only those for whom they or others they trust can personally attest. This need to be known is different from American society where individuals rely much less on personal knowledge and much more on bureaucratic indicators of reliability, such as credit ratings, certification, or, as the request goes, a "picture i.d. and a major credit card."

In India, as in all societies, peaceful interaction requires that people behave for the most part in predictable and reliable ways. Law, enforced by sanctions external to relationships, is one source of reliability; trust, embodied within relationships themselves, is another. In south India, trust still has a major role. An Indian evaluates the degree of trust he or she has in the reliability of a relationship in terms of knowledge of the other party or parties in that relationship. A reputation is the public sense of one's responsibility for one's identity and actions, an assessment of responsibility for past behavior.

One important factor in such an evaluation is the reputation of the other party as a civic individual. Is the other known to be a "good person" and a trustworthy individual, for example? A second factor is the strength and nature of the relationship the parties have, including how enduring and important the relationship is to the parties involved. The underlying assumption is that if a relationship is important to a person, that individual will act in a reliable manner because it will be in his or her self-interest to preserve the relationship. Again, we see here that the Indian view preserves the sense that individuals are responsible for their own actions. Finally, a third factor is whether or not the other party is known to persons of eminence and is vouched for by them. A man or woman of eminence is a person who has an enduring and highly prized relationship with his or her community,[1] one that is defined by the prestige and status the person has achieved in that community. The actions of such men and women are circumscribed by the collective interests that define their prestige and constrain their statuses. Consequently, it is very much in the self-interest of eminent persons to preserve their eminence by vouching only for those they trust. If a person for whom they have vouched betrays their trust, it is in the eminent person's interest never again to act as a guarantor on the betrayer's behalf. This fact is well known in India. It should be clear, therefore, that reputation, eminence, status, including offices, achievement, and responsibility for how one behaves and who one are are highly valued features of identity, defining a person's civic individuality in Indian society.

It should also be clear that eminent individuals play key roles in the regulation of trust within communities. For an ordinary person, known to a limited circle of individuals, it would prove difficult to establish ties of trust that reach beyond the circle without the validation of eminent persons. An eminent person is known much more widely. Indeed, the greater one's eminence, the greater the circle of individuals among whom one is known and can act as a guarantor of reliability. A Tamil's circle forms the context of his or her civic individuality and delimits its spatial dimension.

I remember once sitting in a jeweler's showroom in George Town, the business center of Madras City, chatting with a prominent diamond merchant, when a Viswakarma, or goldsmith, came in. This particular merchant had recently shown me a diamond and gold necklace worth, he told me, $90,000. It certainly looked like it was worth that much. It was a heavy piece with several courses of diamonds. One of his Indian customers living in New York had ordered it made by him, and he was preparing the customs papers for mailing the necklace, which was why, he said, that he had it in the shop rather than under lock and key elsewhere. The merchant had a few goldsmiths who worked at the back of his shop, but according to business custom, most of his work he put out as piecework to artisans who crafted the jewelry in their homes, some as far afield as Bombay. Goldsmiths are poor artisans on the whole, and I remember being impressed that merchants, such as this one, trusted their artisans with gold and gems worth sizeable sums, although not so much as this necklace.

The goldsmith who had entered the shop explained that he was a skilled gem-setter and was looking for work. He was very polite in his demeanor and speech, and in reply, so was the merchant. The merchant explained to the goldsmith that he had no work for him but would keep him in mind. After the goldsmith had left, the merchant said to me that he would never hire the man. I asked if he knew him personally. The merchant replied that, while he did not, he knew his name and reputation. Some time ago the goldsmith had stolen gold he had been given to make a piece of jewelry and had fled Madras. When he had spent what he had stolen and was again looking for employment, he found that no one was willing to hire him in his new locality because he was unknown to jewelers there. As his situation became more desperate, he returned to Madras, but now found that no jewelers would hire him there, either. The merchant explained that he, like other jewelers, never hired a man whom he did not personally know or for whom another trusted jeweler would not or could not vouch. Effectively the goldsmith had been blacklisted, and it was unlikely that he would ever again work as a goldsmith.

I asked if the police had been called regarding the theft. The merchant laughed. There was no advantage in that. Calling the police meant that you would lose twice, once from the theft and a second time from the police, who would require bribes. Basically, the jeweler felt that the merchants' network offered a more effective means of dealing with theft than the police.

The jeweler's sentiment is widely shared. The effectiveness of relying on personalized relationships to regulate behavior in India's cities is attested by the low rates of urban crime, despite high rates of poverty, compared to U.S. cities. For example, with a population of about 12 million people, one third[2] of whom live in slums, Calcutta recorded less than 100 homicides in 1990, compared to New York City's 2,200 (Karl E. Meyer, *New York Times*, Jan. 6, 1991). One Calcutta newspaper editor bragged, "You are safe in the parks. We've had one notorious rape there in 20 years" (Karl E. Meyer, *New York Times*, Jan. 6, 1991). Similarly, in Madras, with a population of 4.2 million in 1981, 15,693 crimes were recorded for the year (*India Today*, 66). This represents a crime rate of one crime per 267.6 persons, although the number of crimes is undoubtedly underreported. This rate compares with one crime per 5.9 persons[3] in 1986 for the university district surrounding my own University of California campus, where underreporting is also common. In the university community the crime rate is forty-five times higher than that of Madras.

Low crime rates relate to neighborhood solidarity and stability. Urban crime rates in India are highest in the new residential suburbs of India's biggest cities. In 1961, before substantial suburbs had been developed in Madras City, the crime rate was one crime per 463 persons, almost half of what it is today.[4] In the old residential areas of an Indian city, the individual has very little anonymity. If a man is not known, people ask who he is, or they note things about him so that, if it interests them, they can follow up on finding out about him. On several occasions I have seen an Indian note the license plate number of someone who has piqued their interest, their intent being to find out who the person is. A week later, through private enquiries, they know. I myself have found that all sorts of Madrasis have known me by my license plate number. It is clear that individuality—expressed here as being known—is considered important in urban India today, and that a reputation for good character and ability is highly prized.

THE "BIG-MAN" VERSUS THE BUREAUCRAT

It would be misleading, of course, to suggest that bureaucracy plays no role in Indian society. In fact, its role is a major one. The police, law and the courts, voter registration and elections, driver's licenses, taxes and fines, examinations and university degrees, bank accounts and applications for loans are familiar components of bureaucracy that regulate the lives of Indians. In contrast to trust based on personalized relationships, bureaucracy depends on depersonalized criteria for determining reliability. For example, a bureaucratic method of determining financial honesty is by rules of accounting that judge honesty by criteria defined in law. A man's civic individuality—who vouches for him, what his relationships are, and what his reputation is—is much less relevant, although it may weigh in decisions about hiring or about how to prosecute law breaking. However, in a trust-based relationship, honesty and reliability *are* evaluated in terms of who a person is. With no direct monitoring, a trusted person has considerable leeway in the use of resources that he or she might control in common trust, that is, so long as that trust continues.[5] The point to be made is that bureaucracy diminishes the importance of individuality and of personalized relationships, whereas in a society that bases reliability on relationships of trust, the importance of individuality, namely, who a person is and what a person does, is stressed.

In a trust-based society, when persons who control desired resources, commodities, and services need to choose who is to get what, then the identity of the individual seeking a benefit and the influence of the people he or she knows can be the critical factors determining how choices are made. For example, a seller often must choose to whom among several potential buyers he will sell, and a banker has to decide to whom to lend money. Under such conditions, knowing eminent persons, people south Indians often refer to as *periyar*, big-men, can obviously be very beneficial. Here I use the term to include influential women, although the reader should keep in mind that their comparative number is quite small. Big-men can wield great influence among members of their communities, because people perceive them as being able to act as brokers on their behalf. The civic attention of the community focuses on the individuality of big-men when community members accord prestige to these community leaders, a public recognition that distinguishes their singularity and agency. These are the individuals who make things "happen" for their followers. By contrast, bureaucracy is designed precisely to circumscribe the influence and agency of individuals by depersonalizing the operation of institutions.

A south Indian friend of mine, whom I shall here call Tambi, related the following story about trying to start a business in Madras that reveals the juxtaposed roles and different styles of the bureaucrat and the big-man in south Indian business and banking. The story has deeper implications than simply how to get a loan in India. It suggests that there is a close relationship between the role of the individual as an agent and the organization of south Indian society. This is a relationship I shall explore in detail in the chapters that follow.

Tambi and three of his friends met as engineering students at the Indian Institute of Technology (IIT) in Madras. When they graduated they decided to start a small industry in Madras City, manufacturing tubular aluminum furniture, an industry that depends heavily on marketing. To finance the initial capital required, Tambi went to his elder brother, Annan, who is himself a wealthy and well connected businessman in Madras. The brothers are members of the Nagarattar caste, a well-known business and banking caste in south India, which also has extensive business ties with Southeast Asia (cf. Rudner 1989). In addition to the businesses that Annan runs in Madras, he is the director of a large textile mill in Kerala and has ownership interests in rubber estates and financial institutions in Malaysia. Annan maintains close contacts with the business moguls of Tamil Nadu, many of whom are also Nagarattars. This he does in part by his active membership in the Cosmopolitan Club of Madras, a men's club that is an important meeting place for the state's business and government elite. Annan also maintains his ties by going on pilgrimage to Kerala to worship the god Aiyappan with a group of his influential Cosmopolitan Club friends every December/January. Pilgrimage groups of this sort are a common feature of the Aiyappan festival, and the shared experience intensifies the sense of fellowship among group members. Members maintain their pilgrimage group year after year.

At the time that Tambi approached him, Annan had an interest in a private lending society, Frontier Investments,[6] a business that was owned by the father of two of his classmates. Annan arranged for Tambi and his partners to borrow Rs. 10,000 on a *hundi* contract, a short-term high-interest promissory note, that stipulated that at the end of three months they would return Rs. 12,000. This was an agreement that required a high rate of profits for the fledgling industrialists. Each partner also con-

tributed Rs. 1,000. The partners' plan was to use the Rs. 14,000 to finance their fixed capital, but they still needed a place to manufacture.
For the time being they rented a small house on the outskirts of the city,
but the structure was inadequate for their needs, and, moreover, they
lacked adequate working capital.

Tambi then discovered that a new shed was being built at the Guindy
Industrial Estates in Madras, which he thought would be ideal for their
needs. The problem was how to win the lease. The estates are an established development run by the state government, and Tambi and his partners knew that competition for the lease was bound to be fierce. Again
they approached Annan. One of Annan's friends was a deputy director
in the Department of Industries and Commerce, which administered the
leases in the Guindy Estates. Annan told the four young men to take their
application to him. Subsequently, they succeeded in obtaining the lease,
although there were several other qualified applicants for the shed.

With their fixed capital and lease secured, they now approached the
branch of the State Bank of India attached to the Industrial Estate and
explained to the loan officer there that they had their own fixed capital
and were seeking a working capital loan. The State Bank, a state-run bureaucratic institution, administered a special scheme for industrial development. They required that applicants be university degree holders
whose application demonstrate that they had a viable project. As grad-
uates in engineering, and with Tambi's elder brother's charter accoun-
tant's help, the partners had no trouble writing a convincing application.
They got the loan. Their successes up to this point were a result of a com-
bination of personalized contacts and appearing to meet bureaucratic
regulations. However, without Tambi's elder brother's personal connections, the four partners would have lacked sufficient fixed capital and
the manufacturing shed, and so would not have qualified as a reliable
risk for the working capital loan under the bureaucratic criteria used by
the State Bank. The State Bank loan officer was also unaware of the high-
interest *hundi* loan, which in fact meant that the partners' enterprise involved very high risks.

Surprisingly, in the year that followed the partners managed to keep
their business afloat, and, seeing their success, Annan personally took over
the *hundi* loan at year's end, allowing the partners to reduce their interest
payments. Financially, things were beginning to look better, but profits
were still slim. By the end of that first year, the four realized that it was
going to take time to develop their market before they could expect to
make any real money. All but one decided, therefore, to go back to grad-

uate school in engineering. The exception was the partner who had been managing the business. He decided to enter management school instead.

The business continued for three more years, each partner attending school and contributing to the business in his spare time. They managed the business out of their dorm rooms on the IIT campus. When at last they all graduated, the manager, who had been talking to some of his management friends, decided to leave the business and to go to Bangalore to begin a new business, which he thought would earn him "big" money. The departure, however, was a tense one. The manager told his partners that they owed him back pay for his four years as manager. Shocked, Tambi told him that if he insisted on back pay, they would sue him for having ruined the business, since it was running at a loss at the time. To give force to his threat, Tambi told the manager, "Go see my lawyer." The lawyer was in actuality a good friend of Tambi's, and also happened to be the son-in-law of one of Annan's partners. The reader should notice how Tambi's access to Annan's veritable "cat's cradle" of social connections begins to emerge.

The manager decided to leave peacefully. However, unbeknownst to his partners, he went to the State Bank before he left and told the loan officer there that he was leaving the business and that, since he was the only one of the four who knew how to run it, the bank would be well advised to call the partners' loan. When the partners next tried to make a withdrawal from their capital account, they found that it had been frozen and the loan recalled. The partners' financial situation was desperate.

After several months of looking for a bank that would finance a capital loan, the three partners again approached Annan. In response, Annan arranged for Tambi to meet with the chairman of the Bank of Madurai, a large private bank founded and controlled by Nagarattars. Annan knew the chairman, and like many other Nagarattars, he conducted his business banking through this same bank. Without Annan's connections, Tambi says he would never have been able to arrange to see the chairman.

Tambi arrived at the meeting prepared with an accounts summary of his business. Annan explained Tambi's situation to the chairman, and then Tambi and the chairman talked informally "across the table." Tambi described his need for a loan to pay off and replace the one that the State Bank had recalled. To a banker, of course, the State Bank's refusal to continue the loan was very damaging information because it indicated that after four years of business the bank judged the partners a bad risk. This simple fact was the reason the partners had been unable to get another bank to consider a loan. The chairman, knowing this, also knew Tambi's brother Annan and that Annan was a reliable business-man of recognized stature in his own right who kept his business ac-counts at the bank and also happened to belong to his own caste. There is a common sentiment among prominent men of a caste that a leader owes it to his community on occasion to extend a helping hand to his caste fellows. Bonds are created that benefit both, the benefactor gain-ing a loyal supporter and the beneficiary receiving the benefaction. Af-ter a short chat, the chairman told Tambi to talk to his branch manager and that "everything would be done."

Reflecting on why he got the loan, Tambi told me that he thought be-ing a Nagarattar was important. "Most people working in the bank are Nagarattars," he said, "and if a Nagarattar with a degree knows some-one working in the bank, he can get a job there. A couple of my cousins work in the bank." Also critical was the fact that his brother had a strong, established relationship with the chairman. Had he been judged purely by bureaucratic criteria, Tambi is certain he would never have gotten the loan. Subsequently, the chairman helped the three partners with addi-tional loans, including capital loans for machinery. As a result, the busi-ness has grown and is now quite successful.

The account of Tambi and his partners reveals not only contrasts be-tween how bureaucratic and trust-based relationships work, but also how trust-based relationships link up with and center on men of influ-ence, "big-men." Consider the organization of the relationships used to acquire the Bank of Madurai loan and the agency of the individuals in-volved. The chairman enacts the role of a preeminent big-man, that is, a man who can make things happen because he controls an institution that distributes resources and services to a clientele. He is also a big-man because he wields substantial influence among prominent men, such as Annan, who are less powerful than he. In contrast to men of Annan's stature, relationships among preeminent big-men tend to be highly com-petitive; they do not help each other. Instead, they try to outdo one an-other, each seeking to achieve the reputation of being first among the preeminent. Annan, by contrast, plays the role of one of the chairman's lieutenants; he is a subordinate big-man because, while he has influence and can affect the outcome of events, his influence is less than the chair-man's. He needs people like the chairman from time to time. Indeed, be-cause he is a beneficiary of the chairman's influence (he benefits as a banking patron and by being able to help his brother), he may be counted a member of the chairman's clientele. At the same time, as a man "with connections," Annan also has his own constituency that incorporates Tambi and his two partners among others. In turn, Tambi is a member of the constituencies of both Annan and, through him, the chairman. Finally, Tambi's connections make him the benefactor of his partners, who in turn are members of his constituency. The relationships joining the men are in each instance unequal and are based on personal rather than bureaucratic ties.

The hierarchical interlinked nature of all of these relationships and how to work them is well understood by all the parties involved; consequently, they go largely unstated. People recognize that the chairman is a big-man because of his preeminent power and control of desired resources, and out of his earshot people will call him a *periyar*. By contrast, "lieutenant," "constituent," and "clientele" are my terms, which I am using to ease the reader's understanding. My informants, while they have an intimate sense of the relationships these terms label, including the subtleties of relationships involved and the degrees of power represented, do not use these terms to refer to one another. Instead, they talk about a person's connections with big-men—how good they are—and who a person knows. They also appreciate a man who helps them and imbue him with eminence because he does. Eminence is the basis of a man's prestige and all Tamils, particularly men, strive for it. And eminence is graded: the eminence of powerful persons who have large constituencies is greater than that of persons who are less influential. A direct measure of eminence is the institutions that a person heads or is an officer in and the size of the population that these institutions serve.

THE INDIVIDUAL AS FOCUS OF ORGANIZATION

In Indian society, pivotal persons such as *periyar* exhibit a special form of public individuality, which I call an "individuality of eminence,"[7] because public recognition of a leader's uniqueness stems in part from the fact that the leader ranks first among his or her followers. This kind of individuality is expressed in part by the special influence and autonomy that leaders have within groups and by their abilities to distribute benefits and command others to do their bidding. The individuality of leaders, therefore, is not that of one unique person among many similar unique persons, as some characterize Western egalitarian individualism. Rather it is a type that is marked by the superiority of leaders over their followers. In the West, leaders often seek to identify themselves as one among their constituents, as expressed in the U.S., for example, by the presidential phrase, "My fellow Americans." By contrast, in Tamil society, leaders are recognized as self-interested patrons who rank above their constituents. Leaders use their constituents who in turn use them.

The individuality of eminence is associated in Tamil Nadu with a special type of group formation, the "leader-centered group." This kind of group is an association that forms around a central figure, a man like the chairman, and his subordinate lieutenants, men like Annan, and is maintained by ties of relationship that link the central leader to all members of his group. The preeminent big-man of such a group is always the controlling officer of corporate institutions that he uses to distribute benefits and attract a clientele. A few of his subordinate lieutenants will be junior officers in these institutions and will serve only him. Others, such as Annan, lack offices in the preeminent big-man's institutions, but are persons who bring clientele into his constituency because of their own personal relationship with him. Lieutenants like Annan may have ties with several preeminent big-men, just as a big-man's ordinary clients may also maintain ties with several preeminent men. A big-man serves different sets of clientele with each institution that he controls. Consequently, the total constituency composing a leader-centered group is an aggregate of his lieutenants, the separate constituencies attracted by each of these lieutenants, and the distinct clientele served by each of the preeminent big-man's separate institutions.

Although leader-centered groups are themselves not corporate, the institutions that the preeminent big-man controls usually are. Nonetheless, these too are the organizations of their central leader, and when that leader dies or grows too old to command, often they decline or splinter into new leader-centered institutions, each organized around a new central figure and his personal following. This pattern is typical of a range of institutions, including joint families, caste associations, community charities (Mines and Gourishankar 1990), cooperatives (Mines 1984), and political parties in Tamil Nadu today.[8] This pattern is also true of privately owned banks such as the chairman's, if to a somewhat lesser degree, despite the direct bureaucratic control over banks exercised by the central government. For example, consider how who the chairman is (a member of the Nagarattar caste) and knows (Annan, himself a Nagarattar) has affected how he conducts business (favoring Nagarattars) and whom he employs (again, Nagarattars). Should the bank fall into the hands of a non-Nagarattar, for example, bank policies will change, just as who the new chair knows and relies upon will change, whatever the new chair's caste may be.

A key expression of a Tamil leader's individuality is the leader's public reputation. In Tamil society, the reputation of a respected leader is somewhat paradoxical. Eminent leaders are often economically successful, reflecting their skill as pursuers of self-interest. However, to avoid accusations of venality, a leader must circumscribe his or her successes with a reputation for altruism, honesty, and a commitment to the collective good of the community. In other words, a leader must achieve a reputation for behavior that is in effect a denial of self-interest. Yet, leaders also want people to know that it is they who are altruistic. A leader's patronage is not given anonymously, but publicly, with the knowledge of his community. It is to commemorate their altruism that community leaders typically engrave their names on the stairs and walls of temples, marriage halls, charitable societies, and libraries. They also publish their names and sometimes their pictures in the posters, announcements, invitations, and book-sized souvenirs that are associated with public events in order to make known who they are and to advertise their individual responsibility for deeds done for the benefit of their public.

Achieving simultaneously a reputation for both success and altruism is difficult because the two are seen as contradictory. Consequently, it is no surprise that the more successful a leader is, the more he or she will be accused of venality and corruption. This helps to explain the highly acrimonious nature of leadership in south Indian society.

In Tamil culture, the archetypal way a leader establishes a reputation for altruism is through patronage and involvement in institutions established to serve the interests of a constituency. By acquiring offices in such institutions and rights to symbolic honors associated with them, leaders dramatize their eminence and place themselves at the center of a clientele that they seek to serve. Competition for offices and honors is a part of the achievement strategy of leaders and would-be leaders alike.

In sum, the individuality of Tamil leaders lacks the characterizing values some scholars (e.g., Dumont 1970a) have associated with Western individualism, notably equality and liberty, which are associated with the sense of the individual as an equal among equals.[9] Nonetheless, the identity of leaders does exhibit several other features of socially significant individuality, including individualistic social identity defined by public reputation, uniqueness marked by eminence, achieved identity associated with a deliberate striving after one's own gain, dominance and prestige, and autonomy marked by responsibility for who one is and what one does. This form of public individuality, the individuality of eminence, therefore, rests on a recognition of achievement and of the individual as an agent.

KASI'S STORY:
A TAMIL BIG-MAN EXPLAINS HIS CIVIC IDENTITY

I interviewed "Kasi," Kasiviswanathan, in his home in 1979, in the town of Trichengode, which is located in the western dry zone of interior Tamil Nadu. The town is a pilgrimage site because of its famous Saivite temple, dedicated to Ardhanariiswarar—Siva represented in a half male, half female form. The temple offers a dramatic sight, located on the top of a giant rock at the town's edge.

Born in 1912, Kasi was sixty-seven years old at the time of my interview and still very much involved in public life. He belonged to a Tamil weaving caste, the Kaikkoolars, and was well known in the region as a caste and political party leader.

As a younger man, Kasi had been a follower of the famous Tamil independence leader, "Rajaji," C. Rajagopalachariya, and until his forty-fifth year, was the president of the *taluk* (subdistrict) Congress committee. The Congress was the leading party of India's independence movement and the dominant political force in Tamil Nadu until the mid-1960s. I had been told by acquaintances of Kasi's that I must go to Trichengode just so I could meet him. Kasi was recommended to me in this manner because his friends considered him an important man, a man of accomplishment, one of the big-men of his caste. In their recommendation, his acquaintances described to me features of his individuality: his importance, offices, and reputation for past actions. Stressing Kasi's eminence, his friends emphasized his individuality.

When I interviewed Kasi, we met at his house. It was after lunch and the atmosphere was quiet; most in the household were taking their afternoon naps, as is the Tamil custom. On the wall was a signed photograph of Jawaharlal Nehru, dated 1929. Kasi had the relaxed manner of someone who had been interviewed many times before, but he seemed happy to be of service to me for a few hours.

When I begin a life story interview, I usually start by asking my informant about family—his or her parents and siblings, date of marriage, children, their education and what it is that they are doing today. Completing this section of the interview, I next ask my informant about himself or herself.

Kasi had a precise sense of what it was he needed to tell me so that I would know who he was and what he did and had done. His approach was identical to the way I had heard others describe themselves when they, like Kasi, had achieved some degree of eminence. He related to me first his status as the head of his family and family businesses. Next, he listed his current civic offices, and then he described the institutional offices that he had held earlier in his lifetime.

He said that he was the proprietor of all his family's businesses, meaning by this that he was still the head of his own joint family. He and his wife lived with their second son, while his three other sons lived separately. Nonetheless, all five men together managed the several enterprises that they jointly owned under Kasi's proprietorship. Kasi also ran a textile sizing business, which he owned in partnership with one of his brothers.

Kasi next described to me the offices he currently held in various civic institutions. At the time of the interview, he was headman (*naaṭṭaan-maikaarar*) of the Kaikkoolar caste council in Trichengode and the joint-headman of the caste's territorial council for a region incorporating seven cities and their surrounding village hinterlands, known as the Seven City Territory (Eeṟuurunaaḍu). Trichengode was the territory's headquarters. In other words, Kasi was telling me that he was one of two preeminent caste leaders for the seven cities area. Next, Kasi said that he was the president of seven religious institutions and the president of a committee that collected construction funds for the Trichengode Government High School. He told me the committee had already built eleven rooms for the school, three in his family's name. When Kasi spoke of his family's name, he meant his name as family head. He had also built under his leadership and in his family's name a marriage hall for his caste, which was located in front of the rock temple, an auspicious location. He said ten to thirty marriages were conducted there by his caste fellows every year. Finally, he said, he was also a member of the Trichengode Rotary Club, an association that kept him in touch with all the associations in town. He kept his finger on the pulse of local events, he said, and remarked that his second son had been the joint secretary of the Junior Chamber of Commerce the previous year.

Next Kasi described civic offices that he had held in the past. Until 1977, he had been the vice president of the statewide handloom weaver's cooperative society, Cooptex, an important post. A friend, caste mate, and close political ally was the society's president. Kasi had also been a member of the state's Handloom Board for ten years and director of three cooperative spinning mills, located in Salem, Tirunelveli, and Srivilliputtur. And he had been the director of the Cooperative Union in Tamil Nadu, which is an advisory board to the government on production cooperatives. Finally, as mentioned above, when he was younger and had political ambitions, he had been the president of the Congress Party Taluk Committee.

At the time, I remember realizing that Kasi's purpose in describing his institutional offices was not simply to list his accomplishments for me, but primarily to describe his role as an institutional leader with multiple constituencies, some small, some large. His description reveals the contextual nature of civic identity and its spatial dimension, which expands and contracts in relationship to the size of a leader's constituencies. Over time, the size of the populations Kasi had served had changed substantially. Once he had been a state-level leader. Until his retirement from Cooptex in 1977, Kasi had served a statewide constituency that he had helped build. The handloom textile cooperative movement took its inspiration from Mahatma Gandhi and was until 1977 controlled by members of the Congress Party, which used it for the distribution of largess and the building of grassroots support. In those days, the handloom weaving industry was the largest category of employment after agriculture in the state, and so Cooptex appealed to what was theoretically a significant pool of potential political supporters. Throughout the state under Cooptex auspices, local leaders founded or managed production cooperatives, which tapped into the statewide association, enabling them to enact roles as patrons within their local weaving communities. Kasi told me that when a weavers' housing colony was built in Trichengode with Cooptex support, it was named after him, although he himself had favored naming it after Rajaji. As president of the Congress Party Taluk Committee, therefore, and vice president of Cooptex, Kasi was for a time a patron of statewide influence and eminence.

In 1979, when I interviewed him, Kasi was a leading townsman and regional caste leader serving a much smaller constituency. As co-headman of the Seven City Territory, he shared his preeminence as a caste leader with only one other man. That night, following the interview (see Mines 1984), I had the opportunity to observe Kasi in his role as headman during a council meeting that the leaders and representatives of the subcouncils of the territory attended. Kasi sat on a raised dais surrounded by the subordinate headmen and representatives of the Seven City Territory, and when I entered the meeting room, I had an immediate sense of his power. He was a chief among his lieutenants, a man with the power to outcaste or impose fines on any local council that failed to adhere to Kaikkoolar caste rules regarding the governing of councils. That night the council of one of the towns that had been outcaste by a previous action came to plead for readmission. Symbolic of its submission, throughout the discussion of the case, a servant of the council lay prostrate on the ground, his arms outstretched before Kasi and his fellow Eeṛuurunaaḍu Council members.

Yet the caste council was only one of the many institutions within which Kasi held a preeminent role at the time of the interview. The other associations he described himself as heading were what Tamils term charitable institutions. The constituencies of these institutions—the seven religious institutions, the school building fund committee, and the caste marriage hall—were much smaller than that of the caste council. Each of these institutions, however, enabled Kasi to play the role of patron. As patron, Kasi cast himself in the role of an altruistic leader dedicated to the service of his community, his clients. He told me that he had donated Rs. 30,000 to the school building fund. Through these many institutions Kasi built for himself a grassroots political constituency, based on his personalized relationship with the circles of clients associated with each of the many institutions he managed.

Listening to Kasi describe himself, I realized that his intent was to make clear to me his public self. He was telling me that his eminence, his institutional roles, and his influence among others distinguished him. These features define Kasi's "civic individuality." Kasi even described his identity within his family in these terms, stating that he was the head of his joint family and proprietor of all his family's businesses. It also became apparent that having control over decisions affecting himself and others, an ability which is associated with statuses of eminence, was an important feature of his individuality because control gave him autonomy.

When a person such as Kasi describes his civic identity, his telling is filled with implied authority, but it is also always impersonal, revealing little about the inner man. This impersonality is a distinguishing feature of the way Tamil men express the civic dimension of their individuality. It was later, when I asked Kasi about his personal goals and dreams that he told another story, the story of his motivations, hopes, and disappointments. In his telling, he revealed himself as an idealistic young man who had entered politics in the heady days of Mahatma Gandhi, Rajaji, and the Indian Independence Movement. Kasi personally had known Rajaji. He told me that politicians then were motivated by ideas and ideals, while today politics is "all personalities." Politicians no longer

care about ideas. He regretted the years he had spent as a politician after Independence was achieved, and he was disgusted with modern politicians. He felt betrayed by them.

The layered way in which Kasi reveals his identity is typical of men
who have achieved some public eminence in their lives: First they tell of
their civic identity. It is later, when they are questioned about their goals
and aspirations, that they reveal the private dimensions of their lives.
Civic lives and private selves are not, then, two separate identities. Kasi
has a sense of himself within society and a sense of how others know
him. He also has an inner awareness of himself. Each of Kasi's senses of
who he is affects the other. Personal talents and abilities, private desires,
hopes, and disappointments drive motivations and give force to achievement in civic life. They energize its drama and pathos. They lie behind
the manifest public individual. (Tamil descriptions of the inner self are
the subject of chapters 7 and 8.)

Finally, it must be noted that Kasi did not describe his individuality
in opposition to groups, but rather in terms of who he was and what he
did within groups. In this context, it is important to distinguish between
Kasi's civic identity and what Dumont labels a collective identity. In the
latter case, the person has the identity of his or her group. In Kasi's case,
his identity is his own, but it is an identity that is built on his eminence
within groups, an aspect of his contextualized identity.

THE COMMUNITY AND THE INDIVIDUAL

The examples of the goldsmith, Tambi, and Kasi illustrate the importance
in Tamil society of personalized relationships and of leader-centered
groups, configurations of interaction that require a close connection
between organization and individual agency. But just how important are
the agency of leaders or the actions of ordinary persons as influences on
the way urban communities are organized and integrated? Part of the answer lies in how civic individuality is valued. I have suggested that eminence implies a community that shares values, as does reputation. What,
then, is the relationship between these values, which are features of the
interaction between individuality and community, and the formation and
dynamics of an Indian urban community? Or, put differently, what does
an Indian urban community look like, and how does its appearance reflect this interaction between shared values and individual interests and
agency? And finally, just how important are communities, castes, and individual identities in a large cosmopolitan Indian city today? What are

the motivations and involvement of ordinary citizens in community, and what are the currents of change?

I argue in the chapters that follow that the relationship between individual and community has been historically dynamic in India, and that, as circumstances change, individuals rework their relationships with their communities. In the process, they transform the meaning of both citizenship and community. Leaders are important agents of this community transformation. Forever competing to enlarge their constituencies, they must from time to time redefine what they consider their own interests in light of changing circumstances and adjust how they make their appeals to ordinary citizens to suit.

The roles and motivations of individuals are reflected not only by the organization of urban relationships but also by an urban community's very structure and layout. I take as the focus of my study the old walled town of Madras City in Tamil Nadu, south India, the area of the city that is today known as George Town. I argue that the organization of George Town reflects the history of a series of Indian solutions to the problem of how, in the highly competitive context of commerce, to guarantee trust and reliability in relationships. What the organization of the urban community shows is that the freedom of the individual is always circumscribed by an ethic that sets the standards by which the civic individual in different roles must behave in order to establish trust-based relationships. Individuality is not eliminated by this imposition of constraints on behavior but, rather, is emphasized, although emphasized differently from the way it is in the West.

CHAPTER THREE

Institutions and Big-men of a Madras City Community

George Town Today

George Town and Fort St. George, just to its south, are the oldest parts of Madras City (see map 2). One can still see fragments of the old wall fortifications that once circumscribed and protected George Town, while the fort still has its walls and traces of its moat. The fort must be entered through heavy iron-studded doors, which remind the visitor of the uncertain peace of former times. Within the old walled area of the Town the streets are narrow, often choked with every sort of vehicle, cycle rickshaws carrying boxes of freight, small children on their way to or from school, and sometimes men holding great sheets of metal, which they have purchased for purposes unknown to the observer, slowly being pedaled among the crowds; there are brightly painted lorries, hand-pulled carts, bullock carts, bicycles, scooters, automobiles, and auto rickshaws buzzing about the Town's outer edges, trying to avoid getting stuck in the traffic jams. Pedestrians clog the streets' remaining spaces.

The Town is the financial center of Madras. American Express has its office here, and so does the Madras Stock Exchange. The Town is where the descendants of Madras City's oldest banks are located; it is also a center of informal banking. The big moneylenders, the "shroffs" of old, dealers in bullion and cash, operate here, so too, the Cashiers, the Kasukaarar,[1] the accountants of the big banks and enterprises. George Town is also the business center of the city. Madras harbor lies just across the railroad tracks on the Town's eastern edge. Once there was no harbor, only the open sand beach on which small wooden boats departed and landed through the persistent surf, ferrying goods and people to and

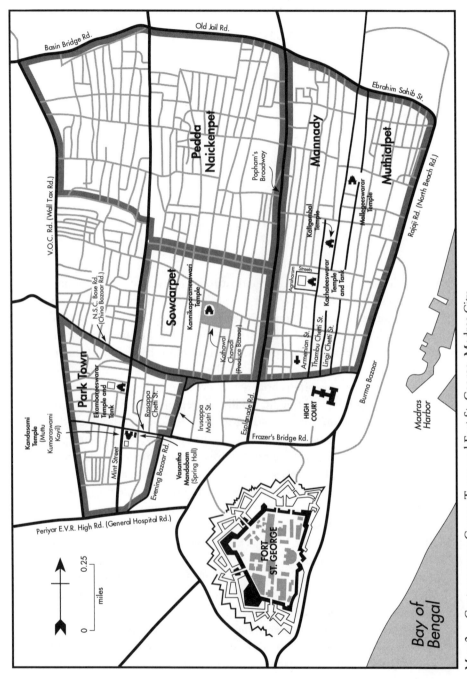

Map 2. Contemporary George Town and Fort St. George, Madras City.

Figure 2.   A view along First Line Beach Road. The photo was taken from the roof of the Beach Railway Station. The large building on the left is the local head office, State Bank of India, formerly the Imperial Bank of India during the colonial period. George Town, 1992.

from ships anchored at sea in the "Madras Roads." Today, Madras has an artificial harbor, which is fitted to receive the giant container ships that ply international waters, although one can still see ships like tiny dashes on the distant horizon, "standing" in the roads waiting their turn in the harbor. For convenience, the Custom House and the General Post Office, the city's main post office, are located near the harbor on North Beach Road, now renamed Rajaji Road.

As the city's business center, the range of enterprises, large and small, located in the Town area is extensive: jewelers, gem dealers, book sellers and publishers, moneylenders and bankers, wholesalers and retailers of iron and steel, nonferrous metals, textiles, fancy feathers for the fly-fishing industry, fireworks, electrical goods, leather, pharmaceutics, locks, and metal hinges—the list is enormous. Several of the oldest business houses, houses whose names reflect their British colonial past, have home offices here: Binny's, Best and Crompton, Castrol, Parry's, Gordon Woodroffe. This area of the Town, just across from the harbor, is called Muthialpet. Mannady, the adjacent area to the southwest, is considered by old residents to be an integral part of the Muthialpet neighborhood. Popham's Broadway, running north and south, marks the western edge of this eastern section of George Town.

Across Broadway, inland and to the west, is the old community of Pedda Naickenpet, although, today, this area, too, is subdivided. The northern section is still called Pedda Naickenpet, but the southern section is now called Sowcarpet. North Indian Hindu and Jain merchants live here in large numbers, and south Indians say that they feel transported to north India when they step into these streets. Sowcarpet is where many of the big moneylenders, gem dealers, and some of the Tamil-speaking goldsmiths live and operate. The buildings are mostly old houses to which one or two stories have been added over time. On the narrow veranda of one, a goldsmith and his three assistants manufacture 22-karat-gold bangles and necklace "chains." Nearby, a Jain gem dealer sits resting against a long white bolster, talking quietly to another man, his wooden desk cum money-box by his side. Large sums of money change hands in these modest surroundings.

At its heart, Sowcarpet incorporates the city's main green grocers market, Kothawal Chavadi, where I once bought one hundred limes for Rs. 2, about U.S. $0.26 at that time. Business is so intense here that wholesalers rent shop space by the hour. A single shop may have several tenants operating in series, each for a few hours, through the course of the twenty-four-hour day.

Just to the south of Sowcarpet is Park Town, famous for its jewelers and iron merchants and the location of George Town's most popular temple, the Muttu Kumaraswami, or Kandasami temple.[2] This is the temple to which I was going on a rainy night in September 1985, to begin my fieldwork in George Town.

It was my plan over the next ten months to study leadership and individuality among two of the Town's prominent castes, the Beeri Chettiars, one of the foremost merchant castes of the Town, and the artisan caste once named the Kammaalans (Smiths),[3] now usually called Acharis or Viswakarmas. The Beeri Chettiars had been close associates of the British, from the founding of Madras in 1639, up to Indian Independence in 1947. I had chosen the Viswakarmas because they, like the Beeri Chettiars, had once been a leading caste of the left-hand section of castes in Madras City. Their historic rivals were the castes of the right-hand section, especially the famous merchants, the Komati Chettiars, the community that owned and controlled Kothawal Chavadi. While these once bitter rivalries and the left-hand/right-hand moiety division that framed them are now memories, and although today's descendants of these castes pride themselves on their friendly relations, the history of Madras is marked and shaped by riots and competition between the two factions. The area east of Popham's Broadway, Mannady and Muthialpet, was once the territory of the left-hand castes, the area to the west, Pedda Naickenpet, the territory of the right-hand castes. What legacy had this old division of the Town left behind to shape the civic communities of today?

A few days before my first night of fieldwork, I had been discussing my research intentions over tea with an acquaintance, C. Gourishankar, and his friend, "Babu." Babu, recently retired, had volunteered that one of his former colleagues at All India Radio was a Beeri Chetti who also happened to be the head managing trustee of the Kandasami temple in George Town. I asked him if he could help me contact this man. I thought he might make a good starting point for my research.

Babu made the arrangements. We were to meet with his former colleague, Tiru P. Balasubramaniyam ("Bala"), at the temple office a few nights later. Babu had explained my interest to Balasubramaniyam, and he, "Bala," had indicated that he would try to have present at the meeting a few knowledgeable older men of the community.

Although it was beginning to rain, the three of us—Babu, Gourishankar, and I—managed to find an auto rickshaw willing to take us to the Town. It was dark and wet when we arrived at the temple. We left our sandals at the sandal concession next to the temple's main entrance and entered through the Raja Gopuram, the kingly tower that faced onto the street. High on the tower's face a neon sign depicted in Tamil the word "Om," the primeval sound of meditation. Inside, the temple was stone and cement, cavernous; we made our way toward the back, past a video shop selling religious films, to the office. Several men, all Beeri Chettiars, sat around a table. Along one wall were large steel cabinets, marked with sandalwood paste and *vibuti*, symbols of Siva.

Over the next two hours, Bala and his associates spoke rapidly, sometimes singly, sometimes several at once, so that it was all that I could do

Figure 3.   Rasappa Chetti Street showing the Kandasami temple entrance tower
or Raja Gopuram. George Town, 1992.

simply to follow what was being said, let alone take the kind of notes I
wanted to. In those two hours, this small group of men outlined what
they thought I should know about the Beeri Chettiars of George Town.
They told me about the Kandasami temple, its history, and why it was
important to the Beeri Chettiars of George Town. They told me the
names, families, and brief particulars of who in their memory had been
the leading men of the Beeri Chettiar community before families had begun to move away from the crowds and congestion of George Town.

Figure 4.   Kandasami temple roof line.

The list included bankers, the cashiers of important British companies, a lawyer politician, and several very wealthy merchants. A few leaders had belonged to families in which sons or sons-in-law had succeeded fathers and fathers-in-law as influential men. I could tell that everyone present knew of these men, including the non-Beeri Chettiar friends who had come with me, even though some of the leaders had been dead for decades. Among those present, there was a shared sense of the George Town Beeri Chettiars as a community distinguished by who its leading citizens had been. It was also clear that several temples and especially the Kandasami temple figured importantly in both the identity of the community and its leading men. Bala then told me who he was and described the schools and charitable institutions that he had helped found as a leader within his community. Next the men told me a little of the history of the Beeri Chettiars in George Town. It was their sense that the community vitality that had prevailed in their youth was weakening. Families had moved away, and now people often did not even know who their neighbors were. Bala said it was a goal of his, as head trustee of the

Kandasami temple, to reestablish some of the old sense of community. Finally, the men described some of the relationships the Beeri Chettiars had with other temples and other neighborhoods in Madras and surrounding towns. What they were describing to me, albeit in outline, was the identity of their civic community—a community that they saw as threatened, a community that was identified with its preeminent men, its temples, and its institutions—and the relationship to that community that Bala and some of the other leading members of the caste held as individuals. These were the topics upon which my research was to concentrate. They were giving me a quick overview. There are several features of this overview that told me much about the nature and role of civic individuality in Madras today.

When I left the meeting at about ten that night, it was raining heavily and the city was dark. The city lights had failed in the storm and the streets were flooded in places. The normally congested streets of George Town were almost deserted except for a few men wading slowly through the deep puddles.

EXPLORING THE NATURE
OF THE "INSTITUTIONAL" BIG-MAN

Later, thinking about what Bala and his friends had said, I was struck by how personalized their description of the Beeri Chettiars in George Town had been. Names had flown about the room as they had described the caste's past and present distinguished men, the caste's *periyar*.[4] They had told me which houses had belonged to these men, who they were related to, what they had done, and what their roles in businesses and civic institutions had been. My friend Gourishankar, aged sixty, obviously had known who they were talking about. He had known some of the men when, forty years before, he had attended Christian College, which in his day had been located in George Town. Reflecting on what had been said, I realized Bala and his friends had described their community to me in terms of its big-men and their institutions. I realized that if I were to share their sense of familiarity with their community, I needed to understand what it meant to be a Beeri Chettiar big-man.

In the months that followed, I was to hear informants use a number of terms denoting leaders. I have listed some of these in my previous chapters. In addition to the term *periyar*, I learned that *periyadanakaarar* (big-gift-giver) is a related term in a class of similar terms for informal leaders, including *talaivar* (headman) and *ejamaanan* (master, headman).

These terms are used to mark the preeminence of persons within their communities and, in some cases of special fame, within the larger society. *Mahatma* is a similar Sanskrit term, familiar as a designation for Mohandas K. Gandhi, and lexical equivalents of the Tamil terms for big-man are general to Indian languages. In fact, Pedda Naickenpet, the name for the area of George Town west of Popham's Broadway, conveys this same sense of big-man. *Pedda* is Telugu for "big," and *Pedda Naickenpet* means the place (*pet*) of the "Big Naicken," the title of the headman who used to control this part of the Town in the early years of British East India Company trade. During those early times, in the shadow of the Telugu-speaking Vijayanagar Chiefdoms, the Naicker caste was politically dominant in the locality.

As the head trustee (*dharmakarttaa*) of the Kandasami temple, Bala is himself an "institutional" big-man among the George Town Beeri Chettiars. As indicated in chapter 2, I add the "institutional" qualifier to the Indian big-man concept because men like Bala attract followers and enact their roles as generous leaders through the "charitable" institutions that they control.[5] For south Indians, a "charitable institution" is a highly personalized leader-centered association or group that is designed by its founder or leader to benefit a particular clientele, constituency, or community. The leader attracts a following by the benefits he provides. In return, his followers reward him with prestige and an eminent reputation, attributes that give him great influence and discretion among his constituents. When his eminence is great and his institutions particularly effective, then a big-man's reputation also spreads among outsiders. People will know that he is a man responsible for getting things done among his constituents. Like Annan's banker of the previous chapter, an important big-man is a very valuable person with whom to have connections. In Bala's case, the Kandasami temple is one of several community institutions that he heads, but he founds his reputation and so his leadership in these other institutions on his role as the head trustee of the Kandasami temple.

Institutional position is a necessary condition for the viability of the Indian big-man, but it is not sufficient. In keeping with their highly personalized nature, Indian institutions, including temples, expand and contract in popularity and membership depending on the idiosyncratic charisma of their heads. Although it is often supposed that local Indian leaders can depend on ready-made caste and kin constituencies, the fact is that even hereditary leaders have few followers when they lack charisma and skill. Indian society is salted throughout by these "hollow

crowns"—would-be leaders, the heads of associations who have little or
no following (see Dirks 1987). In the case of the Kandasami temple,
townspeople told me that they thought Bala a particularly effective
leader and that the popularity of the temple has greatly increased during his tenure as head trustee.

As I reflected further on my hosts' naming of their community's past
big-men, I began to be aware that knowing the names and offices of many
people is a concomitant of leader-centered group organization. I sensed
that if a person wishes to navigate a fruitful public life in a society composed of such highly personalized institutions, then it is important to
know who heads and is responsible for what, as well as who has connections with whom. This is one of the reasons why Tamils keep tabs
on so many people. A person who can claim good connections with influential people finds it is easier to accomplish social objectives and to
influence others. Knowledge of this sort and the ability to claim connections is valuable and can be misused by dishonest persons. Reflecting this, when much later in my fieldwork I was collecting Bala's genealogy, he suddenly remarked that the information I was gathering
could be valuable to unscrupulous persons who might use the information to claim close ties with him. He asked me to be careful to whom I
showed it.

Why, then, did Bala and his friends list the past leaders of their community? It was clear to me from the way they spoke of these men that
they did so in order to stress that who the George Town Beeri Chettiars
are today is in part built upon their community's connections with men
of prominence and responsibility from their recent past. They see their
community as a composite of families and other associations that big-
men head and the connections that exist among these elements, a community centered on eminent persons, their institutions and groups, and
on the connections that link them, forever in the making.

TEMPLE, TRUSTEES, DONORS,
AND THE CIVIC COMMUNITY

A Tamil villager once told me that a community without a temple was
unfit for residence. The temple, he said, indicates that the community is
graced by the presence of God and that its citizens form a moral community. A community identifies and is identified by others with its temples. Bala and other Beeri Chettiars went to considerable length to explain to me the nature of their community's identification with the

Kandasami temple and the role that big-men played as its patrons and managers. The temple and its functions symbolize the caste community, and publicize its leading associations and who its leading men are. Stories about the temple's history and endowments reveal as much.

That night in the temple office, Bala and his friends described the Kandasami temple as a "denominational" temple, meaning a temple controlled and managed by a single caste community, in this instance, themselves, the George Town Beeri Chettiars. What makes the temple a particularly important institution of big-man leadership among the Beeri Chettiars today is that it is the primary and by far the wealthiest institution controlled by the caste as a whole and, in much the same manner that villagers use their temples, it is used by leaders to represent the caste as a civic and moral community to the world at large. It is also importantly a charitable institution, the caste's central repository of resources that exist for the benefit of the caste as a civic community. An individual who is elected to the managing board of trustees of the temple is elected, therefore, to a position of leadership within the Beeri Chettiar community with control over its main assets. Among the five trustees of the temple, the head trustee, the *dharmakarttaa*, is preeminent. It is Bala who holds this position. He is the *periyar*, the big-man, and he is a preeminent figure in his community.

Until 1980, the electorate of the Kandasami temple included only male Beeri Chettiars who lived in Muthialpet, Mannady,[6] and Park Town, but because by that time increasing numbers of families had moved to other parts of the city, caste leaders changed the bylaws of the temple to include in its congregation male Beeri Chettiars living or doing business anywhere in greater Madras City (Madras High Court records). The Madras Beeri Chettiars, therefore, today form the temple leaders' constituency. And this constituency, as a group, constitutes the caste's civic community defined most broadly. But even with this change in bylaws, the Park Town-Muthialpet Beeri Chettiars constitute the core congregation of the temple, and temple trustees have always been selected from among the caste's George Town leaders. It is these leaders who are and always have been the principal donors to the temple and sponsors of temple functions, and it is because of them, and because of the location of the temple, that George Town remains the geographic heart of the Beeri Chettiar's sense of their civic community in Madras City.

Because popular temples such as the Kandasami temple are important institutions of civic leadership, control of them is often contested. In George Town, the leaders of several castes would like to gain special rights in the temple, and some conspire to dislodge the present temple trustees with this aim in mind. These contenders pursue a variety of strategies, among them bringing lawsuits claiming that members of other castes have made donations to the temple and so, since the Beeri Chettiars are not its sole financiers, they should not be its exclusive managers.

In and out of court, Bala and his allies have countered these pleas, asserting that the caste's right to exclusive control of the Kandasami temple is based on what they argue has been more than three hundred years of unbroken management and on a legend that the temple was founded by two old friends, Velur Mari Chettiar, a Beeri Chettiar, and Kandappa Achari, a Viswakarma man. According to this legend, the two friends were on their monthly pilgrimage to worship Lord Murugan at Tiruporur, fifty-six kilometers away, when they miraculously discovered the idol of Kandasami hidden in an anthill and brought it back to Madras. There, on an auspicious day in 1673, they installed and consecrated the deity in a temple dedicated to the elephant god, Vinayakar, located in the garden of one Muthiyalu Naicken of Pedda Naickenpet. Subsequently, when Mari Chettiar sought to build a temple for the deity, funded in part by his wife's generous gift of her jewelry, Muthiyalu donated the Park Town lands on which the temple now stands. When Mari completed the temple, he handed its management and that of its financial trusts to the "eighteen group" Beeri Chettiars, the eighteen named clusters (*gumbuhaḷ*; sing., *gumbu*) that composed the Town Beeri Chettiar community at that time. In commemoration of his services, the Beeri Chettiars installed a statue of Mari Chetti near one of the temple's sanctums, where he is worshiped today as a god. Here we see an individual, Mari Chetti, being commemorated for what he had done.

Aside from this legend, lists of donations, and a few undocumented stories, little specific historical detail is known of the temple. Nonetheless, challenges by covetous leaders of other castes to the exclusive control of the temple by the leaders of the George Town Beeri Chettiars have been unsuccessful so far. What historical evidence there is of Beeri Chettiar control has been too strong.

From archival materials, endowment records, and stone inscriptions in the temple we do know that Beeri Chettiar control of the temple is at least two hundred years old. F. L. Conradi's 1755 map (map 3) of "Madraspatnam," as the city was then called, depicts a small unnamed shrine at what is the temple's location today (Love 1913, 2: endpocket-map). We know that the temple was renovated and sanctified as a brick temple in 1780 by the "eighteen group Beeri Chettiars." We know that

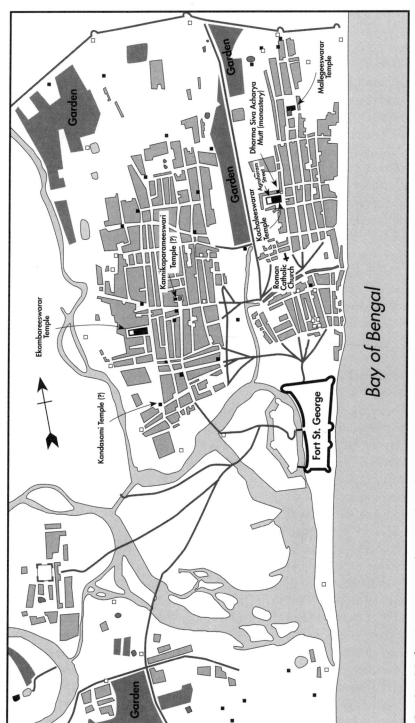

Map 3. Madras in 1755. Based on "A Plan of Fort St. George and The Bounds of Madraspatnam" by F. L. Conradi.

about 1865 the temple was rebuilt of stone in its present form, and that in 1869 a generous man named Vaiyabari Chettiar donated Rs. 66,000, an enormous sum in those days, to establish a trust to fund various temple functions. He also built the large temple car (*teer*) in which the processional idol of the god is carried on the seventh day of the main annual festival (*brahmootsavam*). We also know that around 1880 Akkamapettai Govinda Chettiar and Narayana Chettiar donated the land next to the temple for the purpose of building a large community hall, the Spring Hall (Vasantha Mandabam). And we know that in 1901 Kaḷi Raṭṭina Chettiar, a wealthy businessman and the father-in-law of Bala's father-in-law, donated Rs. 50,000 to build the temple's entrance tower (*gopuram*) and, in a dramatic gesture still spoken of with awe, gave a cup of diamonds for jewelry to decorate the idol.

Richly endowed, the temple today owns more than sixty houses, most located on prime urban land. The head temple priest's house, which is rented to him by the temple, gives an idea of values. In 1986, its worth was estimated at Rs. 10–15 lakhs (1 lakh equals 100,000 rupees), $100,000 or more at a 1986 rate of exchange. A few of the endowments have been especially grand. The previously mentioned gift of a cup of diamonds and Rs. 50,000 by Kaḷi Raṭṭina Chettiar is one of these, a gift that in those days was worth many times the value of a house. Another is Bala's uncle Venugopal Chettiar's gift to the temple of ten grounds of urban land, which are today the site of a one-thousand-student Beeri Chettiar grammar school founded under Bala's administration. Other endowments sponsor particular festivals; they buy flowers and textiles for rituals and clothes for the deity. Yet others fund building, renovations, and cultural events. Today the temple controls hundreds of millions of rupees in assets.

The rich endowment of the temple reflects its popularity and the affluence of the Beeri Chettiars. As a measure of the temple's lively appeal, the temple concession that looks after the sandals of worshipers annually earns about Rs. 36,000 by charging customers a small fee of ten paise[7] for safeguarding their footwear while they go barefoot into the temple. Given that many locals leave their sandals at home when they are going to the temple and avoid the charge, this sum equates with at least 360,000 individual visits to the temple each year. This popularity is especially evident during the Spring Festival (Vasantha Brahmootsavam) when the god, garlanded in flowers and bedecked in gold and diamond jewelry, is taken on lengthy nighttime processions. On these nights, when the processions are longest, crowds gather in the streets for miles. These crowds are the audience before whom the trustees play out temple pageantry depicting the trustees' role as patrons and the wealth and importance of the Beeri Chettiar civic community.

The temple's rich endowment also reflects the sense each endowment donor has of his or her civic individuality, since endowments state something about who each donor is in relationship to the Beeri Chettiar community: that he or she is an acknowledged member of the community and makes his or her gift in the interest of the caste's collective good. Through his gift, the individual achieves for posterity a respected reputation within the community congregation. Over the centuries Beeri Chettiars, singly and as associations, have made numerous donations, both large and small, slowly building the temple's wealth. Individual donors without children who have left houses and property to the temple are commemorated in inscriptions and posters that list donations. Without descendants, their donations must preserve their identity within the civic community and keep alive a memory of who they were.

A Viswakarma once told me that a person with lots of gold has abundant strength and fertility. So, too, a community. On the night of our initial meeting, demonstrating the temple's wealth, Bala first described the gold ritual vehicles and processional objects possessed by the temple, and then, with the others at the meeting, we left the office to examine them in their locked sheds. He made clear the connection between donors and sponsors and particular ritual objects: the Beeri Chettiar Iron Merchants Association donated the gold crown worn by the processional idol and all the gems that encrust it; the Town's betel leaf[8] merchants donated approximately 2.5 kilograms of gold for the gold peacock processional vehicle (*vahana*); the shroff (bankers and dealers in bullion) merchants donated 4.0 kilograms of gold for an elephant processional vehicle. And the Town Beeri Chettiars as a community donated 3.0 kilograms of gold for the processional palanquin of the supernatural warrior-hero and ally of Kandasami, Surabatman.

The temple also has a silver-plated car, strung with colored lights, constructed with temple funds. Temple cars have a pyramidal form, ornately decorated with carvings, temples on wheels. Some are huge juggernauts, towering twenty to thirty feet or more. Electric wires obstruct the passage of these biggest of cars, and today only a few are taken on procession in the city. Others, smaller, are designed to pass below the city's electrical lines. The garlanded and jewel-bedecked idol is carried in the car-shrine during processions, often with priests sitting before it in order to accept and present offerings submitted by worshipers. In

Figure 5.   Gold-plated temple car (*teer*) with the Kandasami *gopuram* in the background. The processional idol of Kandasami may be seen riding in the car.

1984, in his role as head trustee of the temple, Bala himself built for the temple with temple funds a gold *teer* plated with 7 kilograms of gold, one of twelve in southern India, and a significant new expression of the temple's claim to importance.

   In their opulence, each of these ritual objects declares to all who see or hear of them the vitality of the George Town Beeri Chettiars and idealizes the altruistic commitment to the civic community of the associations and leading citizens who gave. Of course, everyone recognizes that the objects also make great advertisements for the donors and the Beeri Chettiars as a community and boost reputations. Bala and the others were showing me that the Kandasami temple is regarded by the Beeri Chettiars as a key institutional symbol not only of their community as a whole, but also of its leading citizens and associations.

TEMPLE PROCESSIONS, COMMUNITY, AND THE EMINENCE OF LEADERS

If the temple is a symbol of the community, then the temple's builders and the officers of the temple and its events are key agents of the community. They take responsibility for the community's image and in doing so draw attention not only to the community, but also to their own individual importance within it. Without leaders, there is no community; without a community, there are no leaders. Civic leadership and community go hand in hand.

During festivals and important times of worship, which are collective community events, temple trustees and other leading citizens among the Beeri Chettiars enact ritual roles that single them out and publicly dramatize their eminence as instrumental individuals within their community. During a special worship, for example, the sponsor stands closest to the deity among the spectators and acts the role of a dignified but humble host to important guests and spectators (fig. 6). South Indian culture values the leader who is generous, who acts on behalf of his followers. The leader's actions and position near the god mark him as responsible for the event and indicate that he is important. It will be known that he is responsible for accomplishing things in other social arenas as well. Should he show special respect to others while enacting his ritual roles, this recognition confers on them public prominence. The sponsor's civic individuality, therefore, is expressed partially by his eminence and his seemingly selfless agency, his status as a temple trustee or as a sponsor of a ritual event. After the worship he will receive tokens of special respect from the head priest, marks of honor, such as a large quantity of *prasadam* (food "left" by the god) that he can distribute, in recognition of his instrumental role as sponsor. When a temple event is important, great prestige is attached to these symbols of respect because they indicate a man's significance within his community, and for all the outward appearance of altruism, the reality is that leading men compete bitterly to achieve or protect rights to them. By the mechanism of his own re-

Figure 6.   Tiru P. Balasubramaniyam, head trustee or dharmakarttaa of the Kandasami temple, shown here with the decorated processional idol of Kandasami, who is flanked by his two consorts. The humble demeanor of Bala is characteristic of a sponsor of worship. George Town, 1992.

distribution, the recipient of honors confers respect on others as well. In a few instances at Kandasami festivals, leaders belonging to other castes are also publicly marked with ritual honors, indicating their status as respected but subordinate allies.

The most important of the Kandasami temple festivals is the annual twenty-day Spring Festival. During this festival the god, Kandasami, is treated like a king, engaged in the activities in which a real king might be engaged at the onset of spring. He leaves his palace, the temple, and goes out on excursions (*maṇḍaga paḍi*), and, symbolizing the annual renewal of life, he reenacts his marriage to his two wives. His love marriage to his second wife, Valli, a mythical tribal princess encountered on one of his excursions, is an especially popular ritual event among women.

The twenty days of the festival are a period of celebration among the Beeri Chettiars, a time of spectacular entertainments and grand ritual events. Under a huge *pandal*, or thatched roof, funded by the Vaiyabari endowment and directed by Bala, the temple and Kandan Arts, an association founded and headed by Bala, sponsor public concerts in the street that runs before it, and the crowds that come out to celebrate and worship are large. The temple processions reach out like tendrils, entwining the constituencies the temple serves, providing leaders associated with the events opportunities to be seen publicly in roles that declare their individual importance as the community's civic leaders. Ideally, the more prominent a leader's ritual role, the greater his fame and influence. In reality, the more important a leader's ritual roles are, the more apt his claim to eminence is to be contested. The politics of temple leadership reflect the competition of local leaders for prominence as individuals within their community. Temple offices and ritual roles are their "badges" of prestige and honor, badges that in most cases must be individually achieved.

Temple processions go where the trustees and sponsors have clientele, persons who will be attracted to the event and among whom the leaders wish to publicize who they are. For example, over the years, north Indians, who do not participate in such festivals, have gradually replaced the south Indians who used to live around the non-denominational Ekambareeswarar temple, just to the north of the Kandasami temple (see map 2). As a result, the trustees of that temple have modified its processional routes so that they leave the area behind and enter the residential area of south Indians. There the roles of the trustees are still appreciated. However, processions cannot go anywhere a temple's management might like to go because other temples and their leaders mark off their own domains. A temple's domain is the constituency area of its leading men, and if a procession were to enter uninvited the domain of a temple controlled by a different set of leaders, the incursion would be seen as an act of aggression, an attempt by the encroaching temple's leaders to poach on the clientele of the other temple. In George Town, where prominent castes control their own denominational temples, an elaborate processional etiquette exists, which historically has been much contested and negotiated. Reflecting the old left-hand/right-hand moiety division that separates Muthialpet and Mannady (the domain of the left-hand Beeri Chettiars) from Pedda Naickenpet (the territory of the right-hand castes), even today no Kandasami temple procession enters or passes through Pedda Naickenpet (map 4).

The Kandasami temple has several processional routes (see maps 5 and 6), which declare the influential reach of the Park Town Beeri Chettiars. One circumscribes the block in which the temple is located, the four streets known as the Chinna Maaḍa Viithi (Little Temple Streets). A second begins like the first but then goes north to the Ekambareeswarar temple along Mint Street, then returns along Nyinappa Naicken Street, Evening Bazaar Road, returning along Mint Street. These streets are known as the Periya Maaḍa Viithi (Big Temple Streets). A third route, now defunct, used to take the idol to the Angalaparameeswari temple for the benefit of the Beeri Chettiars who live in Sulai (Choolai), in west Madras. A fourth route proceeds along N.S.C. Bose Road, Thambu Chetti Street to the Kachaleeswarar temple. A fifth, which used to go to the Harbor Beach, now travels further south to the Marina Beach because the harbor has been closed off, making its beach inaccessible. The sixth runs the length of Thambu Chetti Street, leaves the Town area, and continues north deep into Royapuram. This processional takes Kandasami out beyond the northern border of the Town to what once was countryside. On its return, it travels along Lingi Chetti Street before returning to the Kandasami temple. Bala is now talking about developing yet another processional route that will take the idol to the Kapaleeswarar temple, a major temple located in Mylapore, several miles to the south.

THE COMMUNITY CENTER AND ITS GALAXY OF INSTITUTIONS

In the recent past, the Kandasami temple was only one of several religious institutions that the leaders of the George Town Beeri Chettiars used to organize their community. Although the community is no longer so tightly knit, caste members still understand the organization of their community in terms of these institutions and the framework for leadership they provide. To conjure a picture of community and leadership, therefore, it is necessary to describe these institutions and the relationships that once characterized them.

Although it is today the principal remaining community institution, in fact the Kandasami temple was once merely an important satellite temple of a central aggregate complex of institutions located in Muthialpet that the Town Beeri Chettiars used as institutions of leadership and community during the eighteenth, nineteenth, and early twentieth centuries. That the Kandasami temple is among the last institutions with castewide significance in George Town is an indication of just how much community solidarity among the Town Beeri Chettiars has declined since the turn of the century, a decline that has accelerated since the 1950s.

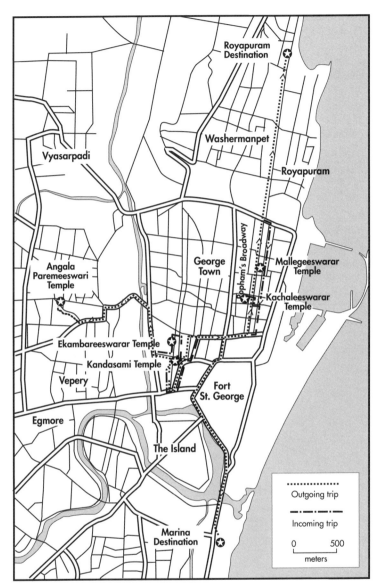

Map 4.   Kandasami temple long processional routes and destinations.

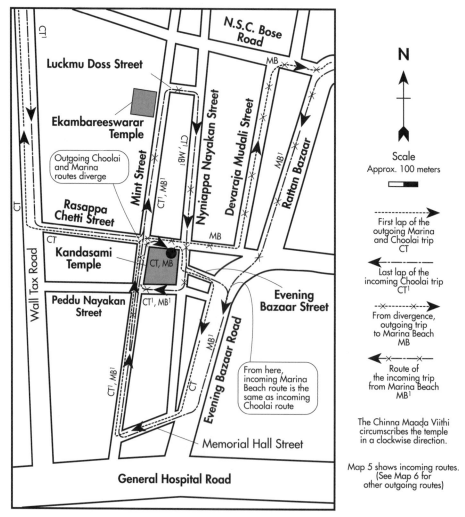

Map 5.   Kandasami temple processional routes to Choolai and to Marina Beach.

Until the late 1950s, caste leaders controlled a big-man centered galaxy of ritual institutions, which together formed a mandala, each point in the layout of which was a satellite that served its own constituency and was headed by a different mix of leaders.[9] In the case of the George Town Beeri Chettiars, this galaxy framed a minipolity composed of the caste's leading members, including caste headmen (sing. *ejamaanan*), and their constituencies, called "clusters," which together constituted the civic community of the caste in the Town.

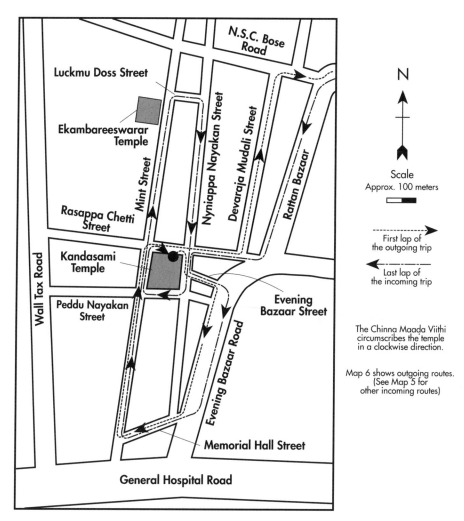

Map 6.   Kandasami temple processional routes to Kachaleeswarar temple and to Royapuram.

In addition to the Kandasami temple, caste leaders controlled two other major kingly temples in Muthialpet, the Kachaleeswarar temple, built around 1725, which, prior to the twentieth century, was the caste's central temple, and the nearby Mallegeeswarar temple, first referred to in British records in 1652 (Love 1913, 1:119n). Each of these temples was an important satellite in the caste's institutional galaxy (see maps 2 and 3), although in the 1950s the caste lost control of both.

Figure 7. The north end of Lingi Chetti Street, with the Mallegeeswarar temple and *maṇḍabam*. The tin shed to the right of the Raja Gopuram houses a large temple car. Muthialpet, 1992.

In addition to these temples, other satellite institutions filling out the Beeri Chettiar's George Town mandala were a large *agraharam*, or residential street of priestly Brahmans, associated with the Kachaleeswarar temple, which was a kind of priestly center to the Town Beeri Chettiar's civic domain; a caste monastery, located within the *agraharam*, the

Figure 8.   A view of part of the *agraharam* that surrounds the Kachaleeswarar temple on three sides. The first building on the right is the Abanatha Dharma Siva Acharya Maḍam, the Beeri Chettiar's caste *maḍam* or monastery. Muthialpet, 1992.

Abanatha Dharma Siva Acharya Maḍam, which housed the caste's celibate Brahman guru and was where leaders of the caste community met in council in the nineteenth century; the caste death-rituals shrine and tank, the Attipaṭṭaan Kuḷam, located some distance from the caste's residential streets, and a host of lesser temples and "public" institutions and locations in the Town area and its surroundings within which caste leaders maintained rights. One of the more important of what I am labeling here "lesser" temples included the Kaalahasteeswarar temple, which the Beeri Chettiars built in 1640, one year after the British founded Fort St. George at Madras (Love 1913, 3:388). The temple is located on what became Coral Merchant Street. There are numerous others, some fairly large, some small, built by the caste.

Institutional galaxies, such as the Beeri Chettiar's, are loosely integrated, since each of its satellites can conceivably stand alone and is typically characterized in the public's mind by its current preeminent leader and lieutenants. These institutions are, therefore, what I am calling big-man or leader-centered institutions, not only because locals sometimes refer to their top leaders as *periyar* or *periyadanakaarar* (big-gift-givers), but also because these leaders use the institutions they control to attract their followers (see Mines and Gourishankar 1990; Mines 1992). It is the pyramidal overlapping leadership and constituencies of these institutions, a layering of alliances and tacit agreements among big-men and ordinary caste members, rather than any overarching system of administration, that makes them satellites in a galactic polity. However, as I describe in chapter 4, in the nineteenth century, the principal headmen of the eighteen named *gumbuhaḷ* of the caste did meet in council, the Periyagramam, to jointly administer caste affairs and to enforce caste codes (ILR, 135). But at that time each of the eighteen *gumbuhaḷ* of the Beeri Chettiars also formed a distinct constituency under its own headman and handled its own affairs with the recognized proviso that when differences between *gumbu* actions and Periyagramam dictates arose, the *gumbu* headman deferred to the Periyagramam.

In those days, it was the Periyagramam council that selected the trustees of the Kandasami temple, while some of their members separately controlled major ritual institutions that extended the influence of the Beeri Chettiar leaders beyond the Town. For example, one Beeri Chettiar headman was the *suroodiriyamtaar*[10] of a major temple in Tiruvotriyur, just to the north of the Town, a status that gave him an inheritable right to the temple's office of head trustee. His descendant is the *suroodiriyamtaar* and head trustee today. Another headman was the hereditary trustee[11] of a major temple in Tiruvanmiyuur, the Murugeeswarar temple, located on the way to Mahabalipuram to the south. Yet another controlled a temple near Poonamallee to the west, while the trustees of the *maḍam* also administered a shrine and shelter (*maṇḍabam*) in Tiruvaalangadu, not far from Poonamallee at the site where caste elders believe the original Dharma Siva Acharya Maḍam was located.[12]

The reader should notice in this description the mandala pattern that begins to emerge, which extends the leadership of Beeri Chettiars well beyond George Town. In fact, according to one informant, himself a descendant from a headman family, when a headman family sponsored an auspicious event, such as a marriage, it was still the custom in the 1920s to prepare twelve offerings of betel nut and leaf (a traditional offering of hospitality, called a *taambuuḷam*) to give to persons who attended as representatives from outlying locations where the Town Beeri Chettiars maintained important ritual rights. A *taambuuḷam* would then be given to the chief visitor from each locale for distribution at their home institutions, a kind of symbolic announcement to the community of the family's auspicious event.[13]

PORTRAYING THE CENTER:
MUTHIALPET'S KACHALEESWARAR COMPLEX

Until the end of the nineteenth century the Kachaleeswarar temple was the central temple of the George Town Beeri Chettiars. Today, despite the popularity of the Kandasami temple and the superior wealth of their locale, the Park Town Beeri Chettiars still portray their former status as a satellite of Muthialpet during the Kandasami temple's Spring Festival when, on the morning of the eleventh day, they take the idol of the god on procession. The god, Kandasami, enacting the role of a living king, travels to the Kachaleeswarar temple to celebrate the renewal of life that the winter rains have brought and to float on a raft in the temple's tank. Today, unfortunately, the tank is dry because the Town's water table has fallen, so, as one informant said with a twinkle in his eye, the idol goes instead "for the stroll."

At the tank, Kandasami is joined by the idol of Kaligambal, the benevolent female deity who gives her name to another nearby temple on Thambu Chetti Street (see map 2), this one controlled by the Viswakarmas, or Smiths, who have carried her here this morning in procession. Like Kandasami, Kaligambal's idol has come to "float" on a raft in the Kachaleeswarar tank and to pay respect to the more powerful god-king, Kachaleeswarar. The two deities coming together like this expresses the friendly relationship that has historically existed between the Beeri Chettiar community and the Viswakarmas who live among them, but it also suggests that the trustees of these two temples were once the subordinate lieutenants of the trustees of the Kachaleeswarar temple.

In British times, older informants say, the Viswakarmas were poor compatriots of the Beeri Chettiars and were often employed by them. One informant told me that forty years ago it was common for young Smith girls to work as domestic servants in Beeri Chettiar households. In yet earlier times, when the temple was built in the eighteenth century, the two castes were leading members of the left-hand moiety of castes that lived east of Popham's Broadway and were allies in competition with the right-hand castes that lived to the west. This is the old division of George Town, which, as we have seen, has left its legacy in the local organization of the Town and in legal rights in institutions. The Float Festival, a day-long celebration that occurs during the annual Spring Festival, continues to symbolize the old alliance between the two castes.

The Float Festival is also associated with two of the Town's most venerable legendary Beeri Chettiar big-men, Thambu Chetti and Lingi (sometimes Linga) Chetti. Two of Muthialpet's main streets today bear the names of these former leaders. In the eighteenth century, the Kachaleeswarar temple was sometimes called "Tambi Chetti's pagoda" (Love 1913, 2:541–2), and according to British East India Company records, the temple and its tank were built by Thambu Chetti in 1725, when he was one of the Company's chief merchants and the premier headman or chief of the Town Beeri Chettiars (Love 1913, 3:387–8, 391). He built the temple on land that had belonged to Lingi Chetti, a contemporary headman-merchant and in the mid-1700s the mint contractor of the British East India Company that ruled Madras at that time (Love 1913, 2:312–13n). Lingi Chetti was a major employer of Smiths in the mint and his relationship with the caste may well have been the source of the connection between the Beeri Chettiars and the Smiths that continues today.

One of the first stories Bala told me, a story others often repeated to me, concerns an attempt by the trustees of the Kandasami temple during Thambu Chetti's reign to carry on the "float" festival independently of the Kachaleeswarar temple. My informants' purpose in telling me the story was to describe the power and control that a preeminent big-man had in former times, power which enabled him to dictate relationships among leaders within the community polity. The story goes that the trustees of the Kandasami temple decided to hold the event at the Kandasami temple itself rather than go to the Kachaleeswarar temple. When Thambu Chetti heard of the plan, he immediately ordered the Town officer to instruct the Kandasami trustees to bring the deity to the Kachaleeswarar tank as tradition dictated. Hearing of Thambu Chetti's displeasure, the persons responsible for the day's festival rushed to him to apologize and beg forgiveness. Thambu Chetti chided them for their presumption and ordered them to renovate the Kachaleeswarar temple palanquin, used to carry the god in processions, as an expiation for their action.

This story, of course, also tells us that the Kandasami temple is seen by today's leaders as once having been a satellite of the Kachaleeswarar temple and that the Beeri Chettiars of Park Town were once under the jurisdiction of Muthialpet's leaders. My informants thought that the story clearly illustrated the great importance of individual leaders, especially the premier big-man of the community, and his dictatorial power.

F. L. Conradi's map of "Madraspatnam" (see map 3) supports this view of the satellite status of the Park Town Beeri Chettiars. The map depicts the Kachaleeswarar temple in 1755 as centered in what we know from records was the heart of the Beeri Chettiar community. The temple is grand, surrounded on three sides by the tree-lined streets of a Brahman *agraharam*. There is no other temple in this section of the Town as large. Only the Ekambareeswarar temple in Pedda Naickenpet, the section of George Town then controlled by the right-hand castes, is comparable. There is a noticeable symmetry in the size of these two major temples, a balanced representation of each moiety's importance and power. By contrast, in 1755 the Kandasami temple is depicted as little more than a small shrine. Kachaleeswarar's size aside, what gives the temple its centrality in the caste's institutional galaxy is its *agraharam* and, located within the *agraharam*, the Beeri Chettiar's caste *maḍam*. The temple, the *maḍam*, and the *agraharam* together constituted the central institutions of civic leadership within the Muthialpet area until the end of the nineteenth century.

The *agraharam* once housed a Brahman priestly community, members of which were supported at least in part by Beeri Chettiar "charity," reflecting both the caste's spirituality and wealth.[14] Endowing Brahmans, for example, by feasting them—sometimes the Beeri Chettiars fed a thousand at a time—was a traditional way of symbolically maintaining the relationship between the wealth and power of leading individuals and the caste community on the one hand and the cosmic order on the other. This public gifting of Brahmans and the large *agraharam* dramatized, therefore, not only the honorable reputation and eminence of the caste civic community and its leaders who endowed Brahmans, but also represented the civic community as an orthodox ethical order. At the center of this urban cosmos was the temple-palace housing the god-king, Kachaleeswarar. Next were the *agraharam* streets that encircled the temple. Finally, came the civic community itself, which was made part of the cosmic fabric by the processional streets of the temple that wove through the community.

As noted, the third institution of the Kachaleeswarar temple aggregation is the caste *maḍam*, the Abanatha Dharma Siva Acharya Maḍam, located within the *agraharam*. Until 1876, the *maḍam* housed the celibate Brahman spiritual head of the caste, the Dharma Siva Acharyar, whose duty it was to instruct Beeri Chettiars on their moral codes. In the nineteenth century, the *maḍam* was also importantly the administrative center of the George Town Beeri Chettiars and the meeting place of their caste council, the Periyagramam, a council of between twenty-one and twenty-two headmen in the 1880s (ILR, 135). This council remained active until near the end of the nineteenth century. In the uses of the *maḍam*, the reader should notice again how the Beeri Chettiars harmonized and dramatized worldly power and wealth with ceremonials and a ritualized depiction of their position in the cosmic order.

Today, the trustees of the Kandasami temple still see themselves as part of the Muthialpet Beeri Chettiar community, but, even so, the George Town community acknowledges few leaders and has nothing like the cohesiveness that it once had. There are still descendants of headman families living in George Town, and among them there are some who are influential public figures. But, as one informant explained, most today are merely ordinary men. Descendants of many of the old families have left business for other lines of work and, no longer so dependent on connections, have moved out of George Town. As they have, the residential composition of Park Town and Muthialpet has changed dramatically. "You do not even know who lives in the next house," one old-time resident told me.

In the late 1950s, quarreling among themselves, Beeri Chettiar leaders lost control of the Kachaleeswarar and the Mallegeeswarar temples to the state run Hindu Religious and Charitable Endowments Department, widely referred to by Tamils as the HRCE Department. In the 1960s, the Kandasami temple was also threatened with takeover by the HRCE Department. First in 1964 and again in 1969 the Department appointed managing boards to the temple. For a time the caste collectively controlled no important big-man institutions.

But in 1967 things began to change slowly. Several Park Town residents petitioned the HRCE Department to allow the caste again to elect their own temple trustees, and in 1976, several residents, including the head trustee of the caste *maḍam* and some of Bala's allies, filed a civil suit to regain the legal right to do so. As a consequence, pending a final decision by the Madras High Court, elections were again held in 1978, the first since 1957, but with the new proviso mentioned early in this chapter: In order to increase Beeri Chettiar involvement in the temple, the temple's charter ("scheme") was modified to extend voting rights to

Beeri Chettiars living or doing business anywhere in Madras City. While Muthialpet still had its core of old Beeri Chettiar families, as it does today, by this time most had relations living elsewhere in the city. One elder Beeri Chettiar estimated that today there remain only about one thousand members of his caste still living in Muthialpet. The decline of the headman system, changes in education and in economic opportunity, high real estate prices, family partitioning, and the desire for more open spaces had dispersed the once compact community.

"It used to be," my elder informant said, "that everyone knew each other, but now often your neighbors are strangers." He then gave me an example to illustrate the extent of the change: People used to lend their jewelry to the temple to be used to decorate the idols during festivals. Donors knew that they would get their jewels back. Now, because the community is so loosely knit, no one lends jewelry, and it is unlikely, my informant thought, that they would get it back if they did. The high level of trust that went with a community organized and constrained by personalized face-to-face relationships has disappeared. To a considerable extent the need to establish trust through enduring personal ties has been replaced by impersonal contractual relationships, law, and governmental bureaucracy.

Reflecting on the institutions that the Beeri Chettiars once controlled in Muthialpet, it is easy to imagine how prior to 1959 the processions of the Beeri Chettiar's three main temples crisscrossed and circumscribed Muthialpet and Park Town. Caste leaders used these temples, in conjunction with the *maḍam*, their Periyagramam council, and the *agraharam*, to define the caste as a community and locality-based political domain. Viewed by all who saw them, the temples and their processions were grand and opulent expressions of the Beeri Chettiar's power and wealth. They stated who the Beeri Chettiar's leaders were, that the caste was a moral congregation, and that Muthialpet and Park Town were their neighborhood domains. Of course members of other communities subordinate to the Beeri Chettiars also lived among them, including the Smiths (Viswakarmas), as we have seen. But the caste that historically had been the Beeri Chettiar's chief rival, the Komati Chettiars, lived with their allied castes west of Popham's Broadway, where they had their own temple domain.

Clearly the Beeri Chettiars saw themselves and were seen by members of other castes as the dominant caste of Park Town and of Muthialpet and Mannady. They controlled a more elaborate ritual structure in those neighborhoods, including denominational temples, than did any other caste, and so they controlled the public symbols of status and prestige associated with these institutions.

TO ROYAPURAM AND BACK,
THE SINGULARITY OF LEADERSHIP

My fieldwork journal for January 30 reads: "Bala tells me that he is now trying to reestablish some of the old etiquette associated with festivals. His aim, he says, is to reinvigorate the sense of community that he feels has been so greatly weakened among the Beeri Chettiars, especially over the last forty years." Prior to the Spring Festival, he had a temple servant personally deliver announcement-calenders of the festival to the heads of some of the old leading families of the Town, showing them special respect and inviting them to be present and honored during the events. Taking the Kandasami idol on procession through the Town, Bala still seeks to weave a community constituency from its residents (fig. 9).

On the night of the fifteenth day of the Spring Festival in 1986, Bala, as he has done every year in his role as head trustee, plans to take the idol through the length of George Town in a procession that will last until dawn. The procession will begin in Kasimedu, a part of Royapuram, the area of Madras City that lies just north of George Town. Here the idol is said to have "rested" during the day at a site owned by the temple, Suriya Narayana Chetti Choultry, named after its donor. The Choultry was once a wooded garden on the outskirts of the city, and the idol of Kandasami has been brought here in procession the night before to enjoy the spring forest[15] and to fetch his bride-to-be, the tribal princess Valli, whom he will marry as his second wife on the sixteenth night of the Spring ritual cycle.

Returning to the Kandasami temple from Kasimedu, a journey of several miles, the procession will proceed down Mannarsami Koil Street, where thousands of celebrators are gathering to watch and make offerings to the god as he passes. When it reaches George Town, the procession will then pass down the full length of Lingi Chetti Street on the way back to the Kandasami temple.

Just prior to the procession, the principal sponsors and participants sit on mats chatting with their guests in a temporary enclosure erected to house the god. Priests dress the god and decorate him with a dense garland of flowers. I want to photograph the process, but after some discussion the priests decide that the deity should not be photographed in

Figure 9.   Kandasami on procession.

an undressed state. When the dressing is complete, the deity is carried to
the front of the enclosure on his palanquin and the procession forms up.
Bala, as the head trustee of the Kandasami temple, stands with a dignified demeanor at the head of the procession. He beckons me to stand on
his right, a position that shows me special respect. The betel nut merchant, who is the chief sponsor of this night's festival, will walk with his
middle-aged son on Bala's left. In his role as head trustee of the temple,
Bala's eminence and authority is expressed by his position at the head

of the procession, and it is in his power to distinguish his allies with symbolic marks of respect such as inviting me to stand by his side. Normally, the other members of the temple's board of trustees would also walk with Bala, but on this occasion they choose not to attend because of an ongoing dispute for control of the temple. They are waiting to see what happens.

Before the procession leaves the "garden" it pauses, and spectators rush to the god to make offerings of fruit, incense, coconuts, and money. Sitting on the palanquin at the feet of the idol, priests take the offerings from the worshipers and present the offerings to the god, then, keeping the small sums of money and a portion of the rest of each offering, they return to the worshiper what remains as *prasadam*.

Entering a broad Royapuram street, the procession pauses again. Traffic has been diverted so that the night-long journey back to the Kandasami temple can be made. The residents of this section of Royapuram are poor. Many are fisher folk, someone tells me. Tens of thousands have come out for the god's passing and they fill the streets. As we stand before the god, a young fisherman approaches Bala and, addressing him as if he were a lord, shows him his shoulder, explaining that it was broken when he was beaten by the police. He asks Bala if he could help him to have his shoulder mended so that he will be able to work again. Observing this, I turn to my research assistant, who is walking with me, and remark that people are treating Bala like a king. "He is king!" my assistant responds.[16]

The god next enters George Town and passes down Lingi Chetti Street. The idol pauses at street corners and before the houses of prominent men who are singled out when the god stops before their houses and the priests perform *aaraati* to them, giving them a coconut and fruit offering. The honored individual makes an offering of money in return. In this manner, the procession stops at the house of the hereditary trustee of the Tiruvotriyur temple. It also stops at the house of the head trustee of the Kaligambal temple, a Viswakarma. Proceeding further down the street, Kandasami again pauses to give respect to the goddess at the Kaligambal temple and then continues on his journey back to his temple. The following night, under the sponsorship of the betel nut merchant and his son, the marriage to Valli is to be staged.

Beeri Chettiars tell me that this grand procession and those of other festivals have been repeated each year for as long as anyone can remember. Sometimes new processional routes are established, which extend the reach of the community into new areas of the city, as Bala is now attempting to do. Other times, old processional routes are given up or lost when a section of the city loses its significance to the caste community. Each procession provides its sponsors and the temple trustees a chance to portray themselves as their community's eminent men. Without community, their roles and sponsorship would be meaningless. The converse is also true: without leaders and their institutions, there would be no community. Not only is civic individuality an important expression of who a person is, but also the very structure of George Town is an expression of civic individuality.

CHAPTER FOUR

Making the Community

George Town in Social History

One of the things that surprised me when I began my research on Madras was how little the local organization of George Town had changed since the start of the eighteenth century. Early maps, such as the one commissioned by Thomas Pitt around 1707–8 (not reproduced here), when he was governor in council at Madras, and that of F. L. Conradi, "Madraspatnam," drawn in 1755, reveal this simple fact quite clearly (see map 3). True, in its early days the Town area had far fewer buildings. In those days, much of the area was garden and open land, a sharp contrast to George Town's density and near complete lack of open spaces today. But already in these early maps the division of the Town into eastern and western moieties is one of its dominant features. In both maps, the Town's two sections are clearly divided by a canal with gardens on either side. In the Conradi map, a line, straight as a ruler, divides the western gardens from those of the eastern section. This can also be seen in J. Talboys Wheeler's sketch map of Madras in 1733 (map 7). Later, Popham's Broadway replaces the canal and gardens as the dividing line between the two sections (map 8).

The maps reveal that even in these early times, the local organization of the Town reflects the division of castes into right-hand and left-hand moieties. This is a distinction that is no longer made in Madras today, although it still affects the Town's layout and the distribution of caste residences. And there are older inhabitants still living who can remember disputes over temple rights founded in the division. As we have seen, the left-hand division to which the Beeri Chettiars belonged lived pre-

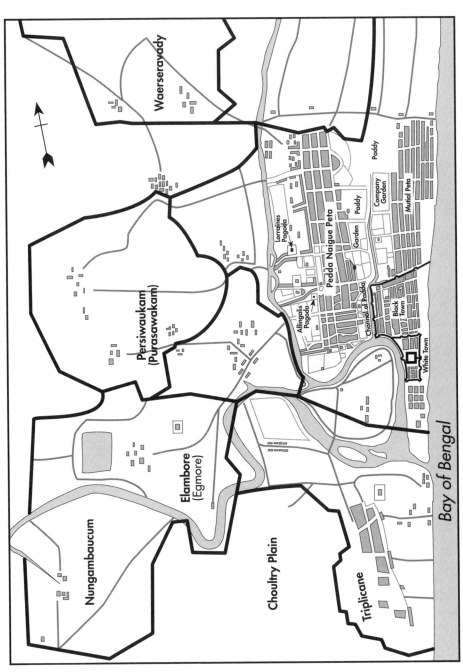

Map 7. Madras in 1733 (based on Subrahmanya Aiyar's enlargement of J. Talboys Wheeler's map).

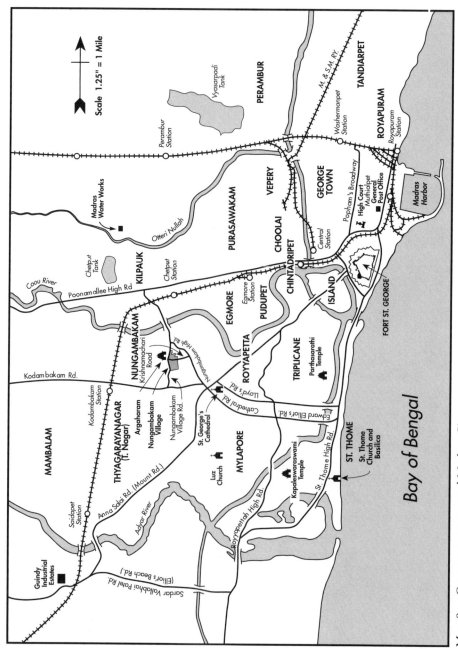

Map 8. Contemporary central Madras City.

dominately in the eastern section of the Town, to seaside, while the right-hand castes, headed by the Komati Chettiars, lived in the western section. Today, should a person stroll the streets of the two areas, the division is still apparent in the location of temples. In the eastern section of Town, temples are Saivite, because the left-hand castes were predominately Tamils, the great majority of whom are followers of Siva. By contrast, Vaishnavite temples predominate in the Town's old right-hand section because its residents were Telugu speakers, a group composed largely of worshipers of Vishnu. But the right-hand/left-hand division was not sectarian based. There are Telugu-speaking Beeri Chettiars who are followers of Vishnu, and while the majority of the Telugu-speaking Komatis consider themselves Vaishnavites, nonetheless Komatis claim a Saivite goddess for their caste deity, Kanyaka Parameeswari. Her temple, located in Kothawal Chavadi market, is the counterpart of the Beeri Chettiar's Kandasami temple.

On the basis of these observations and on the evidence of the maps and the stroll through the Town, it might, nonetheless, appear that the forces determining George Town history and local organization are primarily those of caste and religion. After all, this is what the maps and caste-based residential areas seem to reveal. One would have good company making such an assumption; the supposition that caste and religion are, in fact, primary determinants in Indian social history has long dominated anthropological and historical discourse. Yet, when listening to Bala and his Beeri Chettiar friends explain who they are, it is apparent that they stress the actions and motivations of individuals, not caste and religion, to explain why things are the way they are. To listen to Bala, George Town is organized as it is because leaders have made it that way and because ordinary townspeople have been motivated by self-interest to assist in that construction. Bala's explanation and interpretations that stress caste and religion as the primary agents in Indian history are, therefore, fundamentally contradictory. Why do Bala's and his friends' views contradict those of Western scholars? Might not Bala's explanation of agency be a product of the late twentieth century, when individual responsibility is much more stressed in law and in social life generally than it appears to have been in the past (e.g., Béteille 1987)? In this chapter, I explore the social history of George Town and the role that civic individuality has played in its construction. My aim is to see what explanations persons living in different time periods gave as motivations for their behavior, and why, from their point of view, the Town was organized in the manner that it was. Looking back in time helps us, as observers of present-day George Town, to understand what the interrelationships between religion, caste, and individual interest were and why the community of George Town today is framed in the manner that it is.

THE SOCIAL SETTING

What follows, then, is an analysis of the character and role of individuality among the George Town Beeri Chettiars and its role in the construction of the Town during three time periods: 1652–1708, 1717–1816, and 1876–1890.[1]

At the outset it is necessary to call attention to the fact that Madras City was officially founded by the British when they gained the right to locate Fort St. George at the site for the purposes of trade in 1639 (Arasaratnam 1986:21). It is wrong, however, to assume that from its inception Madras was socially a British city, or that it was framed by a dominant Western-style mercantile economy (Washbrook 1988). On the contrary, "Black Town," the Indian section of the city, was Indian in its organization and reflected the social character of the surrounding region (Lewandowski 1985). Similarly, the organization of trade and production was also Indian. The dominance of Indian ways is hardly surprising, given the small number of English East India Company servants, about twenty-four "exclusive of Apprentices and Soldiers" in the second half of the 1600s, the weakness of British forces, and the Company's policy of depending on local merchants to conduct their trade and manage production (Wheeler [1861–2] 1990, 1:38–39). During the reign of Charles II (1660–1685), for example, when the number of English soldiers in Madras was increased, they still numbered less than two hundred. Rather than imposing Western ways and economy, Company agents tapped into existing systems (Arasaratnam 1986:3; Washbrook 1988:62; cf. Wink 1990:4) and adopted local Indian customs of public interaction, patronage, and display.

For example, during his stay in Madras from 1699 to 1704 Thomas Salmon described how temple dancers

> make up part of the equipage of a great man when he goes abroad; for every man of figure in the country, I observed, had a number of these singing women run before him; even the Governor of Fort St George was attended by fifty of them, as well as by the country musick when he went out. (quoted in Love 1913, 2:75)

The Company Council also made donations toward the maintenance of priests, supported a "water choultry" (a roofed public well and rest place for weary travelers) within the Town, and contributed to ten to twelve temples, including particularly the Company Church, the "Town Pagoda" (Chennai Kesava Perumaal temple), and the Triplicane Pagoda (the Paartasaarati temple) (Love 1913, 2:578). Public giving of this sort marked the preeminent leadership roles Company officers sought for themselves within the local Indian community (see Mines 1984:149). But in these activities the British mimicked the many prominent Indians, whose model for displaying eminence they were following.

As I demonstrate subsequently, Company-Indian interaction had a characteristically dialogic quality (Irschick 1989:490; 1994). In the early years, the Company's main effect on local society was that it offered new opportunities for trade, and Company representatives clearly fanned competition for access to these by favoring different Indian merchants. Consequently, from the beginning competition among merchants was intense.

From the first, Beeri Chettiar merchants were one of the main trading castes of Madras City. Their arch-competitors in the early years of Black Town were the Balijas and the Komati Chettiars, who were the dominant trading castes of the surrounding countryside. This competitive opposition reflected the organization of castes into rival right-hand and left-hand moieties in this region of post-Vijayanagar influence. The Komatis and Balijas were both Telugu-speaking, Vaishnavite castes belonging to the right-hand caste division, while the Beeris were predominantly Tamil-speaking Saivites, belonging to the left-hand section.

1652–1708

During the early period of Madras history, the East India Company relied on prominent Indian traders, called "Company merchants," to contract their trade.[2] When a merchant was awarded the Company investment, or "Prize," his control of contracts and cash advances meant that he stood at the head of an extensive intercaste network of weavers, artisans, service castes, and traders, who produced, processed, and ultimately delivered the goods listed in the Company muster to the Company ships. Consequently, when the Company Council in Madras awarded a contract to an Indian merchant, the contract meant not only that such men stood to become wealthy, but that appointment singled these persons out as men of power who could deny or reward access to trade to anyone wishing to participate. This sanction of denial enabled them to act as arbiters of trust within their communities (Rudner 1989). Essentially, such men were brokers and agents, who through their dispersal of the investment, controlled the logistics of trade from the point of manufacture through to the boatmen, who took the goods to the ships anchored in the Madras Roads (cf. Pearson 1988).

It is evident, therefore, that the mercantile-manufacturing sector of Madras society at this period contradicts a Dumontian interpretation of India on two grounds: first, because the society is integrated by market trade rather than cooperative distribution, which Dumont contends characterizes the Indian economy and is a concomitant feature of India's caste-based division of labor,[3] and second, because intercaste relations are organized by key individuals in pursuit of self-interests. Dumont offers market trade no causal force in Indian history, arguing that economics remain "undifferentiated within politics," which is itself subordinated to religion (Dumont 1970a:164–6). What he means by this is that it is religion that determines the order of Indian society, not politics or economics. Yet in south Indian society the importance of trade is attested by its antiquity (cf. Hall 1980; Gittinger 1982), the receptivity of local polities to European trade, and the ready response of traditional Indian merchants and manufacturers to the opportunities created by the East India Company. Essentially, the Company tapped into what was already a highly developed manufacturing and trading culture, which was, of course, what attracted them in the first place (Arasaratnam 1986:3; Chaudhuri 1985:92–3; Washbrook 1988; Wheeler [1861–2] 1990, vol. 1). Further, the Indian merchant headmen exhibited an individuality that indicates that they cannot be dismissed as mere representatives of collective interests and so lacking real social significance as unique persons.

The individuality of these merchants was especially marked by their *preeminence* as the heads of intercaste constituencies that they formed around themselves in their capacity as the brokers of trade. Expressing the headmen's preeminent roles, the British referred to them as the heads of caste, commonly meaning by "caste" either the right-hand or left-hand moiety, and held them responsible for the behavior of their followers. The headmen's ability to control behavior depended on their pivotal roles as the contractors and financiers of trade, roles that enabled them to demand compliance from allies in exchange for their patronage in trade. In addition, individuality was marked by *achieved reputation*, which depended importantly on the personal ability and successes of a merchant. Finally, individuality was distinguished by *au-*

tonomy, stemming from the headman's achievement of preeminence (he was responsible for who he was) and reputation as a broker-financier (he was responsible for what he did). Headmen exercised this autonomy in their relations with the British as well as in their intercaste and intracaste relations.

As we shall see, religion played an important part in the organization of Black Town society, but religion was not the cause of organization, competition for control of trade was. Relations between the two moieties were determined by competition for trade, and their relative positions in Madras society directly reflected the successes and failures of merchant-headmen, especially in their relationships with the Company.

REPUTATION, ACHIEVEMENT, AND INDIVIDUALITY

For its own part, the Madras Company Council maintained its power over merchants by awarding contracts on an annual basis. The continuity of a merchant's power, therefore, depended on his ability to maintain good relations with members of the Council and in particular with the Council governor. By the early eighteenth century, such relations depended upon the merchant's ability to finance his own trade and also upon his entrepreneurial skills and reputation for being able to meet the Company muster. If a merchant was publicly accorded honors ("tasheerifes," from Arabic, *tashriif*, "honoring," conferring honor[4]) by the Council, and especially by the governor, then his reputation among his production and trade network remained strong. His ties with the Council were confirmed. Conversely, if in public a merchant failed to receive respect from the members of Council, it meant that the favor of the Council had shifted to his competitors. Thus, the standing of Indian merchants within their own communities depended on public knowledge of their individual relationships with the governor and his Council. Respect and ritualized honors singled out individuals and were the barometers of power that signified that their recipients had the connections that made for profitable trade.[5]

Competition among leading merchants was fierce, and the propensity of the British on occasion to favor the lower-ranked Beeri merchants over right-hand Komati and Balija merchants led to heated disputes. The riots of 1652 involved all of these elements. The governor in Council, Aaron Baker, was on the beach embarking on a leave from Madras when he made public his preference for Beeri merchants by refusing the gift of fruit right-hand merchants offered him. Instead, Baker honored the "principalls of the left hand," Beeri merchants, with "tasheerifes," and "after them the Bramanees also, and hee comforted said principalls of the left hand with the Bramanees, that they should have patience two yeares, in which tyme hee would take course to Content them" (Love 1913, 1:123). A Balija, who was agitated by Baker's favoritism toward the Beeris, called a Beeri to his face and in the presence of the English, a man not worth a "cash," and tit for tat, the Beeri labeled the Balija worth less than two cash. Incensed, the Balija went to Town and raised members of the right-hand to attack and plunder the left-hand community, cutting off the ears of two men in the process (Love 1913, 1:120). The Company had only twenty-six English soldiers at the time, and they were unable to prevent the fighting that ensued. Both sides brought in men to carry on their fight.

The aim of the Balijas was to drive the "Chettis" (the Beeri Chettiars) from Town (Love 1913, 1:122). Significantly, this was a trade dispute, although ostensibly the dispute was over "'who should be the more honnourable Cast and have Presidency of the other'" (Love 1913, 1:120). If Baker's public preference for the Beeri merchants were allowed to stand, it would have signaled that they were also to be given precedence in trade. Baker intimated as much at his departure (Love 1913, 1:123). The Balijas struck, therefore, with the aim of undoing all this.

In the end, as had also occurred in the 1640s, the dispute was settled by dividing the streets of the Town, assigning those in the east to the left-hand castes and those in the west to the right-hand. The purpose was to separate the moieties to prevent riots from occurring during ritual occasions, when the leaders of the rival communities claimed ritual honors that expressed their conflicting claims to precedence and public reputation, claims that would single them out, individualizing them as leaders (Dirks 1987; Presler 1987; Mines and Gourishankar 1990). Territorial separation was a standard Indian approach to settling such disputes (cf. Buchanan 1807, 2:268; Appadurai 1974; Mines 1984:45) and indicates that ritual precedence, far from encompassing politics and economics, was limited by these. Separation, however, was a temporary solution because the Company Council created an untenable situation when it contracted exclusively through the merchants of one alliance. Riots were to occur again when the right-hand Komatis were once more excluded from trade.

The next great dispute occurred in 1707.[6] According to the right-hand Komati perpetrators of the riots, the point at issue was again one of ritual precedence. But the actual cause of this great conflict was the Company Council's decision to break off ties with "Sunca Rama and Iapa Chitty," head merchants of the dominant right-hand Komatis, and to award the year's "Prize" to two left-hand Beeri merchant-headmen, "Calloway and Vinkattee Chitty," the "best Chapmen [merchants]" (P.C., July 31, 1707). The Council's reasons were that the finances of the Komati men looked shaky, while Calloway and Vinkattee Chitty had the "money at command to carry on the buisiness [*sic*]" (P.C., Aug. 9, 1707:92–3).

Discounting Komati complaints that the riots were caused by Beeri infringements on their rights to precedence, the Beeri merchant-headmen explained the reasons for the riots to the Company Council as follows:

> The design of the Right hand Cast was no other thn to impede the dispatch of the Companys Ship for England Expecting there was not a sufficiency of Goods in the Godown [warehouse] to Load on thm, which they thought would occasion the Company displeasure against the Governor and councill and utter ruin to the Left hand Cast, as soon as it could come to their [the Company's] knowledge, and that was their [the right-hand caste leaders'] sole aim. (P.C., Nov. 6, 1707:152)

The importance of the Beeri Chetti contention is that it reveals that the Komatis are contesting ritual precedence as a political strategy, revealing that ritual hierarchy is not the cause of Komati-Beeri Chettiar intercaste relations, as a Dumontian analysis would lead one to expect, but that competition for control of trade is. Thus, ritual practice is made part of the politics of trade.

Dirks (1987:261) has criticized Dumont's contention that in India religion has always been a separate and superior force to politics. By contrast, he argues that religion was an integral part of political authority in the ancient regimes of India but became separated from politics during colonial times, when the authority of caste headmen, which had been invested by local kings, declined in the face of British rule. Under colonial rule, temple honors continued to signify local prestige, but the recipients no longer had any political authority. The result: religion was separated from politics. The disputes of 1652 and 1707 support Dirks's assessment of the political uses of religion and indicate that the East India Company was still too weak to force the separation at that time. In fact, as will become evident, one wonders whether at the local level this separation ever occurred fully.

It took the highly vexed British a year to settle the 1707 dispute. For the first several months riots disrupted the peace. At one time the leading Komatis led a withdrawal of right-hand castes from Madras City to

San Thome (P.C., Aug. 20, 1707), while members of the left-hand castes locked themselves in their houses (P.C., Aug. 22, 1707). Life was made extremely difficult for both the British and Indians of the city. Water carriers no longer brought water to Fort St. George. Parayah laborers refused to work, boatmen refused to carry passengers and cargo to and from the ships anchored in the Madras Roads, fishermen refused to fish, and artisans engaged in textile production refused to process cloth (P.C., Aug. 27, 1707). To top it off, the Council determined that one of their number, William Frazer, was in league with the rebel Komatis, trying to engineer his own trading advantage to the detriment of Governor in Council Thomas Pitt (P.C., Dec. 2–6, 1707; Wheeler [1861–2] 1990, 2:41–61).

The manner in which the right-hand traders had achieved all this mischief was straightforward enough. They paid or promised to pay the providers of services, the handicraftsmen, Parayah workers, boatmen, washermen and women (bleachers and preparers of cloth), and fishermen, for the pay they would lose while they were on strike (cf. P.C., Aug. 27, 1707). In other words, society was organized by the market and self-interest—not by cooperative distribution, as Dumont would contend.

The response of the Company to the disputes was multiplex. First, it threatened to use force: "[T]he gov' propposd the attacking of St Thoma [San Thome] the 26th at break of day . . . and [there to] put as many of them ['our Parriars'] as posible to th Sword, but no Inhabitants of any Cast else . . . " (P.C., Sept. 24, 1707:128–9). But this "allarmd Severall" inhabitants of Madras, especially the Armenians and Moors, who feared the Company would not succeed and the "Parriars would flye" into the country (P.C., Sept. 25, 1707:129). Likewise, the "Pedde Naique," the big-man head of the western section of Town, pressed the Company Council not to attack, arguing that it should use milder means to achieve a settlement (P.C., Sept. 25, 1707). He said he knew the governor of San Thome and intimated that he would try to use his influence with him to persuade the "Parriars" to return to Madras. Notice in all these ploys the importance of connections and of key individuals in the organization of early Madras society.

Second, the Company sought to gain control over the loading and unloading of ships by contracting to build twelve of their own shore boats, and by recruiting boatmen from outside the Town, who were independent of the right-hand headmen. Third, they offered to finance the removal of service caste headmen, who had cooperated with the right-hand merchant-leaders, in order to make room for new headmen who promised to show first loyalty toward themselves (P.C., Oct. 20, 1707). Next, they attempted to counter Komati tactics by offering Company support to service castes in substitution for the support the Komatis had provided or promised, guaranteeing employment and protection, in return for the promise of loyalty and a return to work (e.g., P.C., Dec. 2, 1707). Further, in order to control the Kaikkoolar weavers and the "Oyle-men," who had been switching allegiances back and forth, causing trouble to both the right-hand and the left-hand castes, the Council required that these castes declare themselves for the left-hand and the right-hand respectively (Love 1913, 2:29). Here we see the British attempting to place lower-ranked castes under the headmen of the leading castes of the right-hand and left-hand moieties so that they could be controlled.

When, in January of 1708, the Council learned that Sunca Rama, one of the displaced Komati merchant-headmen, with the help of the Indian governor of nearby San Thome had coined money ("coin'd a parall of fanams and cash") to finance his efforts, they banned the circulation of his money in Madras, under threat of severe punishment (P.C., Jan. 15, 1707/8). Obviously, the British thought that the loyalty of the right-hand intercaste alliance was financed by the dispossessed Komati merchant-headmen. Much of the British effort to end the conflict, therefore, was directed at countering the financial power of the right-hand leaders. In effect, many Company efforts were recognizably counterbids designed to buy loyalty for the Company.

But the most effective policy of the Council was its use of the pivotal role of these leading individuals. The Company held the leading caste headmen of the right-hand directly responsible for the uprisings, citing them as the "Chief Instruments in raising the . . . rebellion" (P.C., Aug. 27, 1707) and repeatedly arrested the headmen of both sections to force them to make a settlement (e.g., P.C., Aug. 25, 1707). Sunca Rama was prominent among the rebels of the right-hand, while Calloway and Vinkattee Chitty were two of the four headmen of the left-hand. In effect, while struggling to control these headmen, the Company was also attempting to rule indirectly through them—without great success, it might be added.

In the end, the headmen of the moieties themselves reached a settlement involving the redivision of Black Town into right-hand and left-hand sections. After 1652, the old residential division had gradually been forgotten and members of both moieties had come to live in the streets of the other. Now the streets of the moieties were redefined and the ownership of upwards of five hundred houses were transferred. As in 1652, the purpose of dividing Black Town was to confine ritual activities, which expressed the ritual precedence of headmen, to the localities of each moiety. In essence the purpose of separation was to limit the significance of ritual precedence by dividing it equally between two separate but rival headman territories, reflecting competing domains of merchant-headman authority. It is this division that frames the local organization of the Town area to this day. Its continued importance attests to the renewal of the separation down to the twentieth century.

Like the earlier riots of 1652, this dispute and settlement reveal several features about the organization of society at this time. It reveals, as we have seen, that the headman-merchants had great social authority, and that the British relied on headman-brokers to manage their trade and to regulate society. The Company participated in establishing authority by awarding contracts to headmen, which in effect defined the strength of their political and economic influence. In turn, headmen created the local organization of Black Town, and they divided it into two domains as a compromise solution that allowed them to preserve their preeminence and so their reputations among their separate constituents. The separate domains of the moieties, therefore, reflect the merchant-headman basis of organization. It was not religious hierarchy, then, but competition and the broker system of trade and finance that were the causes of local organization and caste relationships. The acquisition of wealth, reputation, and power were key motives behind organization. Finally, the division of the Town into domains of precedence indicates that local organization centered around the pivotal role of headman-brokers, rather than around a single encompassing ideology of hierarchy. This is apparent because separation offers no solution to contested hierarchical caste rank. However it does offer a solution to headmen threatening each other's preeminence among their constituents because it distinguishes constituencies as distinct territorial domains. Under conditions of separation, conflicts would only arise in situations where headmen either usurped the precedence of their rivals within their domains, or where they attempted to penetrate their rivals' domains without acknowledging their preeminence (Mines and Gourishankar 1990). Indeed, as we shall see, these are precisely the kinds of causes of conflicts that characterize the Town through most of the eighteenth century.

To summarize, when the role of headmen is understood in the organization of society, the causes of disputes and the local organization of the Town become apparent. Disputes were generated by headmen competing to control production and trade for their own interests and reflected the pervasive influence of the market at all levels of society. Town organization was created by the headmen themselves, in order to perpetuate their own roles and reputations as key individuals among traders and producers. The headmen resolved the dispute of 1707 by demarcating exclusive constituencies for themselves, dividing the Town into distinct territorial units. Their aim was to give themselves permanent social arenas within which they would stand as the central figures. These territories formed their constituency domains, and it was within them that their individuality as the leaders of their communities was now to be defined.

1717–1816

Conflicts led by the headmen of the two moieties did not stop with the resolution of the 1707–8 dispute. Riots (Love 1913, 3:385; P.C., 391A, Mar. 6, 1812) or the threat of riots occurred again in 1716–17, 1728, 1750, 1752, 1753, 1771, 1789, 1790, 1795, and 1809, and then, throughout the nineteenth century and into the twentieth century with less frequency. But from around 1716 the scope of disputes in Black Town changed. Altercations now arose for a variety of more limited reasons than those that had led to the all-out "wars" of earlier years. They occurred when members of one moiety threatened to enter the domain of the other with their ritual processions (e.g., the disputes of 1728, 1752–53), when the caste members of one moiety usurped the symbols or rights of a caste of the other (e.g., the caste flag disputes of 1771–90), or when members of one moiety created innovative ritual displays that were seen by their opponents as overreaching their own markers of preeminence (e.g., the dispute of 1790, occurring when the Viswakarmas created an innovative "brass disc" temple cart, and in 1809, when they introduced the grand pretension of using five *calasams* [pots] on their funeral biers). The instigators of all these disputes were the headmen whose reputations were threatened.[7]

By eighteenth century's end, the role of the Company in local society had also dramatically changed. As a result of the Company victory in the Carnatic Wars, most of south India now came under its rule. In the early years of the nineteenth century, the Company consolidated its administration and developed bureaucratic principles that directly affected the role of headmen in society. When the riots of 1809 disrupted the peace of Madras City, the Company resolved no longer to mediate such disputes but to treat breaches of the peace as matters for the police (P.C.,

391A, Mar. 6, 1812:1444). This is the historical point at which the police, as a bureaucratic arm of Company policy, effectively disrupted the
power of headmen to manipulate public peace for their own political
ends in the name of caste tradition. Nonetheless, headmen continued to
play important roles as brokers and arbiters of social trust among their
own constituents.

Reflecting the importance of caste headmen, the eighteenth century
was a period when a variety of leaders and their caste constituents built
new temples in Black Town (Lewandowski 1985). Both Appadurai
(1981) and Dirks (1987) attribute this proliferation to the displacement
of Indian kingly political authority by the Company. They reason that
ritual honors received during temple events are important public expressions of the relative status of local leaders. Therefore, as an extension of their own authority, kings would have prevented the proliferation of temples controlled by different castes in order to avoid confusing
the ladder of local authority.

It is possible, however, that Appadurai and Dirks have misread the
reason for the proliferation of temples in Madras when they take it to
indicate the fragmentation of governing authority. True, temple honors
did single out individual merchants and establish their relative dominance within a temple community. But the goal of merchants who controlled honors was not political rule, it was to use temples to establish
their own public reputations and influence in order to facilitate their enterprises (Haynes 1987; Rudner 1989; Mines and Gourishankar 1990).
The division of the Town into moieties and of the moieties into caste locales, each with its own set of temples, created limited constituency domains, as we have seen. This enabled a different set of prominent individuals to lay claim to temple honors in each domain. Opportunities for
establishing reputations by building temples and public works, spon-
soring festivals, and administering community occasions were consequently multiplied. Indeed, the multiplication of temples in urban set-
tings is characteristic of south Indian commercial towns prior to the
coming of the British, and the division of towns into right-hand and left-
hand sections is also well known.

In Madras, therefore, the proliferation of temples represented several
things: the replacement of what had been a small number of Company
merchants by a much larger number of men of diminished prominence,
the narrowing of social domains so that they corresponded more closely
to caste domains (Bayly 1984), and the decreased reach of headman constituency networks. Therefore, what the proliferation of caste temples in

Black Town indicated was less that central political authority was diminished, than that the number of merchants and prominent individuals seeking to establish public reputations had increased.

The Company Merchant system was abolished in 1771. Its function was divided among several types of prominent men. Primary among these were merchant-headmen, who organized around them constituents drawn from their own trading castes; "dubashes," who were powerful personal agents usually drawn from non-trading castes and employed by British individuals and enterprises to mediate interaction with Indians (Neild-Basu 1984), and "shroffs" (sarrafs), the cashiers of banks and companies, and the financiers of Indian and often British enterprise. Shroffs and dubashes were influential both among Indians and the British. For Indian entrepreneurs, they were the points of access to business with the English, while for the British, they brokered and guaranteed the Indian merchants and businesses with whom English companies contracted.

Should an Indian merchant fail to fulfill his obligations, the Indian dubashes and shroffs could and did deny further contracts. In this manner, these key individuals monitored the reputations and achievements of individual merchants and enforced public trust. For each of these types of pivotal figures, maintaining good public relations with the English was an important determinant of his influence. Nonetheless, since dubashes (Irschick 1989:477–8) and shroffs served competing interests, the British considered their loyalty highly problematic and used a variety of techniques designed to encourage them to make British interests their first priority, including requiring sizeable bonds, holding out to would-be miscreants the threat of dismissal for life, and guaranteeing to those who loyally served them the employment of a son upon retirement. The linkage, therefore, between individual identity and the trust or predictability upon which business exchanges necessarily depended is obvious, as is also the fact that social relations depended on individual reputations and achievements. Among merchants, dubashes, and shroffs individuality was expressed in the importance of who one was and what one did and was a determinant of social relations both within the British and Indian communities.

Both the increased control of the British over Indian society and the displacement of Company merchants narrowed the scope of authority and influence of merchant-headmen. Headmen were no longer responsible for maintaining law and order within their moieties, but as merchant-headmen they retained the power of patronage. For example, if a caste member sought employment or a merchant sought a loan, then the word of one of these men was sufficient to establish his trustworthiness or credit or the lack thereof. Consequently, in their roles as broker-guarantors headmen continued to establish among their constituents the conditions of social trust needed to conduct business.

In sum, during the eighteenth and early nineteenth centuries headman-broker leadership continued to be important, and authority, though continuing to be equated with ritual status within caste communities, was closely linked to the quality of relationships a headman established with the British. If a headman were able to claim the respect of the British, his ability to do business was enhanced; he was in a position to claim apical ritual status within his own caste community, and his influence consequently earned him immense authority and power among his caste fellows. The actions of Collah Singana Chetty, the great Komati headman of the early nineteenth century, are illustrative.

Collah Singana Chetty (alias Rownappa Chetty) was the brother of Collah Moothoorama (d. 1804), the founder and head trustee of the Sri Kanyaka Parameeswari temple and Kothawal Chavadi, Madras City's wholesale vegetable market. On 22 February 1816, Collah Singana made a permanent loan of Rs. 40,000 to the Company Government for the maintenance of four choultries (rest houses) in return for a suitable show of appreciation—that is, an expression of public honor—from the Company. The Company Board of Revenue agreed to Collah Singana's wishes, reasoning that accepting the gift might encourage others to make similar "benefactions" and that the offer publicized the honorable reputation of the Company among locals. Notice the dialogic nature of Indian-British interaction. Both needed the other. The Company needed the recognition of big-men like Collah Singana to establish its reputation, and Collah Singana needed the Company to establish his eminence and prestige. The symbolic forms for initiating and expressing this public recognition were, given the context, necessarily Indian: Collah Singana's generous gift and the governor in council's public giving of honors.

In appreciation of Collah Singana's gift, the Board of Revenue recommended that he be given "some approbation of the Right Hon'ble the Governor in Council" (Madras District Records). And on 13 September 1816, the Company publicly honored him with gifts of a gold medal and chain, a palanquin, and a "cowle" (from Arabic, *kaul*; an Anglo-Indian legal term meaning a "lease or grant in writing" [*Hobson-Jobson* 1986]), the latter framed and still preserved by his descendants in Kanchipuram (field notes, 23 Mar. 1986). Later, he was made the *suroodiriyamtaar* of

Enadur; that is, he was given the right of management and maintenance of temple land in Enadur. Honor received and a strong relationship established, the Company seems subsequently to have facilitated Collah Singana's purchases of land in Madras, while among his own community he established himself over a rival faction as head trustee of the caste temple (field notes; Madras District Records).

The continued importance of the headman model of preeminence also remains evident in the behavior of some English Company officers at about this time. In other words, rules for establishing identity and individuality as a leader are still Indian. Thus, during the 1790s, Lionel Place, the Company collector of the district surrounding Madras City, commanded great pomp at major festivals in nearby Kanchipuram. Adopting

> the role of an indigenous king . . . Place would call for "all the dancing girls, musicians . . . elephants and horses" attached to the temple at Conjeevaram, a temple city in Chingleput District. "Attending in person, his habit was to distribute clothes to the dancing girls, suitable offerings to officiating Brahmins, and a lace garment of considerable value to the god." He also used Company troops and sanctioned the prayers of Brahmins "to propitiate the deity for a good harvest or for good trade." (Irschick 1986:12)

Place's purpose in acting the role of a headman was to establish his public reputation as the preeminent figure of the district that he administered as collector. He sought a public identity both as commander and patron of the people.

1876–1890

In the mid-1870s the headman-centered organization of Beeri Chettiar caste leadership came under attack from within. This occurred when some of these men, whose personal interests were no longer served by the merchant-headman system of organization, were outcaste for breach of caste codes. In defense, the outcastes responded by setting out to destroy the dictatorial autonomy headmen enjoyed as the arbiters of public trust and conduct within the Beeri Chettiar caste.

Between 1876 and the first years of the twentieth century, these rebels successfully undercut the headman system of authority and administrative style. They did this by limiting the autonomy headmen enjoyed as administrators of caste affairs. The rebels used the civil court to circumscribe with law the power of headmen to enforce caste behavior codes with outcasting; they made offices in caste temples and institutions contestable by election, thereby weakening the hold caste headmen had on the institutions of leadership, and public reputation. And they made headmen accountable under law for their management of institutional funds and assets—the community's resources—in effect substituting audits for reputation as a determinant of trustworthiness. In other words, the rebels forced a redefinition of leadership which curtailed it and made it conform to limits set by bureaucratic standards of administration. Here again we see individuals, motivated by their own self-interests—in this case the desire to relax caste conduct codes—initiating actions that led to the transformation not only of caste leadership, but also of the organization of the Beeri Chettiar caste.

In the 1870s the Town Beeri Chettiars were divided into "18 or 20" named endogamous subcastes, which informants today call *gumbuhaḷ* (clusters), each headed by one and in some cases two headmen (*ejamaanan*) (ILR, 150). According to Beeri Chettiars today, the membership of each *gumbu* was small, numbering a few hundred to a few thousand families. *Gumbuhaḷ* were named after village-centered locations (e.g., Poonamallee *gumbu*, Iḷḷatuur *gumbu*), after the headmen who founded them (e.g., Periyaswamy Chetty *gumbu*, Kasappa *gumbu*), after their relative status (Koṛuvu Viiḍu [lowly house] *gumbu*), or after a trade specialization (e.g., Tin-Sheet *gumbu*, Araca-Nut *gumbu*, Tobacco *gumbu*, Kasukaarar *gumbu*). The *gumbuhaḷ* were ranked by wealth, and the headmen of wealthy clusters, such as the Poonamallee *gumbu*, were the most prominent among the Beeris.

Numbering twenty-one or twenty-two in 1876, the headmen of the *gumbuhaḷ* met to administer the affairs of the caste in the council called the Periyagramam (ILR, 135). These council meetings were held at the caste *maḍam*, the Abanatha Dharma Siva Acharya Maḍam. Headmen also conducted separate subdivisional meetings to decide the affairs of their own cluster constituents, but the Periyagramam meeting held the power to override divisional decisions. *Gumbu* headmen enforced caste codes for behavior but rarely expelled anyone from caste before the 1870s. They had no need to because, as the monitors of public behavior, headmen ensured that the cost of deviating from caste norms was high: loss of reputation. Therefore, incentives favored compliance with headmen in return for the benefits of a good reputation vouched for by one's headman. Without the word of headmen attesting to their reliability, individuals were at a definite disadvantage in economic and social exchanges. For example, people would hesitate to employ such a person, give him credit, or arrange a marriage with him or his family members.

The Indian Law Reports (ILR) describe the clusters in 1886 as very much like guilds and the Periyagramam as like a federation of guilds. In the ILR, the Periyagramam is described as "concerned at least as much with enforcement of social observances and of conduct deemed to be for the good of the community—and possibly for regulation of its trade . . . —as with the punishment of ceremonial offenses" (ILR, 150–51). The comments of the judge here reflected his awareness, gained from witnesses, that by monitoring public behavior headmen played an important role, ensuring a high level of public trust within the George Town Beeri Chettiar community.

Prior to 1876, only two cases of outcasting among the Beeri Chettiars of the Town were known, one in 1864 involving the son of Mylapore Kandasami Chetti, who was expelled when he became a Christian, and one in 1874–5 involving Pakam Sabapathi Chetti, expelled for an illicit sexual relationship with a low-caste woman (ILR, 138). The absence of prior outcasting suggests that the customary sanctions wielded by headmen were sufficient to punish deviants without resorting to expulsion.

By 1876, these circumstances had changed and the first of a series of outcastings occurred. In that year Ratnavelu Chetti, a member of the Madras Civil Service, was outcaste upon his return to Madras for having travelled to England. Overseas travel was still an outcasting offense at this time. But opinion about the outcasting was divided. Ratnavelu's father, Ramasami, a headman of his cluster and a member of the Periyagramam, opposed the outcasting, causing a division within his cluster between those who supported readmission to caste and those favoring the outcasting. The split quickly spread to members of other clusters, and the headmen of the caste were soon divided among themselves.

The first casualty of the dispute was the caste guru. From court records and modern informants it can be surmised that proponents saw the outcasting as legitimated by the caste guru, who was employed in part to interpret the religious basis of caste codes (O.S., 12). Opponents, it seems, countered that the guru had no authority in the decision. Caught between the two factions, his position as a servant of the Periyagramam was untenable. He left the caste *maḍam* and site of Periyagramam meetings on pilgrimage. He never returned and the Beeri Chettiars of the Town were never to replace him, although they continued to maintain the *maḍam* building as a caste institution. Informants today explain why the guru position has been left vacant: they oppose a priestly definition of caste codes.

Next, in January 1877, Ramasami, Ratnavelu's father, was expelled from caste for associating with his son, then readmitted, and reexpelled in 1878 and 1881 respectively. In 1879, Subraya Chetti, the headman of the Periyagramam, considered twenty-eight men outcaste (ILR, 138–9). Suits and countersuits in the civil courts followed.

There are a group of court decisions in particular that unraveled the authority of the Beeri Chettiar headmen. The allies of Ramasami brought suits to gain control of the caste *madam*, which as the site of the Periyagramam and the dwelling of their spiritual teacher, represented both the spiritual identity of the George Town Beeri Chettiar caste and their corporate center. This identity was expressed in part by the caste codes for conduct sanctioned by the Periyagramam under the spiritual aegis and teaching of the caste guru. The aim of the suits was to force

> an account being taken of properties constituting the endowment [of the *madam*], for their being secured for the benefit of the institution, for a scheme of management being settled for plaintiff No. 1 [one of Ramasami's outcaste allies, Krishnasami Chetti] and other competent persons being appointed trustees, and for adequate provision being made for the due administration of the endowment [of the *madam*]. (ILR, 135)

The plaintiffs' purpose was, of course, to control the administration of the *madam*. Control meant it would be they who were first honored during *madam* events, and they who scheduled Periyagramam meetings and defined who was invited. Imposing the *madam* management scheme, therefore, was designed to upstage the moral authority of the conservative headmen and to nullify their efforts to exclude the rebels from participating in caste assemblies.

In 1883, as an outgrowth of these suits, the High Court framed a new administrative scheme for the *madam* in which the rebels had a role (O.S., 4, 11–12). This was challenged by the conservatives, who argued that the rebels had no right to bring the suit because they were outcaste. But in 1886, the outcasting was itself invalidated by the court on the principle that the rebels had been absent from the Periyagramam meeting that had expelled them and so had been unable to face their accusers as was their civil right, under the maxim, *aude alteram partem* (ILR, 145). Western law here defined the civil rights of individuals set against the legal corporate right of a caste to expel members.

By wresting control of the *madam* from their opponents on the Periyagramam and eliminating the caste guru, the rebels were in the position to validate their own more liberal codes and to successfully challenge the prerogative of the conservative headmen to enforce caste codes of behavior. Reflecting on these events today, aged informants recall their elders' attitudes and put the matter bluntly: educated men were no longer willing to accept the reactionary authority of uneducated caste headmen (field notes).

These lawsuits mark the end of the headman system of caste organization among the Beeri Chettis in Madras City, but they do not mark the end of caste leadership nor the end of the role leaders as individuals play as a cause of caste organization. In chapter 6, I continue the story of these issues and the changing nature of individuality in Madras society.

In the last quarter of the nineteenth century, the rebels had achieved a rapid and fundamental shift in social organization from a headman-centered system of caste, well suited to a mercantile lifeway that benefited from a high level of social control, to a caste society organized by general bureaucratic principles of law, better suited to a more open, less personal society. For educated civil servants and professionals the headman system of organization had become too restrictive.[8]

The degree to which the caste organization of the Beeri Chettis has been that of headman sodalities is made clear by the fact that the demise of headmen has also meant to a considerable extent the end of the overall corporate organization of the caste within Black Town. This demise should not be surprising, since the institutions of corporation were the Periyagramam and the clusters, which were orchestrated by headmen. Today, caste members still have rights in the skeleton institutions through which headmen once implemented their leadership: the caste *maḍam* building, the one remaining caste temple—the Kandasami temple—the caste funeral rites tank, and the endowments associated with these. These legally constituted rights are the legacy of the bureaucratic management schemes the rebels and their associates implemented at the end of the nineteenth and the beginning of the twentieth centuries. But no one considers that either these institutions or their elected officers represent the identity of the Beeri Chettiar caste as a community today.

CONCLUSIONS

Do individual uniqueness and achievement play a role in the history and organization of Indian society? The history of the Beeri Chettiar caste strongly indicates that they do. During each of the time periods considered, key individuals play a primary role in determining the organizational form that caste society takes. Further, recognizing the importance of individual achievement in Indian society allows the highly competitive and pragmatic nature of much Indian interaction to find its rightful place in the portrayal of Indian public life. Thus, the role of achievement is readily apparent among the Beeri Chettiars when the highly competitive nature of intercaste and intracaste relationships is recognized as stemming from the competitions of merchant-headmen spurred by individualistic desires to achieve wealth, power, and prestige.

In the pursuit of these goals, headmen created the organization of Black Town society, and as circumstances changed, modified old organization and created new. This appears to have been true to such a degree that one might contend that among the Beeri Chettiars at each period of history caste organization was identical with the organization that headmen created in the course of their leadership. During the period 1652–1708, the moiety division of castes reflected the primary competition of individual headmen-brokers, each of whom stood at the apex of an intercaste production and trade network that he organized as a trader-financier. This headman-broker system of organization was set against a legacy of Vijayanagar rule that gave social precedence to its chiefly allies, the right-hand castes, and subordinated in social esteem the traders of the left-hand. During the period 1717–1816, headman-traders segmented the Town into constituency domains. This enabled the heads of the moieties to compete within their own territories for economic and social preeminence, while to a considerable degree avoiding the issue of relative precedence between the two main trading castes, the right-hand Komatis and the left-hand Beeri Chettiars. Finally, during the period 1876–1890, their interests no longer served by the headman system of maintaining social control and spurred by their expulsions from caste, leading men garnered allies and forced a restructuring of the Beeri Chettiar caste, curtailing the autonomous authority of headmen in the civil courts and imposing bureaucratic standards of administration that deflated their power. The history of the Beeri Chettiars, therefore, directly contradicts Dumont's characterization of Indian society as ignoring the individual. On the contrary, individuals are the agents of organization and their interests and achievements play clear roles in the transformation of Madras society.

How then are we to understand and characterize individuality in Indian civic society? Certainly throughout the history under consideration, Beeri Chetti headmen have striven for and have achieved a type of socially significant individuality based on preeminence. Equally clearly, this has been an individuality unsupported by the values of equality and liberty that Dumont stresses in his characterization of Western individualism. What Beeri Chettiar history has illustrated is that individuality may take a different form than Western individualism, involving, nonetheless, a mix of traits, some of which Western notions of individuality also share, notably: (1) individualistic social identity that is recognized, evaluated, and considered instrumental within the context of groups, a contextualized individuality that is spatially defined; (2) an identity defined by eminence within groups, an individuality of inequality; (3) uniqueness marked by public reputation; (4) achieved identity associated with a deliberate striving after one's own gain, dominance, and prestige; and (5) autonomy marked by responsibility for who one is and what one does. Because context defines the spatial dimension of a person's individuality, and it is within particular contexts that features of identity are known, as noted in chapter 1, I have proposed the label "contextualized individuality" to characterize this particularly Indian type of politically significant individuality.

Recognizing the essential role individuality plays as a cause of organization and as an integral feature of leadership greatly affects how Indian society is conceptualized. The societal order that individual pursuit of advantage begets, while it exists within the context of castes, expresses a distinctive form of traditional organization in which the paradigm of society is not caste hierarchy, nor conceptualizations of purity/impurity, nor even priestly versus kingly modes of behavior, but that of *constituencies*, which form around dominant individuals and their patronage. It is these groupings that I have labeled "leader-centered" or "headman associations." Throughout history and at every level of Indian society leaders have achieved public recognition as individuals. It is they who have created, managed, and transformed the institutions that give Indian society its corporate frame and Indian history its political and economic drama.

CHAPTER FIVE

A Portrait of Change

The 1870s and 1880s are too distant in the oral histories that George Town informants relate for me to flesh out the lives of Ramasami and his son Ratnavelu, the headman and his son, whose outcasting led to the nineteenth century lawsuits just described. I wonder about the specifics of their motivations and what their goals were. Were they merely concerned with reversing the Periyagramam's decisions to outcaste? Or was their vision more far-reaching? Did they personally feel that *gumbu* headmen and the caste council no longer served the interest of men like themselves?

I am fairly certain that they were motivated by both reasons. Their actions show that they wanted to nullify the decisions that had outcaste them. And clearly they found the rule of the headmen too restrictive. Circumstances had changed. Education and broadened opportunities had created a new social order and a need to travel and form alliances beyond the locality. I find evidence that corroborates these inferences in more recent experience. Very similar changes occurred in the lifetime of an elderly informant of mine, Natarajan,[1] a member of the weaver caste (the Kaikkoolar), who began his adulthood in Kanchipuram, an urban hinterland of Madras City some fifty miles to the west. In towns located away from Madras, the kinds of changes Ramasami and his son experienced occurred many years later. I present Natarajan's story here as a cameo study of these kinds of changes.

Informants had told me that I should interview this man, an elderly lawyer practicing in Madras City. They told me that he was an important leader of the Kaikkoolars, who in his youth had been at the center of a controversy that led to what my informants described as progressive changes in the organization of his caste.

Successful lawyers like Natarajan are busy men. I arranged to meet with him at his office in his home one night at seven o'clock. A bald, round-faced gentleman with wire-rimmed glasses met me at the door. Age slowed his movements and he seemed tired, but he was keenly interested in telling his story, and his animation during its telling was demonstration that he cared deeply about the principles he had spent his life living and advocating. Sometimes, when he related an episode in his life, he would fall silent for a moment, reflecting on what had happened. There was a sadness about him.

Describing his youth, Natarajan (b. 1907) told me how his future father-in-law, Murugeesan,[2] an engineer and architect in Madras, approached his father to seek his, Natarajan's, hand in marriage for his daughter. The year was 1932, and at the time Natarajan was away from his family in Kanchipuram studying law in Madras. What made the proposal unusual, indeed revolutionary, was that his father-in-law's family belonged to a different locality-based endogamous subgroup. In 1932, locality endogamy was still the custom among the Kaikkoolars in Kanchipuram, as it was for the caste throughout the state.

Kaikkoolars adhered to the custom of locality endogamy not because they feared "excommunication" (outcasting), but because the custom corresponded with their own individual motivations to maintain their community connections and their family's good-standing within the locality. After all, it was on these that their successes and reputations depended. Nonetheless, since it was the caste headman's role to act as guarantor of his constituent's behavior, everyone also understood that if anyone did transgress the locality marriage rule, they could expect the headmen of the subcaste to outcaste the culprits. According to the locality rule, a Kaikkoolar who belonged to the Kanchipuram subcaste might move anywhere he wished, to Madras City, for example, but when he married or his descendants married, they were required by custom to make an alliance with someone belonging to the Kanchipuram subgroup. Murugeesan's marriage proposal, therefore, was a rebellious bid aimed at overthrowing one of the central rules of Kaikkoolar marriage custom.

Natarajan said that in the early 1930s, there were only thirty to forty Kaikkoolars statewide with university educations. One knowledgeable informant told me that as recently as 1927 there were only fifteen Kaikkoolars with bachelor degrees. Natarajan himself was one of the first degree-holders from Kanchipuram. Acting through a newly founded statewide Kaikkoolar caste association and its publications, this small body of university-educated men strongly advocated discarding locality endogamy rules. Their motives for doing so were twofold. First, with university educations their occupational opportunities extended far beyond the locale, and they sought new extralocal connections that would help them to exploit these opportunities. Marriage offered them a way to start. In south India, a man's wife's relatives are supportive kin, and marriage ties create strong bonds upon which to build new relationships of trust. Second, and this is the reason informants stress, they wanted to arrange marriages with educated families, who shared their perspectives. They saw themselves as "progressives" and as "advanced" thinkers. But, because there were so few educated men in the state, as Natarajan said, it was necessary for them to "come out of their localities" in order to find educated families with whom to arrange marriages.

At about this time, 1932, the caste association held a statewide meeting in Kanchipuram. Natarajan's university education qualified him as a member of his caste's small progressive elite, and, eager to serve his caste, he was elected secretary of the association. He was also introduced for the first time to his future father-in-law. During that meeting, some association leaders renewed the call for "breaking out" of the locality restrictions that prohibited free intermarriage among Kaikkoolars. It was in this atmosphere of "advanced" ideas that, after meeting Natarajan, Murugeesan approached the young man's father and mother. He found them receptive to his marriage proposal. Natarajan's father was himself a progressive who wanted to arrange a marriage with an "educated and advanced family," knowing full well that this would mean breaking locality endogamy rules. Natarajan's mother and father also believed an alliance with one of the leading members of the Kaikkoolar community in Madras City would be to their son's professional advantage.

Natarajan related that it was his "desire in life" to become a lawyer. "I wanted to lead an independent life and to have scope for doing social services and joining public activities." The Great Depression was in full swing when he told his parents of his career wish. At first his father opposed the idea because, as Natarajan recalled, he "thought the lawyer's profession an unsteady one." In his mother, however, Natarajan had a strong advocate. She persuaded his father by threatening, if need be, to sell her jewelry to finance her son's law studies.

Natarajan must have been exaggerating slightly when he described his father as having been a poor man. At the time of the proposal, he ran a small jewelry shop in Kanchipuram, while earlier he had been a small-scale silk dealer. Kanchipuram is famous throughout India for production of handloom silk saris. But certainly Natarajan's father was not wealthy. Nonetheless, by local standards he must have been reasonably successful because he was a respected member of his Kanchipuram community. An indication of this is that, prior to Natarajan's marriage, he had arranged the marriage of his only daughter to the brother of the caste headman. Thus, although his economic status may have been modest, he was well connected within his own caste locality. Accepting Murugeesan's proposal meant for him, therefore, putting in jeopardy his family's community standing and straining his ties with the headman, a man he could be sure would oppose the marriage. Perhaps he believed he could dissuade the headman from outcasting his son because his daughter was married to the headman's brother. Whatever the reason, Natarajan's father and mother's individual motivations for accepting the proposal had to have been strong.

Natarajan says he himself was personally amenable to the marriage but thought it would be necessary to put it off until he had finished school. He knew his father was too poor to support both Natarajan and a wife while Natarajan was studying in Madras. However, after being made aware of the problem, Murugeesan offered to provide board and lodging for the couple for as long as Natarajan needed to finish his studies and establish himself as a lawyer. Murugeesan's offer made the marriage possible.

Natarajan was the first Kaikkoolar from Kanchipuram to attend law school. When he graduated, he was to join one of a small handful of Kaikkoolar lawyers in the state. But because law in the 1930s was dominated by Brahmans and law practices required connections, Natarajan needed his father-in-law's support and social network to survive his early years as a lawyer. In the end, Natarajan says, his father-in-law supported him for seven or eight years with occasional help from his own father. During the interview, Natarajan spoke about his father-in-law and wife, both of whom were dead, with deep affection. It is apparent, therefore, that while Natarajan's and his father and mother's individual motivations for accepting the proposal were complex, ultimately they rested upon the fact that, given Natarajan's desire to be a lawyer, advantage lay more with aligning with an educated progressive Madras family than with a locality-constrained conservative Kanchipuram family.

Natarajan says his father-in-law's motives for proposing the marriage were of this same sort. He wanted an educated and "advanced" son-in-law who shared his progressive views. Education was what mattered, not wealth. After meeting Natarajan at the Kanchipuram statewide caste assembly, Murugeesan apparently deemed Natarajan an ideal choice.

But there were problems. For all the liberal talk by the young caste association intellectuals supporting free inter-subgroup marriages, according to Natarajan, the reality in 1932 was that interlocality alliances were very rare and widely opposed. When his family indicated publicly their intention to go ahead with the marriage, as expected, his father was told by the Kanchipuram caste headmen that, if he did so, Natarajan would be outcaste.

In the end, however, Natarajan said, he was not outcaste. He was threatened, but his father's influence in Kanchipuram saved him. The marriage took place at his father-in-law's on Pycroff's Road in Madras. But, said Natarajan, "even close relatives refused to attend the wedding." Natarajan paused and became very still for a moment, thinking about his marriage. I could tell there was something in this boycott of relatives that still hurt him. When I asked him who these close relatives might have been, at first he hesitated, and I thought he might not want to tell me. But after a moment, he explained that the absence that mattered the most to him was his sister's. It was clear that all these years later, her absence still disturbed him. His sister's husband's brother was, of course, the reigning headman of the Kaikkoolars in Kanchipuram at the time.

Although tensions ran high for a time and the marriage divided the Kanchipuram Kaikkoolars into progressive and conservative camps, Natarajan's marriage, nonetheless, did constitute a successful rebellion. With a law degree, Natarajan's statewide connections were more important to him than those of his locality, and his father-in-law more helpful to him than the caste headman. Natarajan says his marriage spelled the end of the office of headman. His singular defiant marriage reflected a new reality, namely, that the influential educated members of the caste—the men who many thought were to be the future leaders of the caste—no longer supported the headman's authority. There was never another Kanchipuram Kaikkoolar headman.

Several important conclusions can be drawn from the story of Natarajan's marriage. For all the headman's seemingly dictatorial[3] power, his authority proved surprisingly fragile. This was in part because his authority was based less upon sanctions than it was upon the incentives that motivated individual compliance with his bidding. Individuals complied as long as they saw it as in their interests to do so. This fragility was also in part because the headman's authority was a feature of community and depended upon the community locale continuing as the primary arena of social interaction. The headman, in other words, was a consensus leader whose arena of influence was limited to the locale. That consensus was abruptly withdrawn when Western-style education expanded opportunities beyond the town. Suddenly Kanchipuram was too small a pond for the fish that education had created.

Motivated by new possibilities for achieving wealth, prestige, and influence, individuals with the support of their families restructured the organization of their caste (subgroup locality endogamy was abandoned) within a very short time-frame, reinvented the arena of social interaction (the statewide caste community replaced the local community), and, completing the revolution, displaced the dictatorial headman. In fact, education, and the new occupational opportunities being opened by education, were creating a new elite within the caste. Natarajan and his father-in-law saw the new circumstances. Like other "progressives," they recognized that to succeed in the new arena, new kinds of alliances would be needed. In this new arena, they also hoped to "serve" their caste community, that is, to play the role of big-men. Their intent was to develop the statewide caste association as an umbrella institution that would engineer the transformation of locality groups into a statewide caste constituency. The resulting galactic polity would be composed of the local satellite caste associations that made up the membership of the statewide association. In fact, they and their fellow leaders were to prove remarkably successful (Baker 1976:199; Mines 1984).

Natarajan's 1932 election to the secretaryship of his caste's statewide association was his first step toward establishing his civic identity as an eminent leader within this new arena. At the same time, he was also designated the honorary editor of the association's magazine, the *Senguntha Mittiran*, a position he held until 1960, when he was elected vice president of the statewide association.

The influence and eminence of the civic individual expands when, as an officeholder, he or she extends control to other satellite institutions, each appealing to its own constituents whom the officeholder seeks to serve. In 1953, Natarajan became the secretary of a devotional society, the Sri Balasubramaniam Baktha Jana Sabha, located in the Royyapet section of Madras City and dedicated to the worship of Murugan (map 8). As I have noted earlier, participating in the management of a religious institution helps validate a leader's altruistic concern for constituents. Since Kaikkoolars consider Murugan their caste god, Natarajan used the society to further establish his singularity as a leader among Madras City Kaikkoolars, particularly those living in the south-central part of the city where the society was located. In 1960, Natarajan was elected the society's vice president, and then, in 1972, its president. In 1970, he also became the president of the Siva Subramania Baktha Jana Sabha, another devotional society dedicated to promoting worship of Murugan, this one located in Pudupakkam, just to the northeast of Royyapet. From 1953, he was also president of the Pudupakkam Permanent Fund, Limited, a private lending and banking company. While this was a position for profit, the company may also be seen as a satellite institution in the galaxy of institutions upon which Natarajan built his role as a leading civic individual. Finally, in the 1970s, Natarajan was designated executor of the Annammal estate, a trust that ran a middle school of about two thousand students in Saidapet, a section of Madras City that lies to the south. Located in the south-central and southern parts of the city, these institutions and offices constituted Natarajan's institutional galaxy, the mini galactic polity within which he constituted his identity as a civic individual and as a lawyer. In 1976, when the statewide association met again in Kanchipuram, Natarajan was its associate president (*tuṇai talaivar*) and a recognized and honored pioneering member of his statewide caste community. By that time the caste headman was all but forgotten. By contrast, there were numerous Kaikkoolar big-men in attendance at the meeting.

CHAPTER SIX

The Decline of Community and the Roles of Big-men

I want to return to Bala and George Town in order to explore what has happened to the Beeri Chettiar community and civic individuality during the twentieth century. But in order to put George Town into perspective let us look for a moment at another section of Madras, which, after all, is a city of about five million. My purpose is to demonstrate how the forces that wed neighborhood and community, that motivate the union of big-men and their constituencies, have determined the organization and character of not just George Town, but of other parts of Madras City as well.

As we have seen in previous chapters, times change and what it is that people want and leaders can accomplish changes with them. Big-men and their clients respond by renegotiating their relationships and by redefining their roles. In the process, the character of the neighborhoods of the city change also. In the second part of the chapter, I return to George Town to describe its evolution since the nineteenth century lawsuits. There, today, Bala is trying to pull together a neighborhood that is coming apart. The forces of change that Bala confronts are broad-based and are impelled by shifts in the needs and motivations of ordinary people.

Looking back over the past one hundred years, I see three major changes in community leadership and in the integration of George Town, each of which is associated with changes in the meaning of civic individuality. First is the period of *gumbuhal*, headman, and the headman council, the Periyagramam. Second is the period of a looser form of leadership, a period of big-men, their institutions, and constituencies. Third is the present day. Big-men still exist, but there are fewer of them, and they are redefining their roles and relationships among a shrinking clientele. Neighborhood localities are losing their community integration. An evolution is occurring that affects the entire city, every neighborhood, old and new. Madras City has begun to change rapidly. It is entering a new period.

Today, a drive down any major street in Madras City reveals clear signs of a vigorously developing metropolis. Consider Nungambakam High Road, which cuts through one of the city's old residential districts: vehicular traffic is congested; diesel exhaust hangs heavily in the air. Lining the road are apartment buildings, a multi-storied, "five-star" Western-style hotel called the Taj Coromandel, new businesses, restaurants, and shopping centers. Then, turning down Krishnamachari Road,[1] a side street, the driver enters an older world. At first the driver passes old houses set in large garden compounds. A few of these are posted with signs indicating the businesses they now house. Traveling further, the driver suddenly finds himself in the center of what was once a village, the "village" of Nungambakam. In the small bazaar, street vendors sell vegetables and rolled sets of banana leaves to be used as dinner plates. A small village-style temple dedicated to the elephant god, Vinayakar, is located there (see fig. 10). A second structure not far away is a devotional society dedicated to the god Ram, and not far from that is a third small temple.

When I first visited the village with a Nungambakam friend, it was September, just prior to my beginning work in George Town. We had gone because it was a festival day, Vinayakar *cathurthi* (Full-moon Day). In the street near the Vinayakar temple, children clustered around a man selling small, brightly colored paper umbrellas, symbols of the god. Next to him a vendor was molding and selling clay copies of the god for people to take home for their private worship. Later they would drop the mud idol into their household wells or into the sea, the proper methods for disposing of these clay images. The central event of the temple festival occurred when the bronze temple idol, garlanded in flowers, was taken in procession, carried on his palanquin through the village streets.

The names of these streets recall the castes and the big-men who once lived here: Krishnamachari Road, a Brahman Iyer name; Kumarappa Mudali Street, the name of a high caste agriculturist; Mangadu Sami Aiyar Street, another Brahman Iyer name (Nungambakam is known as a Brahman Iyer village); and Rama Naicken Street, the name of the mem-

Figure 10.   The Vinayakar temple in Nungambakam, Madras City, 1992. The photo shows the village-like quality of the neighborhood, which is located in the heart of the city.

ber of yet another dominant agriculturalist caste. Here the houses are not set in large compounds; instead, their verandas line the streets so that their inhabitants can sit out in the evenings and talk with passers-by, much as in a village or small town. In inner-city villages like this, there may even be an agricultural plot or two. Called "gardens," these bits of agricultural land, now behind walls, are remnants of the time when the area really was a country village. Madras was once known as the

"Garden City" because of these plots, and in the 1960s when I first lived there, urban agricultural "gardens" were still fairly common. Now, land values and urban growth have eliminated most of them.

Should the driver continue his short journey through the center of the "village," he will leave these traces of a rural past. Suddenly, just as abruptly as he entered, he will pass a wall and emerge once again onto a major road, Nungambakam Village Road, and into the bustling metropolitan present. The village, after all, lies in the heart of Madras City.

What the driver has experienced on his short drive is evidence that Madras's urbanization has been a process of the city spreading and engulfing the villages and towns that once surrounded it. Today Madras City is an agglomeration of villages and towns, each of which retains characterizing features of its own. J. Talboys Wheeler's map of Madras as it was in 1733 (compare maps 7 and 8) depicts the villages and small towns that today lend their names to the municipal districts surrounding George Town at its core: Egmore (Elambore), Nungambakam (Nungambaucum), Purasawakam (Persiwaukam), Vepery (Wepery), Triplicane, San Thome. Unlike the new outlying residential suburbs of the city, where neighbors are strangers and proximity is a product of class, these urban "villages" preserve their small-scale atmosphere. Residents know one another—if not always intimately—and strangers are noticed when they enter. Caste, too, remains an important determinant of residence. The identities of these localities have yet to be lost to the homogenizing forces of urbanization. As in George Town, it is in the context of places like Nungambakam that civic individuality finds expression. It has always fascinated me that these urban villages still influence the atmosphere of the city and leave traces in people's lives.

The experience of a graduate student of mine, who comes from Nungambakam, provides one sense of this influence. Her family has lived in Madras for nine generations. Recently her father and his brothers sold the family's ancestral home in the old "village" center. My student's father, mother, and brother were the only ones living in the house at the time. The father's brothers, who jointly owned the house, had for some years lived elsewhere, in Bombay and Delhi. In old age and in a cooperative spirit when they sold the house, the brothers had all agreed that the time to partition family holdings had come. Like many inner-city houses, it has now been converted into a business. When the house was sold, my student's father and mother rented a nearby house, owned separately by one of the brothers. There, today, they live modestly, a seemingly ordinary middle-class family, neither poor nor rich. They own a scooter, but frugality dictates that they rarely use it. However, if, as observers, we change our perspective so that we see them, not as a single family, but instead as a household at the center of an extended circle of kin, our understanding of the status of the family changes dramatically. My graduate student's extended family is well known in Madras and claims within its circle several highly placed and influential members both in its past and at present. It is no ordinary family.

One summer my graduate student returned to Madras to marry. When she came back to the university in the fall, I asked her about her wedding. "How many people came?" I asked. "Oh," she replied, "it was strictly a family event." "How many attended?" "About a thousand," she said with a smile. Curious about the extent of her family ties and knowing that her family was widespread in India, I asked her further, "If you were to walk down the streets where your father and mother have lived, how many houses would you still pass in which relatives of yours reside?" After reflecting a moment, she said, "About seven." Later, I learned from her father that about 1,200 relatives and close friends had attended the wedding. When I mentioned this to another Tamil friend, he had replied matter-of-factly, "Yes, that's her family."

Among other things, what this story reveals is that kinship ties are still important in Madras and its inner-city village localities. Until relatively recently, locality and kinship were overlapping categories for all castes in Tamil Nadu. For many they still are. When personal connections are important to social success, extensive kinship networks are an outcome, and community localities such as Nungambakam and George Town tend to persist. It is within the contexts of kinship circles and community localities that civic individuality finds expression. Without such contexts, there would be no civic individuality, and without a need for knowing who people are, the ties that unite a community, including those of kinship, need not be strong. It behooves us, therefore, to understand the forces that have contributed to the maintenance of these contexts and to their change so that we can understand how the role and nature of civic individuality is changing in the twentieth century.

Four factors in particular reinforce the association of kinship with locality or contribute to the continuity of urban localities as communities, notably: (1) locality-based marriage rules, (2) the roles that personalized trust and connections (including kinship ties) continue to play as determinants of social and economic success, (3) the community-making roles that big-men play, and (4) the presence of "charitable" community institutions—"big-man institutions," such as temples, production cooperative societies,[2] schools, and scholarship funds—which are the institutional contexts in which local big-men define their roles as community leaders and shape their followings. Like kinship and trust, big-men and their institutions are defining elements of community and social locality. Because big-man institutions have geographic location and often a distinct and sometimes impressive architectural form (e.g., temples, marriage halls, schools), informants describe them as key features of the physical layout of their own community and as distinguishing features of other locales. When institutional management is "denominational," that is, when it is controlled by a single locality-delimited caste, the connection between institution, locale, leadership, and kinship is further emphasized, even when the clientele the institution serves is not caste exclusive, as few are. But keep in mind that all of these forces and connections are weakening in the face of changes that are diminishing the role that communities play in people's lives in Madras City today. When community ties weaken, the spatial context community provides for expressions of civic individuality loses its significance, and the role that civic individuality plays changes.

Consider the nature of the four forces strengthening the association of kinship and locality and of those countervailing forces that are weakening community. First, locality-based marriage rules: Even today within Tamil castes most marriages still occur within recognized locality-based endogamous subgroups. This is true despite the fact that locality rules are no longer enforced and inter-subgroup marriages are increasingly accepted, especially among elite families. Smartha Brahman (Iyer) elites in Madras, the Iyers of Nungambakam included, were among the first to discard subgroup marriage rules. However, working to counter trends toward interlocality marriages, many south Indians still prefer marriages that maintain kinship ties by uniting related individuals: Tamil culture specifies cross-cousins and sister's daughter/mother's brother marriages. In fact, the mother's brother's daughter is called "*murai peṇṇu*" by her father's sister's son, a term that means the girl over whom the son has a right [of marriage]. Genealogies that I have collected reveal that in fact Tamils often do marry relations, if not always these specific ones. My own assistant married his elder sister's daughter in 1986, for example. In some communities, the majority of marriages are among relations (Mines 1972). When I seek motivations for these preferences from informants, south Indians have ready answers: they stress the desirability of arranging marriages with families with whom they share custom and outlook, the better to avoid incompatibility and conflict. However, even when great care is taken to ensure suitability, marriage is fraught with difficult adjustments. Families are naturally concerned about the welfare of their children, especially daughters, who will leave the family when they marry. Consequently, mothers and fathers feel more secure when their children marry into families that they know intimately, and they like their children to live close by so they are able to see them frequently. In part, therefore, these marriage patterns reflect matters of trust, a much cited concern of informants. It is easier to trust people you know and with whom you have continuing relations than those who lack these traits.

But as we have seen, the need to establish trust through personal knowledge is diminishing in India today, and reflecting this in south India, community ties are weakening and strict subgroup endogamy rules with them. The disbanding of subgroup endogamy rules is closely associated with the spread of Western-style education and modern occupational diversity that has led to occupational mobility. Family heads prefer to marry their children to spouses with similar educational backgrounds, to avoid matching a person with a progressive outlook, for example, to someone whose outlook is narrowly circumscribed. Opportunity and territory are closely linked, and education expands opportunity well beyond the locality. Members of educated families tell me that subgroup endogamy rules work against their alliance-making interests because they restrict the field of suitable families too severely. Consequently, as soon as families in a caste begin to educate their children, they begin to chafe at locality-based subgroup endogamy restrictions. If there are no other reasons for restricting marriages to their locality, elite families soon begin to arrange interlocality marriages, although the majority still arrange marriages within their subgroups. In some instances, full-blown intercaste marriages begin to occur as well, but the number of these marriages is small. Usually these are "love marriages," arranged by the partners concerned.

Since the 1960s, my data shows that the numbers of intercaste marriages have increased in Madras City; by 1986 every genealogy I collected in George Town included one or more. What is important is not the number of such marriages, which is still small, but the change in attitude toward them. Twenty years ago families cut off ties with intercaste couples and were reluctant to discuss them. Today people acknowledge them as part of life, something with which kin have had to learn to live. But informants privately tell me they still dislike them. They say their caste community disapproves of them, and families become quite upset when they occur. In George Town, the family priest, *puro-hit*, who conducts marriages for the Beeri Chettiars, told me that twenty years ago if he had conducted an intercaste marriage, he would have been boycotted by the caste. Intercaste marriage ceremonies were then small private events. Today he performs intercaste marriages at five-star hotels. However, despite such evidence of growing tolerance, continued reliance on personalized trust among business and artisan castes acts as a countervailing conservative force that works to preserve subgroup caste marriages. So do the personal preferences of individuals. In fact, I found among the Beeri Chettiars of George Town the vast majority of marriages still unite families that belong to the same *gumbu* subgroup.

Also reinforcing the association of kinship with locality are the roles that personalized trust and connections continue to play as determinants of social and economic success: locality integrity is maintained because castes whose members still rely on personalized social trust to regulate their economic relationships also tend to see advantages in maintaining close community ties. Business and artisan communities are of this sort, although there is considerable variation among them. Take the case of the merchant. Community membership facilitates business because it enables the merchant to achieve a reputation for trust and establish enduring social and economic ties. Within his community he may achieve a reputation for credit-worthiness, for example. This may enable him to enact verbal contracts among his fellows at will. "His word is money," is highest praise for the Tamil businessman because it attributes great integrity, and large sums are sometimes exchanged on the basis of such a word. A merchant's reputation in India is worth money. Further, knowing the members of the community, a merchant has a sense of whom to trust, mistrust, or be cautious about. Of course, any merchant will also tell you that you can never really tell about anyone. But, among people he knows, or knows indirectly through big-men, the merchant who maintains strong community ties has the advantage of greater information with which to assess risks compared to one who lacks such ties.

Another factor strengthening the association of kinship and locality is the community-making roles that big-men play. In particular, this includes the various ways in which big-men and personal relationships are put to use to support reputations, to determine social trust, and to organize the ways and means of accomplishing ends. These uses together create forces that contribute to the preservation of neighborhood localities and the urban village phenomenon. Communities are preserved because people preserve and use personal ties as means to achieve an ordered social life and other important social ends. Knowing this, whenever I set up household in India, I make an effort to obtain most of the household services I need through a big-man or woman. This helps ensure for me the reliability of the service providers, because they choose not to abuse their relationship with me lest they jeopardize their continuing relationship with the big-man/woman through whom I made my contact.

Of course, relations with big-men and women are two-way streets. Such leaders also make deals on behalf of clients who seek to negotiate their relationship with me. I remember once, while conducting research among Muslim merchants, wanting to do a survey of Muslim women in their houses. I checked with a number of the community's leading Muslim men before beginning, explained to them that I had hired a female Muslim social worker to administer my survey—*purdah*, the seclusion of women, precluded my personally conducting the survey—and began the survey when I thought I had the support needed. I had been conducting fieldwork in the town for over a year and thought I knew my way around. Two days into the survey, the religious head (*moulvi*) of a small but conservative faction objected strenuously to the survey and demanded that it be stopped at once. I went back to the Muslim big-men with whom I had first consulted and asked their advice. In a most friendly manner, they explained to me that while they personally thought the idea of the survey was fine, after I had gone back to the U.S., they were going to have to live with the conservative members of their community. Perhaps it would be better, they suggested, if I gave up the survey. I did.

The fourth factor reinforcing the association between kinship and locality is the presence of charitable, big-man institutions. The big-man institutions that mark and delineate distinct communities reflect the important roles that big-men play in these social formations. However, when people rely on education and new occupations, such as government service, to achieve success, their need for big-man connections to establish their trustworthiness or to act as brokers on their behalf lessens. Bureaucracy, measured in terms of standards established by certification, law, and codified procedure (e.g., diplomas, the courts, elections), grows in importance as a mechanism for maintaining reliability and provides alternatives to the wrath of big-men for countering transgressions and restoring order. Consequently, people are less willing to submit to the personal dictates of big-men and there is less reason to maintain community membership. Concomitantly, reputations and community identity become less important, and individuality is muted. When in association with Western-style education caste members also pursue new occupations monitored by bureaucratic controls, then the roles of big-men are challenged and diminished at the same time as subgroup endogamy rules are abandoned. There is even less motivation for individuals to maintain their community ties.

To understand the impact of the historic spread of bureaucracy and the decline of community, a distinction needs to be made here between "big-man," which I am using as a generic term, and "caste headman" (*ejamaanan*). A caste headman is merely one type of big-man, the recognized head of a caste subgroup. As we have seen, many castes in Madras City and elsewhere once had, but no longer have, headmen, although members of these castes do continue to recognize men and women whom they consider big-men and big-women. A consequence of the growth of bureaucracy is that over the last one hundred years, communities have been rebelling against the dictatorial control that caste subgroup headmen once were able to wield. For castes such as the George Town Beeri Chettiars that had families who turned to education early, rebellions began in the nineteenth century. For others, rebellions began later. A few castes still have recognized headmen, although their power is considerably curtailed.[3] Recall Natarajan: Since the power and authority of a headman depends on consensus, once that authority has been successfully challenged—by even one individual—the end of the office of headman is at hand. This is because without consensus, anyone can disregard the headman's commands. The way former headmen explain the disappearance of their role is that they are no longer given "respect," the respect that they need to command others. However, this does not mean that big-men no longer have a role in community life. On the contrary, if caste members continue to pursue occupations that rely upon high levels of personal trust, then subgroup endogamy may persist and, while the dictatorial headman will disappear from the community stage, big-men will continue to be influential arbiters of trust and manipulators of connections. As such, they continue to play similar roles to those that headmen once had, but without the dictatorial authority to command others to do their bidding. In Madras City, since the nineteenth-century lawsuits, individuals have sought to limit the personal autonomy and power of big-men, using bureaucracy to curtail their independence. They have done so by limiting the big-man's control over institutional offices by converting these into elected positions with defined terms of office. And they have circumscribed the big-man's independent control of institutional funds by implementing bureaucratic checks such as public audits and governmentally instituted and court-reviewed management schemes. Institutional big-men who used to have great entrepreneurial independence in the way they used their institutions have now been entangled in the web of law. As a result, the importance of their civic individuality has been diminished.

THE DECLINE OF THE BEERI CHETTIARS' GEORGE TOWN COMMUNITY

In order to understand the role and nature of civic individuality in George Town today, it is necessary to understand how the community has changed. Although, as described in chapter 4, the nineteenth-century lawsuits mark the end of headman leadership among the George Town Beeri Chettiars, the caste community remained strong and *gumbu* subdivisions, which headmen had controlled, continued as an important feature of social identity and community organization. Beeri Chettiar informants say that it was not until the late 1950s and early 1960s, when inter-*gumbu* marriages started to be common in the Town, that *gumbu* distinctions finally and precipitously begin to lose their social importance. Among the Town Beeri Chettiars, therefore, transgressions of endogamous cluster distinctions were unusual until seventy years after rivals had successfully challenged the dictatorial powers of the Beeri Chettiar headmen in the High Court lawsuits of the 1880s. Today, while informants can still recall *gumbu* names, and a few elderly people still use the initial of their *gumbu* as part of their name, most people agree that memory of them is fading and that they are no longer socially very important. Why, then, did *gumbuhaḷ* persist for so long after the demise of their headmen and of the Periyagramam council, their collegial body? And what finally brings *gumbu* endogamy to an end? The answers to these questions help explain the decline of the Muthialpet–Park Town Beeri Chettiar community at the end of the 1950s and the changing importance of individuality in the Town and city. In hindsight, the answers also reveal the historic relationship between caste organization and agency among the Beeri Chettiars. A caste is a mutable association, reflecting symbiotic interaction between leaders and members, whose organization reflects the purposes to which it is put.

One reason the Beeri Chettiar *gumbuhaḷ* persisted is that the economic and social value of *gumbu* membership continued unabated in the George Town Beeri Chettiar community until the late 1950s, long after the disappearance of the Periyagramam council and headman offices. It is easy to understand why this was true. For one thing, the Muthialpet–Park

Town Beeri Chettiars were still predominantly a business community operating on connections and trust. Each headed by its own big-man, a *gumbu* was a small, tightly knit grouping composed largely of interrelated business families. The strong sense of *gumbu* identification and the need to maintain one's good name helped to create the high levels of public trust that elder informants still talk about. The nineteenth century lawsuits had left this linkage between family and business unaffected. Continuing *gumbu*-locality endogamy ensured, therefore, that relationships among families were enduring and that the trust and connections that facilitated the conduct of business were maintained.

The son of Natesa Chettiar (Natesa Chettiar [b. 1890 - d. 1964]; Kandasami temple trustee 1918–24, head trustee 1931–36), himself a descendant of Ramsami and Ratnavelu, two of the progressive big-men of the nineteenth-century lawsuits, told me that until the late 1950s Beeri Chettiars married street to street, with no intermarriage between Park Town and Muthialpet, even when families belonged to the same *gumbu*. People liked to marry people they knew intimately and with whom they had enduring relations. Known to one another, these were families that would have something to lose if they were to act dishonorably, namely, their reputations and the trust of others, losses that would carry high costs in business and social networking.

Informants also describe a strong desire for the families linked to them by marriage to share their interests and lifestyles. But the Town Beeri Chettiars were a heterogeneous community. In the twentieth century, Park Town had the highest concentration of prominent business families. Muthialpet also included business families but was occupationally and socially more diverse, counting among its numbers families in prominent service with the English in business and government as well as increasing numbers of new professionals. Complicating marriage matters, in Muthialpet, several prominent families were also considered to have traces of English blood, the result of generations of close association with the British. In the eyes of many, this tinged their eminence with a strong sense of ambiguity, and Park Town's elite avoided intermarrying with such families. Some members of these families are said to have had blue eyes and light skin, and, as several informants remarked, they preferred tea to coffee, as their descendants do now—"just like the English." It is also true that some of the most prominent families counted Christians among their kin, as the nineteenth-century lawsuits, my genealogies, and public knowledge of family histories bear witness. Descendants from among these families continue to be among today's most prominent big-men, nonetheless.

The hereditary family priest serving the Muthialpet Beeri Chettiars once remarked to me that the meaning of "gumbu" was a group doing a *single* type of business. Although an exaggeration, the families of each *gumbu* did tend to specialize in particular businesses—a matter of fathers teaching sons their line of work, Bala told me. For example, the Poonamallee and Salem *gumbuhal* were known as dealers in iron and steel and as wholesalers and retailers of betel nut. But they were also coconut, provision, and rice merchants in Kothawal Chavadi, the city's wholesale produce market, and wholesale and retail textile merchants. Kasukaarar *gumbu* families were known as close associates of the British and, as I have noted, were distinguished as cashiers and bullion dealers, although they too counted families engaged in a variety of businesses. Similarly, the leitmotif of "Tobacco" (Pangaiyalai) *gumbu* families was tobacco, while nonferrous metals were the specialty of the "Tin-sheet" *gumbu*, the Tagararkaarar Chetti *gumbu*. Again, families belonging to both these *gumbuhal* pursued other enterprises as well.

Another reason for the preservation of the Beeri Chettiar *gumbuhal* and the Muthialpet–Park Town community was that under British colonial rule, Madras City was the capital of Madras Presidency, and George Town was located at the center of business, finance, education, and government. Situated at the Town's southern edge, the High Court of the Presidency was literally just across the road from Muthialpet (see map 2), which was a short walk from the Secretariat in Fort St. George. Next to the court was the Law College. Across from it and also in the Town were Christian College (founded 1837), and later Pachaiyappa's College, although subsequently both moved to less crowded quarters.[4] These three colleges played important roles in the late-nineteenth- and early-twentieth-century creation of a Western educated Indian elite in the Presidency.

The listing of a few names illustrates the growing presence in the twentieth century of Beeri Chettiar big-men among this educated elite. The *purohit*[5] of the Muthialpet Beeri Chettiars says that in pre-Independence Madras, Soma Chettiar (Kasukaarar *gumbu*), who was head trustee of the Mallegeeswarar temple on Thambu Chetti Street (see map 2), was also a president of Pachaiyappa's College as well as a "director" of Binny and Co., one of the major English companies. The priest says Soma Chettiar was a descendant of the Thambu Chetti family. His grandson still lives in Muthialpet today, although he is an ordinary person without claims to big-man status. Soma Chetti's sister's husband was the hereditary trustee (*suroodiriyamtaar*) of the Tiruvotriyur temple to the north of George Town. His sister's son is the head trustee and *suroodiriyamtaar* today. Another family, well known prior to Independence, was that of

O. (for Ottakaḍu *gumbu*) Tanikacalam Chettiar, descendant of Lingi
Chetti. O. Tanikacalam was for a time a small-causes court judge, a
Madras Legislative Council member, and president of the Madras City
Corporation. One of his brothers, O. Kandasamy Chettiar, was a student
of Dr. William Miller, the highly respected founding principal of Christian College. O. Kandasamy Chettiar himself became a well-known
teacher in the college. His daughter, O. Jeevarathanam Ammal, B.Litt.,
was the first non-Brahman woman graduate in the Town. Other members of the family were advocates, doctors, engineers, military officers,
and bank officers. V. Chakra Chettiar was yet another prominent graduate. He was the brother of Venkal Sundara Ramanujam Chettiar, a
trustee of the Kandasami temple from 1930 to 1935. According to the
purohit, V. Chakra Chettiar was an advocate, a well-known labor leader
in Madras, and for a time its mayor. He was also a convert to Christianity. In addition to the Kandasami trusteeship, his brother was the president of the Beeri Chettiar caste *maḍam* and founder of the Muthialpet
Benefit Fund, a charity serving the community's poor. In 1910, Natesa
Chettiar, the grandson of Ramasami Chettiar—the man whose outcasting led to the nineteenth-century lawsuits—became the first Poonamallee
gumbu college graduate. His *gumbu* was and still is the dominant business *gumbu* among the Beeri Chettiars in Park Town. To this day his
house is known to old residents as "B. A. House" ("B. A. Viiḍu"). Later
Natesa was a trustee of the Kandasami temple between 1931 and 1936,
and an adjunct professor of physics at Pachaiyappa's College. What is
apparent from this listing of prominent Beeri Chettiar names is that
George Town was a center of new opportunities, and, consequently, big-
man institutional leadership, achievement of Western-style education,
and eminence in enterprise had all become intertwined.

The big British and Indian banks were also located in George Town,
and Beeri Chettiar leaders were prominently associated with these. The
elder sister of one of my retired informants married P. Cittaraman, who
became the head cashier of the Mercantile Bank (now the Hong Kong
Bank). His father before him had also been a cashier in the bank, while
his father's brother was the cashier of Binny and Co. Marambuttasamy
Chettiar, the grandfather of another informant, was an agent of the
M.C.T. Bank, an Indian bank run by Nattakottai Chettiars on Coral
Merchant Street. Nattakottai Chettiars were the premier Indian bankers
of south India (see, e.g., Rudner 1989). Beeri Chettiars, especially those
belonging to the Kasukaarar *gumbu*, were prominent cashiers in other
banks, offices, and important British businesses as well: the Imperial

Bank (now the State Bank of India), the National Bank of India (now Grindlay's Bank), government offices (the *tahsildar* office and the Collectorate),[6] and in Wilson and Co., Shaw Wallace, Best and Co., Parry and Co., Burma Shell, and Binny. Positions were often passed from father to son, because, as my informants explained, families had established traditions of "trust and heredity" with these companies. What they meant by this was that so long as a cashier served his company honorably, his son could succeed him. As we have seen in chapter 4, this reflected employment practices dating back to the early days of British East India Company rule.

We see, therefore, that individual Beeri Chettiars were influential leaders in their community and often close associates of the British, employed in government, banking, and business, right up to Independence. If it is remembered that personal reputations, relationships of personalized trust, and "connections" with people of influence were important determinants of how things were done and of how relationships were established in business and government, then it is clear that maintaining community ties would have proved valuable in this special urban environment, especially for Beeri Chettiars, who were members of a caste that was not only wealthy and well connected, but also the dominant caste of the Muthialpet and Park Town sections. In short, George Town was and continued to be a place where people of influence lived. If, in towns outlying Madras, people left their localities seeking to achieve influence and wealth, then Madras City was where the most ambitious were likely to go. The George Town Beeri Chettiars were at the center of things in Madras Presidency.

Nonetheless, there were significant changes in the organization of the Beeri Chettiars after the nineteenth-century lawsuits. True, the eighteen *gumbuhaḷ* that composed the Beeri Chettiar caste in George Town continued to divide the caste into leader-centered constituencies. But these leaders lacked the authority of headmen and, Bala tells me, were now called *perundanakaarar* (syn. of *periyadanakaarar*) rather than *ejamaanan*, headmen. Further, the Periyagramam, which had been composed of headmen and had given the caste its administrative unity, was now defunct, as was the post of caste guru. The failure to replace the caste guru, the guardian of the caste's ritual identity and behavioral rules, who had gone off in the midst of the nineteenth-century disputes, is also a clear indication that leaders remained divided among themselves and that, internally divided, they were never again able to establish their collective authority.

But the *perundanakaarar* still had an important role to play, which was similar to that of headmen, even if they no longer administered the caste locality as a unit. As headmen had done before them, these leaders used caste institutions—especially the three big caste temples, the Kandasami, Kachaleeswarar, and Mallegeeswarar temples—as institutions of leadership. Genealogies indicate that some of these preeminent men were former headmen, their descendants, or the offspring of marriage alliances with descendants of headmen. Indeed, as noted, Natesa Chettiar was one such leader, and Bala's father-in-law's father-in-law was Natesa's kinsman, Kali Rattina, the "diamond-giver." In the last years of the nineteenth century, probably most temple trustees and preeminent *gumbu* leaders were either ex-headmen, kin to them, or their close allies.

Kaattavur Subramaniam Chettiar (hereafter, K.S.) was such a twentieth-century big-man. A wealthy iron and steel merchant and the recognized *perundanakaarar* of Salem *gumbu*, he was a man of humble origins who came to Madras to work for a Salem *gumbu* big-man family and, proving his worth, ended up marrying the boss's daughter. Later, he started the South India Corporation with Raja Annamalai Chettiar, a company that subsequently grew very large under Raja Annamalai's direction. K.S. was the head trustee of the Kandasami temple for three consecutive terms, from 1941 to 1958. In addition, he was trustee of the Mallegeeswarar temple and of the caste *madam*, and, with four other big-men, served as a trustee and member of the caste funeral shrine and tank (the Attipattam Kulam) building committee. An elderly informant[7] told me that K.S. was among the last big-men to hold regular *gumbu* community meetings. He called his meetings at the caste *madam*, sending meeting notices to Salem *gumbu* families living in Muthialpet, Park Town, and Chintadripet.

Another big-man and contemporary of K.S. was Maangadu Ellappa Chettiar (Maangadu *gumbu*), prominent member of a low-ranking *gumbu* that counted a number of wealthy families among its members. Although not the preeminent leader of his *gumbu*, Ellappa worked hard to establish his status as a wealthy and eminent businessman. He built temple cars for both the Mallegeeswarar temple and for the Tiruvotriyur temple located in north Madras. He also built a choultry in his name at the Tiruvotriyur temple, and he built the Mallegeeswarar *gopuram*. With K.S. he served as a trustee of the caste burial shrine and tank and renovated the burial shrine building. These two men may be taken as examples from a lengthy list of twentieth-century *gumbu* leaders residing in

Muthialpet–Park Town prior to the 1960s. Their generation was the last before the breakup of the George Town Beeri Chettiar community.

Thus, although headmen and their Periyagramam council had ceased to function, eminent men, including ex-headmen, continued to play big-man roles. Asserting their generosity and altruism, some of them made spectacular endowments to community temples, as my now familiar example of the cup of diamonds that Kaḷi Raṭṭina gave to the Kandasami temple in 1901 illustrates. But where previously the Periyagramam had appointed the trustees of community institutions from among their number, now trustees were elected. Then again, big-men acted as brokers and arbiters of social trust on behalf of their *gumbu* constituents, just as headmen had done, but without the overarching authority of the Periyagramam. In other words, *gumbu*s persisted in George Town because endogamy did not stand in the way of new paths to success, and because, even without the office of headman, *gumbuhaḷ* continued as groupings of social identity and prestige, constituting important contexts within which individuals organized action, manipulated connections, achieved reputations, and managed personalized trust outside the law courts.

But despite the persistence of *gumbuhaḷ* and the importance of the Muthialpet–Park Town caste domain, the Beeri Chettiar's nineteenth-century lawsuits do pinpoint the period of transition from headman rule and corporate community to what might be described as a more informal period of big-man influence, when the caste was no longer corporate, but still retained a strong community identity. Not surprisingly, this transition also marks the period when the integrity of the Town Beeri Chettiar community began to unravel. And unravel it most certainly did. Today, under Bala's headship, the Kandasami temple complex and its endowments are the only institutional aggregate left that still provides a base for castewide big-man leadership. And as we have seen, only a fraction of the Beeri Chettiar families that used to live in George Town still do.

What happened that would explain this near-collapse of what was once one of Madras City's most powerful caste communities by the end of the 1950s? The answer is that with few exceptions *gumbu* leadership simply failed to reproduce itself. This was not for the lack of sons, but because for several reasons the locale had lost its importance as the locus of interests and influence among caste members. In part, this was a result of Independence, which removed the British, with whom Beeri Chettiars had for so long maintained symbiotic ties, from a major role in the area. And in part, it was a consequence of the declining role business played in the lives of caste members. My genealogies show that the sons and daughters of prominent families were attending school and, in most cases, university, but sons were not returning to run the family businesses or to take over roles in George Town-based enterprises. Instead, they were taking jobs in government service or in professions which offered secure employment but lacked significant centers of influence in George Town. As a result, families no longer felt compelled to live in their old neighborhoods, and in increasing numbers, when brothers partitioned, they sold their ancestral homes in the Town and, each taking his share, moved separately to what each considered more desirable, less crowded, less expensive residential areas of the city. The role of the Town's remaining big-men was diminished by this process and their hold over their constituencies weakened. Elder Beeri Chettiars explained to me that educated caste members often felt little compulsion to subordinate themselves to *gumbu* leadership. Why should they? Their successes depended on education and were no longer embedded within the caste community. The community's decline was a result, therefore, of the changing manner in which Beeri Chettiars made a living. While business was potentially far more lucrative than bureaucratic employment, it was also much riskier.

In 1939, emerging from the world Depression, secure employment was new and novel, and jobs that Beeri Chettiars would consider not very desirable today seemed wonderful opportunities. When K. Sundaram (b. 1921), a retired General Post and Telegraph officer and scion of a once influential family, told me his own story, he laughed good-naturedly at what he clearly saw as the irony of his own career choice. Sundaram comes from a prominent Kasukaarar family that counts caste leaders among its members and once had close ties with the British. I have already mentioned his maternal grandfather, O. Tanikacalam (d. 1929), who was a lawyer and judge of the Madras Small-Causes Court, as well as a Justice Party[8] leader. Sundaram is an only son, but reflecting the family's prominence, one of his sisters is married to an advocate who practices before the High Court, while another is the widow of a former appointed trustee of the Kandasami temple, P. Seetharama Chettiar, M.A. (trustee 1964–1969; 1969–1977), who was cashier of the Mercantile Bank prior to his death.

Sundaram told me that he graduated in 1939 with a B.Sc. degree in chemistry. After graduation, without giving it much thought, he applied to medical school and was accepted. In those days, he says, it was relatively easy to gain admission. Now, of course, medicine and engineering

are regarded by most south Indians as among the most desirable professions one can pursue. But in 1939 that was not the case. He discussed
his options with his family and with them decided that instead of pursuing medicine he should take a job with the postal service, which he did
in 1940. He says being an only son married to a woman who was an
only child factored into the family decision. His father and in-laws
wanted him to lead a "quiet life," one that would keep him near.

Sundaram told me with a chuckle that, given the prestige and earnings associated with medicine today, it is hard to imagine that the postal
service could have actually appeared the better choice. But in those days
many still considered medicine an unclean profession, and government
service was desirable and secure work. He says his starting salary was
Rs. 40 per month. In 1940, you could get a meal for 20 p., a small fraction of a rupee. "Now you cannot get an egg shell." When he retired in
1977 after thirty-eight years of service, he had risen to assistant director
of the General Post and Telegraph Office in Madras. A good position,
but one that has no constituency within the Beeri Chettiar community.

Retired and receiving a pension of Rs. 850 per month when I interviewed him, Sundaram is an ordinary man, well liked, but without the
wealth and connections that he could call on to make himself an important leader among Beeri Chettiars. Yet, for all his ordinariness, in a
neighborhood emptied of Beeri Chettiars, he holds a number of positions that once would have marked him as an important and influential
big-man: he is a trustee and treasurer of the caste *maḍam* located in the
Kachaleeswarar agraharam off Armenian Street and the locality representative to two other *maḍams* in which the Beeri Chettiars have interests, one in Tiruvaalangadu, some twenty-plus miles from Madras, and
the other in Nerinjipet near Bhavani to the south (see map 1). In addition, from 1962 until 1985, he was first the joint secretary and then general secretary of the Tamil Nadu Ayira Vaishya Sangam, the statewide
association with which Beeri Chettiars are affiliated. And he is a lieutenant and ally of Bala's. Nonetheless, despite his offices, Sundaram is a
minor leader with limited influence. None of the institutions in which
he holds offices attracts much interest from George Town Beeri Chettiars today and none of his offices gives him control over significant assets. In other words, his offices are "hollow crowns"—markers of status that lack substance.

Sundaram's story points up the relative absence of preeminent big-men
in George Town today. The big-man form of organization had been well
adapted to the high levels of personalized trust that facilitated business,

but for university-educated professionals and government employees big-man leadership is unnecessarily restrictive and personal. Elder residents in George Town explained to me that by the 1950s big-men were finding that the community was no longer willing to give them the respect they needed to carry out their leadership roles. There were still community giants in the 1920s, 1930s, and even 1940s, but by the late 1950s, the link between claims to eminence and strong community constituencies had weakened to the point where conflict between contenders was rampant.

This was especially true with regard to temple trusteeships, the institutions that gave leaders communitywide recognition. Unlike Sundaram's offices, temple trusteeships were not hollow crowns. Education, occupational diversification, and the dispersal of Beeri Chettiar families meant that too few men had constituencies large enough or cohesive enough to enable them to claim the preeminence needed to defeat or discourage contenders in competition for control of the caste's denominational temples. Seen from the perspective of leaders, the fabric of community had become thin. Looked at the other way around, Beeri Chettiars no longer felt a compelling need to support caste leaders, since big-men now played a much less important role in their lives. When, in the late 1950s, heated squabbling over control of caste temples erupted among Beeri Chettiar residents, the Hindu Religious and Charitable Endowments (HRCE) Department, a state agency, stepped in to fill the leadership vacuum, first taking direct charge of the management of the Mallegeeswarar and Kachaleeswarar[9] temples.

By the early 1960s, trouble was also brewing over management of the Kandasami temple. Symptomatically, in 1962, the man whose symbolic role it was to call temple elections, the man who would have been the head of caste in the nineteenth century, the head trustee of the caste *madam*, resigned his *madam* position. I suspect he did so because, although there were vacancies on the Kandasami temple board that should have resulted in a call for elections, the two temple trustees remaining in office, P. A. Ragava Chetty and K. Venugopal Chetty, instead entered into an agreement with the HRCE Department wherein the department was given the right to appoint the temple's board, with the stipulation that appointees should be drawn only from the Beeri Chettiar community. Why they made this agreement is not completely clear today, but it appears that they may have done so as a bid to maintain Beeri Chettiar involvement in the management of the temple. Because of temple leadership disputes, the HRCE Department had been at the time actively considering taking over management of the temple. The result of the deal they made was that for a time it looked as if the Beeri Chettiars, while they would remain temple trustees, nonetheless would lose direct control of the last remaining important institution of big-man leadership in George Town. With this loss, the crucial social roles that Beeri Chettiar big-men had for so long played as the organizers of their caste corporate community within the city seemed at an end.

BALA TRIES TO REBUILD THE COMMUNITY: 1964–1987

In keeping with the deal, the HRCE Department selected P. A. Ragava Chetty in 1964 as a returning member of the first appointed board of the Kandasami temple. Of K. Venugopal Chetty, however, we hear no more. P. Seetharama Chettiar, Sundaram's brother-in-law, was among the four other appointed members.

But big-men dislike HRCE Department control because bureaucratic constraints inhibit the personalized and entrepreneurial nature of their patronage. By giving the department control over the appointment of trustees, the Beeri Chettiar caste had in effect lost its right to select its own leading men, including who among them was to be preeminent, the head trustee. Even more important, HRCE control greatly curtailed the ability of big-men to compete for temple offices and resources. Since the HRCE Department was a state agency, its control of appointments also meant that party politics would play an important role in the future selection of trustees. The HRCE takeover marked the low point in Beeri Chettiar community integration. It looked as if the community had lost its last institutional context in which meaningful eminent civic individuality could be achieved and expressed.

Three years later, in 1967, several residents rallied to regain control of the temple. Sundaram was a key figure among them. On behalf of the community, he and three like-minded Beeri Chettiars[10] filed a petition with the HRCE Department requesting that the right to conduct temple elections be returned to the caste, arguing that the agreement that had been made was without the consent of the Beeri Chettiar community and that the two trustees purported to have made the deal, in fact, never signed the agreement. Sundaram told me that only the lawyers of the two men had signed. He insisted that because of that fact the agreement should not be binding on the caste community.

In due course, the HRCE Department ruled that the issue of control could not be decided by a writ petition, but would have to be settled by

a civil suit. Accordingly, in 1976, Sundaram and his colleagues filed suit
and requested the court to allow the caste again to hold temple elections
until such time as the case could be decided. This request was granted,
and elections were called in 1978, the first since 1959. As a result of those
elections, Bala was elected to his first term as head trustee.

Like the generation of leaders who immediately preceded him, Bala
straddles the worlds of education and enterprise. He is both an engineer
employed in a government undertaking, All India Radio, and, succeeding his father, a successful businessman, the proprietor of a retail iron
and steel enterprise. He is a man of enormous energy, intelligence, and
accomplishment with extensive ties within the Beeri Chettiar caste community in Madras City. In part, as mentioned before, these ties stemmed
from his links to preeminent men of the past. In particular, he counts
among his wife's antecedents a number of prominent community leaders
including Kaḷi Raṭṭina, the diamond-giver, his wife's grandfather. Although he is himself a member of the Salem *gumbu*, Bala, who married
in 1959, belongs to the first generation of Beeri Chettiars among whom
inter-*gumbu* marriages were common. His wife's *gumbu*, like that of Kaḷi
Raṭṭina, is the top-ranked Poonamallee cluster. Bala also counts among
his affines Natesa Chettiar, whom I have described above, a link that ties
him to the progressives of the nineteenth-century lawsuits. Through these
ties, Bala is related to a number of former Kandasami temple trustees,
both in the distant and more recent past, and he traces kinship ties to
some of his closest allies as well as to some of his most dedicated enemies.

But Bala's success in the 1978 elections was by no means merely a
matter of connections. Already by that year, he had earned a reputation
of his own, one which he had achieved as a community leader among
the Park Town Beeri Chettiars. Key to this reputation was the "arts" association that he had founded in 1969 to promote music, drama, and
literature, the Kandan Arts Academy. Bala says he founded this association with the aim of bringing the Beeri Chettiar caste community together again, uniting them through patronage. Today the Academy has
four hundred members, drawn mostly from the Park Town Beeri Chettiar business community. It annually sponsors two major public concerts, held each year on a platform erected in the street in front of the
Kandasami temple under a huge thatch *pandal* (roof) constructed for the
occasion. The concerts are grand events that bring well-known music
stars to perform, and they are extremely popular. Spectators pack the
street. During the concerts, Bala plays a prominent public role and is
seen as its organizing patron.

Leaders like to sponsor dramatic events to attract public interest. In 1974, the arts academy gave two cash prizes of Rs. 51,000 to artists it judged up-and-coming, one to the music director S. B. Subbaya Naidu, the other to the poet S. D. Sundaram. Artists like these two men are low-income people, Bala says, so the prizes gave them a boost. The prizes were raised by the academy's performances and were a gesture of grand patronage that attracted a great deal of public attention. Bala told me in 1986 that he hoped to make similar awards in the near future. Through the academy, therefore, Bala successfully organized the Park Town Beeri Chettiar merchant community as sponsors of what have proved to be very popular annual events. Doing so, he earned a reputation as a hard-working altruistic community leader as well as the backing among his fellow merchants that enabled him to win his first trusteeship election.

In 1978, the extent of Bala's ties within the caste community was reflected in the 1,062 votes he garnered. The election was a close race in which he won the head trusteeship by a mere 28 votes. The nearest contender was his ally, K. Kesavalu Chettiar, who had served as an appointed trustee since 1964. Twenty-two candidates had contested the election, competing for 2,667 voters, each of whom voted for five candidates, five being the number of board members to be elected. Bala's detractors put this 1978 election in perspective by noting that less than half of the 7,500 eligible voters voted. But the electorate had to travel from all over the city to the Kandasami Spring Hall next to the temple where ballots were cast. This is more than a small inconvenience in a city the size of Madras, and indicates that Bala and his runner-up did well to rally the supporters they did.

Big-man politics accentuate personal rivalries and are typically contentious. It is hardly surprising, therefore, that Bala was to have enemies even among his fellow elected board members. As it turned out, his key rival was the younger brother of P. A. Ragava Chetty, a man whom I shall call Kaliraja. Recall that Ragava Chetty was one of the men who originally made the deal with the HRCE Department and was then reappointed by the department to the temple board. After the 1978 election, as Bala's successes as a leader began to mount, Kaliraja was to do his best to unseat Bala through a steady barrage of charges of wrongdoing, including a lawsuit accusing him and his temple board allies of malfeasance in the administration of temple affairs (Mines and Gourishankar 1990). Kaliraja's aim was to succeed Bala as head trustee. Failing that, he hoped to weaken Bala's influence by supporting increased HRCE Department involvement in temple management, including as a last resort a department takeover of the temple. If Kaliraja could not be head trustee and thereby enhance his own civic individuality, then he wanted to destroy the temple as an institution of leadership for others.

In the context of these conflicts, the case to return temple elections to the caste community finally came to trial in 1986 and, despite Kaliraja's efforts, was decided in favor of the Beeri Chettiar community in 1987. During the trial, Sundaram and his associates were de facto representatives of Bala's factional interests, while Kaliraja backed HRCE control. As events transpired, Bala's allies were able to discredit Kaliraja in court and so disarm his charges against Bala while simultaneously undercutting Kaliraja's claim that HRCE control was needed. During the course of the trial, Sundaram told me that no one was taking Kaliraja's charges seriously, including the HRCE Department. If they had, he said, the department would have intervened in temple management.

The turning point in the trial seems to have come when Sundaram was able to impugn Kaliraja's integrity by gleefully countercharging that Kaliraja was apparently not even a Beeri Chettiar and so should not be involved in Kandasami temple affairs. To Kaliraja's great embarrassment, Sundaram documented in court that Kaliraja had fraudulently registered his son as the member of another caste in order to lay claim to special educational benefits. The court burst into laughter at this piece of evidence. Following that court session, to this enthnographer's eye, Bala and his friends could only be described as in the highest of spirits. They were absolutely tickled with the way their enemy had been trapped by his own indiscretion. Some months later the trial concluded, and in September 1987, for the first time in nearly a decade, new elections for the temple board were held. Bala was again elected the head trustee of the temple board, this time in what amounted to a landslide victory. His contentious opponent, Kaliraja, failed to be reelected.[11]

Since his first election, Bala has dreamed of using his status as the head trustee of the Kandasami temple to revitalize the sense of community among Beeri Chettiars. His motivations for doing so are a mix of community spiritedness and his self-interested desire to strengthen his own leadership, which is necessarily caste-based. His motivations, therefore, are somewhat paradoxical, just as they are also inseparably intertwined. In this regard at least, Bala is probably much like his predecessors. His success as a leader depends on displays of community spiritedness, which earn him a reputation and civic stature. These are attributes that in turn distinguish him as unique, as an individual. But Bala is also aware that conditions and leadership roles have changed since the times of his predecessors. He is moved by a nostalgia for the glory days of the old caste neighborhood, which he would like to recreate. But the conditions that in those days gave authority and power to caste headmen are gone, and the caste neighborhood has dispersed. Bala can build a reputation as a civic leader, and as such, he has influence, but he has little authority over his caste fellows. He can influence, but outside the context of the temple, he cannot command.

Today in Madras, few Beeri Chettiars would say that there are any recognized leaders of caste. Not even Bala gets that recognition. Yet, if Bala could, he would have the galactic polity that he controls be the organization of the Beeri Chettiars in Madras. In fact, built as that polity is around the Kandasami temple, the caste electorate is his constituency, and so, in point of fact, his polity is an important part of what constitutes the organization of the Beeri Chettiars in the city today. But for most, that organization and leadership only lightly touches their lives.

Bala sees himself as a leader struggling to pull together a disintegrating community. He would like to reinvolve community members—to create the conditions where caste members would have a renewed stake in their relations with each other and would again turn to the big-men of the caste for leadership. He would also like to bring all the institutional interests and assets of the caste under a single administrative structure, which he envisions himself as heading. But there are few Beeri Chettiars who share Bala's vision or who see real benefits in the community organization of old. They no longer need *gumbu* headmen and are glad to be free of the constraints that the old system imposed on them. Nearly every Beeri Chettiar in Madras knows Bala. Many have even voted for him. But they do not think of him as someone who has power over their lives, nor do they envision him ever having such power.

Among his caste fellows, Bala is a *perundanakaarar*, a big-gift-giver, an influential big-man, and the preeminent trustee of an important Beeri Chettiar caste temple, but that is it. To be effective he must appeal to followers as an altruistic benefactor, but there is a halo of suspicion that always surrounds public altruism when it is associated with achieved charismatic preeminence and control of public resources. After all, the more a leader benefits his followers, the more important his own individuality becomes. Who is he helping more—himself or his constituents? In Bala's case, the suspicion is mild, but it is there. Tamils think it naive to presume that any public figure's actions are moved purely by altruism. One elder informant, a retired municipal politician and something of a self-styled skeptic, summed up his feelings about Bala's leadership this way: He did not know what went on behind the scenes at the Kandasami temple (meaning that, for all he knew, Bala might be mismanaging temple funds, as his enemies charge), but as head trustee of the temple, Bala had done good work and the community had benefited. This was high praise from a man who for philosophical and political reasons had not entered a temple for over thirty years.

Today, the central institution of Bala's galactic polity is, therefore, the Kandasami temple. And it is in his role as head trustee of the temple that Bala enacts most broadly his role as patron, struggling to recreate his community. The Kandasastri Festival (Kandasastri Kotti Arccanai), a six-day period ending the day after Deepavali, the fall "Festival of Lights," may serve as a brief reminder of the breadth of appeal that the temple has among Beeri Chettiars and so its importance to Bala. During this festival, Bala says, about twenty-two thousand families visit the temple to make an offering and to sit and be greeted by Bala, the head trustee. For Bala, this is exposure at the grassroots constituency-building level. Moreover, it is exposure in an important ritual context that depicts him as the preeminent big-man within his community. The worshipers get the prestige of being seen with him, and he the opportunity to provide them the honor of his presence. It is in public contexts such as this that Bala makes himself most visible as a leader and builds his reputation as a civic individual. Bala's desire, therefore, is to achieve as much exposure of this sort as possible. This means attracting crowds to temple events.

A chief aim of Bala's is to increase the popularity of the Kandasami temple—to make the Kandasami temple *the* Beeri Chettiar temple—the most popular of all the temples controlled by the Beeri Chettiars in Madras City. To do so, Bala pursues two primary strategies. His first is to maximize the spectacular in temple events. Temple trustees have always used grand display and ritual innovation to attract crowds and dramatize their patronage. His second strategy is to reinvigorate the sense of community among the caste, as he says, "to get the community together." For this purpose, Bala uses the institutional resources that he controls to create benefits for as many people as possible. Again, his aim is constituency building.

A popular name for Park Town, the location of the Kandasami temple, is Kaṇḍakottam, "Kandan's Place," reflecting the landmark importance of the temple to the area. Since 1980, Bala has invested over two crore rupees (a crore equals Rs. 10,000,000) of Kandasami temple funds in projects designed to enhance the prestige of the temple and benefit the Beeri Chettiars in the city. During each of his terms in office, Bala has completed a temple project with high spectacle value. His first, completed in 1984, was to build the gold-plated temple car. Covered with seven kilograms of gold and costing twenty lakhs[12] (Rs. 2,000,000), it is a rarity in south India. The gold temple car has added significantly to the fame of the temple and to Bala's reputation as head trustee. Today, the splendor of this magnificent car is a major feature of temple processions in which it is used. Who would want to miss seeing it? His second project, carried out in 1989, was to orchestrate and conduct the ritual purification and renewal of the temple, a *kumbabisheekam* ceremony, an elaborate and expensive consecration ritual of major importance, the performance of which seems to be one of the dream goals of most temple head trustees. As part of this latter event, Bala published a commemorative volume, which documents the spectacle and describes the history of the temple and the George Town Beeri Chettiars. The volume includes numerous photographs portraying Bala himself as a principal figure. It also includes congratulatory advertisements from businesses and community institutions, some of which are Bala's, and a large collection of color photos depicting the wealth of the temple, the crowns and jewelry of the Kandasami idol, and the many golden processional vehicles that Beeri Chettiars have built for the temple. In effect, the volume is a statement that the George Town Beeri Chettiars are a wealthy and influential community and Bala is a central figure within it.

Together these two projects, the gold temple car and the *kumbabisheekam*, have kept Bala and the Kandasami temple in the eye of the public both because they are spectacular and because they are major projects that build on anticipation and require a great deal of community involvement. They have enhanced the reputation of both temple and leader. These projects have also been community building, increasing the pride Beeri Chettiars feel in their temple, which they equate with their collective identity.

Using the popularity of the temple as a resource, Bala is also trying to revive the tradition of giving first honors to the heads of the old leading families of the various *gumbuhaḷ*. In this instance, first honors consists of sending a temple employee to the houses of these men to present them personally with invitations and announcements concerning temple functions. It also involves publicly offering them special respect when temple processions pass in front of their houses. Bala feels that too many of the old prominent families who used to handle *gumbu* affairs have become "just average" people and so no longer claim eminent status nor feel that they are in a position to help others. Nonetheless, he reasons that it is these men who could bring the community together again. If they are again given respect within the community, then ordinary people may once more turn to them for help in their affairs; for example, in settling a dispute, arranging a marriage, or finding a job. Make these men eminent within the caste, reasons Bala, and they will form points of influence around which the community can coalesce.

But even Bala is skeptical about whether this can be done. Too many families, both influential and ordinary, are moving out of George Town. High real estate costs and a desire for more open surroundings are frequently cited incentives. Bala uses his own family as an example. He says his ancestral home is worth ten lakhs. Since he is one of five brothers and his father is deceased, when his mother dies, he and his brothers will sell the house. Each will take his two lakhs, Bala says, and go his own direction. Real estate is too expensive in Park Town, and his brothers already live elsewhere. It used to be, Bala says, that all of his neighbors were Beeri Chettiars. Now most have sold their homes or let them out, some to businesses. It is getting so now there is very little neighborhood left.

But, although sometimes discouraged, Bala has not given up. The temple resources that are at his disposal as head trustee have been particularly important to his community-building efforts. Using temple funds, Bala has founded a number of satellite big-man institutions designed to benefit the caste community and extend its collective reputation. Using donations collected at the temple, for example, he has founded and built two schools and is planning the development of a polytechnical college. One of the schools is a high school, open to all communities, which enrolls one thousand students. It is located in Periswakam to the west of George Town on land valued at ten lakhs. The land was donated by Bala's deceased affine, P. Venugopal Chettiar. The other is located in Park Town itself. Called "Hindu High School," it instructs children from nursery school through high school and is housed in a new two-story building, which Bala says cost seven lakhs. In conjunction with Kandan Arts, Bala has also started a small music school, which at present trains students in vina and singing.

Located to the front of the temple's kingly tower (Raja Gopuram), the main entrance into the temple, Bala has also founded a free library, featuring magazines, dailies, and more than four thousand books concerned with literature, religion, and how to start small industries. The latter category of books reflects an ideal of Bala's. He believes that all Beeri Chettiars would benefit if caste members shared a community interest in helping their poorer caste fellows. An aim of the library is to provide a source of information for the average Beeri Chettiar seeking ways to come up in life. Bala points to the Komati Chettiars and Jains as examples of communities that have successfully pursued self-help strategies in Madras.

Since the 1950s, Jains have been particularly successful in their competition with Beeri Chettiar merchants in George Town, and Bala feels they are out-competing and gradually displacing Beeri Chettiars in part because they lend money to their caste fellows who want to start businesses. The Beeri Chettiars should do the same, Bala feels.

Bala has also founded two free medical dispensaries, one on Thambu Chetti Street, the Muttu Kumaraswami Devasthanam [Kandasami temple] Chamundi Iswari Ammal Free Medical Dispensary, named after the woman who donated her house for the dispensary. The second dispensary, the Kaṇḍakottam Free Medical Dispensary, is located opposite the temple on Rasappa Chetti Street in Park Town. Within the temple itself, Bala also manages the rental of the temple's sixty-plus properties and sells at concession rates *prasadam* (savories "blessed" by the god) and prayer-offering (*arccanai*) packets for the benefit of worshipers. And— a sign of the times—another temple concession sells religious videos.

Bala is also the managing trustee of the Vasantha Maṇḍabam, the Spring Hall, which abuts the temple, and of a marriage *maṇḍabam* on Mint Street, which is owned by the temple and rented for wedding parties and other important family occasions, such as the seventh-month ceremony celebrated on behalf of a woman by her parents during her first pregnancy. The Spring Hall is a well-endowed institution that serves as a community meeting hall as well as an institutional extension of the temple. I have mentioned, for example, how each spring the idol of Kandasami is taken to the hall to "rest." The hall is used by Bala for Beeri Chettiar Association meetings, for community meetings, for example, to select caste representatives for the Nerinjipet *maḍam*, and as the voting place for temple elections. The hall also funds a charity, the Vasantha Maṇḍabam Arakattalai, which each month gives Rs. 500 to poor Beeri Chettiars to assist them in starting a business, finding work, or meeting marriage expenses.

Bala has also founded several other associations, independent of the temple, with the aim of serving his community and strengthening grassroots support for his leadership. I have already mentioned Kandan Arts. In 1984, he organized the Park Town Benefit Fund, a financial institution offering secured and unsecured loans to middle-class Beeri Chettiars, as well as a deposit scheme designed to assist parents saving to meet dowry expenses. The fund was created to provide a means by which Beeri Chettiars could help one another. Bala is the fund's "honorary advisor."

In 1985, Bala also organized a new Beeri Chettiar Association (*sangam*) with himself as president. Initially, the rationale for the *sangam* was to certify the caste identity of members who wished to register for "backward class" benefits. These are government benefits aimed at assisting educationally disadvantaged communities.[13] This service, however, has failed to induce many Beeri Chettiars to join, and the *sangam* remains a "hollow crown" at present. Nonetheless, Bala has aspirations for the association. He feels if he can get enough of his caste fellows to join the *sangam*, he can claim for it the right to represent caste interests generally. His goal is to make the *sangam* the premier institution overseeing all organizations and endowments controlled by the caste, including the Kandasami temple. This would provide him with an institution that would administratively unify all caste assets and organizations, including the caste *maḍam*, giving him control of resources worth many crores. This kind of integrated institutional control, however, has never before existed, not even in the nineteenth century, when the Periyagramam board, composed of caste headmen, used to meet to administer caste affairs at the *maḍam*. In those days, the Periyagramam and *maḍam* were the premier institutions of caste.

Today, there is no chance of the *maḍam* regaining this premier institutional role. The symbolic head of the Beeri Chettiar's *maḍam* normally should be its Brahman guru, a part of whose function it is to instruct his Beeri Chettiar disciples about what for them is an appropriate code for behavior. As we have seen in chapter 4, by the 1870s both the role of caste guru and the enforcement of strict caste codes clashed with urban needs for behavioral flexibility. In 1876, when the Beeri Chettiar's guru left the *maḍam*, he was never replaced. Today, persistent anti-Brahman attitudes continue to make the *maḍam* unsuitable for the role that Bala has in mind for his *sangam*. It is likely, therefore, that the caste *maḍam* itself will remain a hollow crown. The current head of the *maḍam* is Bala's lieutenant, Sundaram. Bala's plan would give his *sangam* control over *maḍam* interests and would subordinate the trustee who oversees them. Sundaram told me privately he doubted the consolidation would ever take place.

Nevertheless, Bala is currently attempting to make *sangam* membership attractive to Beeri Chettiars. He has sent his supporters on a door-to-door campaign championing the benefits of a reunited community and soliciting members. But Beeri Chettiars are not attracted to join abstractions; they join when they calculate that there are real benefits to be gained. In 1985, therefore, in the name of the *sangam*, Bala also founded a form of financial institution known as a "chit fund," the Kandan Financial Corporation, this for the benefit of wealthier Beeri Chettiar merchants. The hope was that if the caste's *perundanakaarars* joined the fund, they might be persuaded to join the *sangam* as well. If they did, then ordinary men might also see benefits in joining the *sangam* in order to be able to associate with such influential men. In point of fact, however, the fund is not really under the control of the *sangam*, although Bala tries to play up connections between the two.

Businessmen join chit funds of this sort to self-finance lump-sum business expenses (see Mines 1972). To begin the fund, Bala brought together twenty founders, each of whom gave between Rs. 20,000 and 25,000 to establish a reserve fund. Each of the Financial Corporation's "chits" is for Rs. 100,000. A chit-fund group consists of forty members, each of whom contributes Rs. 2,500 for forty months. Month by month, members pressed for cash bid to buy the fund, members being eligible to buy once in every period of forty months. At month's end, the month's bid is distributed as earnings among fund members and at the end of the forty-month period, when the chit is completed, members are each given a silver tumbler or other silver utensils. By 1986, the corporation had twenty groups of forty members each. Bala told me that in business, people tend to borrow outside the caste community for fear of spoiling their reputations. The chit fund, which is seen more as a risky form of investment[14] than a form of borrowing, serves a valuable function among wealthy merchants, providing them with both earnings and a source of unencumbered cash, which they can access quickly with a high bid, if need be.

Bala's abounding personal vigor and determination can be seen in all these efforts described here. His efforts also illustrate how a leader who wishes to expand his civic identity must multiply the contexts in which he attracts and serves different clientele. A community is composed of such multiple contexts. In each new institution that Bala founds, he seeks to attract a constituency of followers, who together will recreate the community that has been lost. But except for the temple and Bala himself, there is really very little that connects the different groups that constitute his following. In 1978, when Bala was first elected head trustee of the Kandasami temple, he was, as he is today, a caste leader of a new generation, a generation that lacked a strong connection between caste identity and neighborhood community. Without this connection, Bala has been constantly faced with the challenge of how to pull together a constituency he could serve. His response has been to attempt to revitalize his caste as an integrated community, not as it was—that would be impossible—but as a citywide community, founded on shared interests in the Kandasami temple and the institutional galactic polity that surrounds it. If successful, the caste he would create would be a community only weakly integrated by a shared need to control social trust; the new community would not be a phoenix, therefore, raised from the ashes of what once was. Although Bala does not fully realize this, and despite the fact that he would still use temples and institutions to attract constituencies, much as his predecessors did, the new community would necessarily be a new kind of organization. But despite his efforts, it seems unlikely that Bala can succeed. The conditions that created tight-knit organization are past. Although he believes he is trying to revitalize his caste fellows' sense of community, what he has done in fact is to put together successfully a coalition of constituencies within his caste without recreating the community for which he nostalgically longs. Grappling with a variety of approaches to recreate community integration, Bala is succeeding as a big-man but failing to recreate the caste community. Although caste neighborhoods still exist, they are disappearing. They no longer reflect the dynamics of city organization, which, after all, reflect the needs and interests of the city's inhabitants. The city is undergoing profound change and the organization of civic leadership is changing with it. Big-man networks are still important, indeed central to city organization, but the caste neighborhoods that leading individuals once created to organize their affairs and regulate social trust are no longer essential.

Private Voices

CHAPTER SEVEN

Themes of Individuality in Private and Public Lives

Personal Narratives

If I were interested only in social history, I could end my narrative here—after all, I have now told the story of George Town and its leaders. But my purpose has been more than this; it has been to explore the nature of individuality in Tamil society, and in this endeavor there is more to be done. Until this point in my discussion, I have focused on what is known about the public person—the external manifestations of who a person is, the strivings of leaders, the roles that eminent individuals play in the making of a community. But what of the private self—the personal thoughts and aspirations of an individual, of a man like Bala, or of more ordinary men and women? What does the Tamil individual look like to his or her own mind's eye? Shifting perspective to examine the dialogue between self and society from the vantage of private concerns and inner voices, it is important to bring clearly to mind that the manifested public individual (what is known about an individual), the social being (the fabric of the individual's social ties), and the inner voice are components and dimensions of everyone's individuality. There is an interconnectedness and interaction among all these aspects of the individual that is only revealed when we listen to the stories people tell about their own lives. Each person carries these dimensions of private identity and must work out his or her own orchestration of social and private identification. If we ignore these personal stories, then we ignore the articulation of self, culture, and society that makes each person unique and individuation possible. But we also deny the active agency of the subject in the making of culture, society, and consciousness (cf. Mines 1990, 1992; Obeyesekere 1992:17).

By this point in my discussion, it should be very clear to the reader that in civic society the individual establishes his or her uniqueness in the context of groups. Everything that distinguishes the person and gives him or her identity as an individual is defined in relationship to others—reputation, eminence, leadership, altruism, ability to command others, role as an agent in society, everything. In Tamil Nadu, civic individuality is distinguished by a person's status within groups, and the greater the person's eminence, the more that person's individuality is stressed and valued by others. And it is also true that the greater a person's notoriety, the more his or her individuality is stressed. Bala's enemy, Kaliraja, is distinguished by his unscrupulous efforts to unseat Bala, at least among Bala and his supporters, who form the social context of Kaliraja's notoriety.

Tamils consider the individuality of different people, therefore, to be of unequal worth, and to judge the individuality of another, a Tamil must know who that other person is within a given social context. This is different from individuality in the United States, where, defined in law and in the dominant ethos that supports individualism, each is valued equally—at least notionally—and where a person need not know another to value him. In the United States, a concomitant feature of equality is that each is judged an independent, self-contained agent. There is a uniformity to the idea of the individual.

A dominant American belief is that all persons share a common humanity. By contrast, a Tamil's civic individuality is not an outcome of a sense of common humanity. The value of a Tamil's individuality is a variable thing distinguished by several mutable features: ancestral home, *jati*, or caste, family reputation, status within groups, age, control and responsibility for others, size of following, and the sense others have of one's character. What is being estimated is the importance and nature of a person and his or her agency. In addition, in Tamil culture, civic individuality is circumscribed by ideas that stress altruism and in effect subordinate the self-interest of individuals to groups. An individual is neither independent nor a self-contained agent, as in the American sense. Yet every Tamil would think it ridiculous to assume that persons are not self-interested. Indeed, it is clear from what I have so far described that civic individuals are understood by their fellows as motivated by self-interest and, as we have seen, are constantly jockeying for position. The successful construction of a civic identity requires, therefore, that a leader mediate both public and private interests, while seemingly subordinating private interests to those of a superior public good. To successfully pursue private interests, a leader must demonstrate through patronage of others that he puts group interests before self-interest.

In private life, this same juxtaposition and mediation of self and other, of self and group, exists. As in public life, Tamils believe that in private life a person should subordinate self-interest to the collective interests of those groups with which he or she is most intimately involved, those of family and caste. The ideal is to live in harmony with others, to avoid putting oneself first, and to comply with the decisions of elders and superiors. Because of this, a major psychological challenge of private life is to achieve meaningful control over one's own life.

Public and private individuality represent, therefore, different, sometimes conflicted dimensions of the person. Natarajan's telling of his wedding, a mixture of triumph and sadness, in chapter 5 is a case in point. Consequently, individuality may be understood from more than one perspective. Thus, if big-man status stresses a person's civic individuality within a community, personal narratives or life stories reveal private expressions of individuality and individuation. But it should also be kept in mind that the two dimensions of an individual's life influence and affect one another. They are the interior and exterior dimensions of a single individuality.

It follows, then, that individuality has multiple aspects, and because it does, there are many ways for an informant to tell his or her life story and many ways for an anthropologist to elicit such a telling. It depends on the focus of one's questions. How do I do it? Usually I begin by asking particularistic questions about age, marriage, number of children, caste, place of birth, and places where the person has lived. These questions help me to understand the framework of the person's life and "prime the pump," so to speak, for the interview that follows. Having done this, I have found it very productive next to ask my Tamil informants, "Think back and describe for me the first personal goal or dream you remember having and what happened."

After a moment's reflection, my Tamil informants begin to explain with animation a history of their lives. The depth and intensity of their responses have surprised me and, as a fieldworker, delighted me. Often in response to this key inquiry, an informant has talked for half an hour or more, and in some instances for well over an hour, before my next question, usually a request for elaboration on something said earlier. Judging by my informants' animation and absorption in their responses, asking Tamils to talk about their goals reveals a natural way they have of thinking about themselves and of explaining who they are, what they have done, and why. Describing their goals, how these goals have evolved and changed, and the decisions they have made both to achieve and to change them, Tamils explain their sense of responsibility for their lives and something of what their lives have meant to them. They also describe the evolution of their individuality, revealing how their sense of themselves has evolved through the course of their lifetime. They are at pains to show how their view of themselves, their reasons for action, and their sense of what is meaningful to them has so changed with age and experience that they believe that who they are today hinges on key experiences and choices that they have made in the past. They give to their life histories a strong sense of key periods and continuity. What they are less conscious of is that, when their life stories are viewed chronologically, a clear periodicity in their evolution is revealed. The Tamil's sense of self and culture changes with age (Mines 1988). Each person's sense of individuality and culture is age-layered.

But what do personal life stories have to do with Tamil social history? For their tellers, life stories serve multiple purposes. Among these are the tellers' attempts to make sense of experience and to interpret how they affected the direction that their lives have taken. Older persons naturally have more to say about such things than younger persons. By the time they approach age thirty, they begin to describe situations that they feel have compelled them to mediate between their inner senses of themselves, their private interests, their social circumstances, and their sense of cultural dictates. But, as the life tellings presented below reveal, personal stories, like other kinds of stories, are also tales of self-discovery that reveal how the individual assigns meaning to events, how cultural understandings frame the individual's own understandings, and how the individual interprets his or her life in relationship to society. Private expressions are not separated from public life. They are single voices seeking to make sense of the junction between the self, life experiences, culture, and society. Individuals are the makers of micro-history—modifiers of the given order, subtle re-inventors of cultural meanings. Even when they think they are conforming to society and replicating its order, individuals produce metamorphosis. But they are also products of their time, what Tamils sometimes call the flow of circumstance. And their lives are framed by the historical period in which they live.

One must also keep in mind that the private expressions of men and women are in important ways distinct. Their tellings reveal different problems of being, even while their stories also contain shared under-standings and values. Because society and biology dictate different roles for men and women, the issues and problems that women and men de-scribe receive different emphases. Among my informants, men and chil-dren play bigger roles in women's life-tellings than do women and chil-dren in the stories of men. So, too, psychological struggles for a sense of control over one's life are central to women's stories, whereas goal achievement and issues of public identity are more prominent in many men's tellings. For men, meaning is closely associated with honor and prestige, with leadership, with public reputation, with service to one's community, and with responsibility. For women, meaning is also asso-ciated with attaining responsibility, especially for oneself and for others, but most ordinary Tamil women acquire responsibility in the context of their families. Women are also concerned with the maintenance of af-fectionate family relationships, especially with their children and grand-children. They are concerned with orchestrating the well-being of their children and of their children's families—the direction of concern fol-lows the descent line. Preoccupied as men are with public identities, men rarely mention affection, children, or the illnesses of their children. These are the concern of women and are of the private realm. It is not that the concerns of women are not valued by men and vice versa—they both are involved in the concerns of the other, affected by each other's worries and desires, gaining from each other's successes and suffering from each other's failures—but that what they imbue with special meaning in their stories reflects sex and gender and the effects of cultural meanings and social order. Pivotal points in the life stories of men and women—the crisis points—are different. And so in this chapter and those that follow both men and women reflect on who they are. Both must tell their tales.

C. SIVAKUMAR

I contacted Sivakumar at the recommendation of a friend of his. I made an appointment to meet him at his office, and it was there that I inter-viewed him—in English. We were alone, and my memory is that we were not interrupted, even though we talked for over two hours. We must have had coffee, but I don't recall it. We later became friends, and when I left India, he and his mother presented me with special Tamil sweets, made with jaggery—unrefined cane sugar.

Sivakumar is a man of accomplishment, university educated and very intelligent; my field notes indicate that he likes to enter contests. The director and head of a Tamil Nadu State institution, at forty-eight Sivakumar is professionally a successful man. Yet, when I ask him to tell me about the first goal he remembers having for himself, his manner and words express a deep melancholy. He says, "Life has turned out disappointing for me." He is single and would like to marry, although now the prospects seem slight. When he was younger, he felt vital and life seemed to hold out many exciting possibilities. "The best time of my life was my last two years at school when I was successful in my studies and extracurricular activities. I won awards writing essays and as a debater."

Responding to my question about first goals, he states, "When I was twelve years old, I wanted to get into the IAS [the Indian Administrative Service, India's elite civil service], that's why I stood for the exam when I was twenty-three. I qualified, but didn't get through the interview.

"But at twelve, I was also always thinking about being a writer of short stories—I started at twelve to write poems and stories in English and Telugu for the school magazine. I still write short stories and have published a few . . . but mostly not. Because of work, I can't do much."

He remembers his father giving him a sense of possibilities. "My father was a short story writer on the side and published some, and that inspired me. He sent them to England, but he published in India only . . . but [he] always had the desire."

Clearly upset by his present situation, Sivakumar, describes his life as "stuck"—stuck in a job in which he feels little interest, but one that is too good to give up, stuck in a profession that has nothing to do with his lifetime aspirations, and stuck in social circumstances that depress him. He knows he could change his circumstances, but does not.

He feels unfulfilled. He tells me that his job provides him with a large bungalow. With a wife to run the household, he says, he could live there. But as it is, he lives with his mother in the family home. Later, explaining how she had asked him to return to Madras City after his father's death, he quietly describes her as "an interfering type," which his deceased father was not. The way he says this, mixing repressed resentment with guilt, expresses a central conflict in his life. He is caught on the one hand blaming his mother, while almost in the same breath denying his resentment because it is an Indian cultural ideal that a son should show first loyalty to his mother and that she has the right to ask to come first in his life. On the other hand, Sivakumar recognizes his own responsibility for how his life has turned out. He has experienced periods when he was able to live in the manner he likes, and he knows that it is within his power to do so again. But although he expresses strong feelings about how he would like to live, he himself recognizes that he denies the validity of these feelings as a basis for action. Instead, he gives priority to criteria that make his life secondary to others, particularly the cultural ideals that place his mother's interests before his own, and as we shall see, his view that professional success comes before his own emotional fulfillment.

He describes a number of opportunities that have arisen in his life, but he says that he was always too diffident. "Now my life is stabilized as director because I got stuck here."

At twenty Sivakumar graduated with a B.Sc. honors degree in chemistry and then at twenty-three took his M.Sc. in chemical engineering. Chemistry had not been his first choice, and he says that he really was not interested in his postgraduate studies. He had wanted to study engineering for his B.Sc. degree, but had only secured admission in engineering at a university in Andhra Pradesh State, three hundred miles from his parents' home in Madras City. Guided by a desire to maintain strong family ties, as many south Indians would have been, his mother had thought that too far away. Consequently, as his second choice, he joined the chemistry program in Madras from which he took his degree. It was shortly after his Master's that he failed to win the IAS position that he coveted. Without any real alternative, he took a temporary one-year post at a Madras museum as his first job.

His father was retired, and being the eldest son, Sivakumar had to find a job after his one-year position ended. But jobs were scarce. The one area of employment that looked promising in India at the time was accounting; because of a shortage of accountants, the central government was offering training to qualified candidates. Sivakumar took the opportunity and trained for two and a half years before being posted to Bombay as a central government employee. He was twenty-eight. Again his mother objected to his living so far from home, and hating his job himself, he returned to Madras City and job hunting, this time looking for something closer to chemical engineering.

He tells me that he was still thinking about the possibility of a writing career, and on an off chance he applied for a position as a popular science writer in New Delhi. As luck would have it, he received three job offers, including the New Delhi one. Sivakumar really wanted the job and says that he regrets not following it. The difference in pay was not great, although the pay and status of the job his parents wanted him to take—a civil service job—was marginally better. But his parents were especially against his going so far away, and so he took the job in Madras.

He was thirty-five before a job opportunity arose that was good enough for him to rationalize moving away from his parents. The post was as a chemist in a central government institution in Hyderabad, Andhra Pradesh. He took the job and stayed nearly seven years until his father's death in 1971, when once more his mother called him home. Free of family for so many years, he says he did not want to return to Madras.

He describes his years in Hyderabad with animation. "[It] is a gay place. People are very sociable happy-go-lucky people," he says. "In Hyderabad people move more freely, more openly than Madras, even if they are from different religions or strata."

He had liked debating in college and so joined a speakers' club in Hyderabad. And he won awards as a speaker. "I like to compete and succeed," he says. "I entered slogan contests and did some essay writing." He also says he felt some fulfillment in his work, which he describes as the satisfaction he had of having done a good job.

Sivakumar describes how he and his Hyderabad director began their jobs within four days of one another. Soon a close bond formed between the two. The director was an older man, a diabetic, who needed someone in his house, so Sivakumar stayed with him for a month or two after he first arrived. Sivakumar says the director took to him. He taught him about administration, and gave him a great boost by telling him that he was too diffident. "He told me that you must ask for things. Don't expect things to come to you. I even have trouble now." He describes his mentor as very big and tall, "forbidding and masterful with a terrible temper." But he never directed this at Sivakumar. The director was dynamic and got things done. Even though they were friends, Sivakumar says he never asked for favors, and that was why the director had said that he should ask for things, that he was too diffident. "Even now I think of him as my mentor."

Sivakumar discussed the director near the end of our interview, when I asked him to tell me about anyone he considered his mentor. The director's words gave Sivakumar a sense of justification and moral courage, that it was all right for him to pursue his own interests. The significance that Sivakumar attributes to the director also suggests that it is at this point in his life that he realized his own responsibility for how his life was turning out. He was responsible for himself in Hyderabad, and liked his life there.

He was forty-one when he returned to Madras. He describes the period while he was trying to decide whether to stay in Hyderabad or return to Madras as the most difficult time of his life. "I thought I would do better there [in Hyderabad] and possibly marry there." This was the first mention of marriage and of his feelings about marriage since his brief comment at the beginning of the interview about the bungalow that came with his directorship. He says that his youngest brother is mentally retarded and lives at home. As a result, his family has been unable to arrange marriages because prospective families shy away when they learn about his brother. Only one brother among five siblings (four brothers and a sister) has managed to marry.

But in Hyderabad, living the single life, Sivakumar says that he had a large circle of friends. "There people are more vivacious." He joined the YMCA and a German cultural society, the Max Müller Bhavan, and through a friendly Bengali, he met others. The Bengali was a Hindu who had made a "love marriage" with a Muslim. Another of his friends had married a woman from a different caste.

In time, encouraged by the examples of his friends, Sivakumar himself considered making a "love marriage" with one of the employees at his YMCA, although she, too, belonged to a different caste from his. Then, when his father died and his mother wanted him to return to Madras, he found himself in anguish. He liked his life in Hyderabad and the fact that he could move freely there. But he also felt it was his responsibility to care for his mother and retarded brother. Nonetheless, his director had helped him learn that he needed to assert himself. Finally, under great stress he told his mother that it was not possible to return to Madras because of his job.

It was then that he learned that he was in line for a directorship in Madras City, a status he knew he would never achieve in Hyderabad. In the balance, setting the personal advantages of Hyderabad against the professional advantages of Madras, he was like a man looking for signs, and this one—the chance of a directorship—told him that career and mother outweighed his own emotional interests.

Telling me about his life, Sivakumar juxtaposes his sense of responsibility for his life with his belief that his studies and career have been governed by circumstance. His role has been to take what others have defined as the correct choices. Only once, when he pursued admission to the IAS, had he done what he really wanted for himself or what was in fact within his ability to do within India's restricted opportunity structure. For all his talk about competitiveness, he has always chosen what has been the safer path, the one that has conformed with the ideals of his culture and his parents' wishes. As a result, he feels trapped and depressed, and although he knows it is he who is responsible, he judges himself as "too diffident" to assert himself. He told me that when he left Hyderabad, he lost the chance of marrying the woman he had wanted. He said it was impossible because she was employed there.

When I met him again seven years later in 1986, little had changed. He was still director of his institution, still lived with his mother, had never married, and seemed a very unhappy man. In "big-city" south India, although there are many more intercaste marriages than there were twenty years ago, most people still remain critical of them. Electing to comply with tradition, Sivakumar nonetheless clearly laments his lost chance.

The dilemmas of Sivakumar's life, as he explains them, draw into sharp contrast his own sense of his self-interest and his compliance with cultural and social dictates, especially the wishes of his parents and the priority he has given to socially valued "oughts." His emotional dilemmas are culturally conditioned, of course. Tamil culture and values favor the kinds of choices he has made over the self-interested choices he would have liked to have made. But what Sivakumar's story also reveals is that there are great psychological costs, felt as depression, anger, and grief, which stem from his resulting sense of being trapped. Sivakumar is perfectly aware of his own responsibility for his condition, that if he so chose, he could rebel against compliance and pursue his own goals. His mentor and Hyderabad life made that clear to him. But he is unwilling to pay the price of choosing his own way. He fears what others will say of him, and so he conforms and suffers enormously because he does.

One or another variety of this sort of dependence—conforming to the dictates of others—is a common condition of young adulthood in India. Srinivas, for example, writing about father-son relationships in the village Rampura, describes how Swamy, the adult son of a leading villager, hid his smoking from his father for fear that

> he would be sent out of the house if his father came to know about it. . . . He lived in fear of his father. There were hundreds of others like Swamy in Rampura and neighbouring villages, young men who were husbands and fathers, but who had to behave like children before the head of the family. They increasingly resented their dependence. (Srinivas 1976:100)

The life histories I have collected reveal that, unlike Sivakumar, most individuals do reach a point in life when they choose to give their own goals greater priority, in many cases only after great emotional and sometimes social struggle. To gain control of their lives, individuals must either have responsibility thrust on them, as may occur, for example, when a family head dies or retires and abnegates his or her responsibilities, or they must rebel against their seniors and the values that support compliance, perhaps forcing the partitioning of their family or other jointly owned family enterprise. Indians constantly weigh in their minds the costs of rebellion against those of compliance. Both men and women engage in these calculations and, in the course of adulthood, most describe themselves as coming to recognize that they alone must be responsible for what happens in their lives. It is perhaps no surprise that they often begin adulthood believing just the opposite, that if they comply, then they will be looked after and things will go well for them. But many older informants say that the death of an elder or the misery they felt being controlled by others—either gradually or abruptly, but inevitably—forced them to recognize that they had to take responsibility for themselves. Lakshmi represents a case in point.

S. LAKSHMI

If she had known Sivakumar, Lakshmi might have said that he "lacked guts." Lakshmi is a Tamil Brahman woman, who was fifty-two years old when I first recorded her life story. As a daughter-in-law in a large extended household, she had learned through years of emotional suffering that a person must stick up for herself. But it was not easy. "It takes guts."

When I asked Lakshmi to describe what she remembered as her first goal in life, she responded that as a teenager her dream was of marriage. She herself had grown up in a large extended family, one of seven children (five daughters and two sons). Her father was a leading lawyer in Cuddalore City in southern Tamil Nadu. Characterizing her household, she says her parents and especially her grandfather v ̣ ̣ very orthodox. If, as a small child, she ran into her grandfather's room, then he would bathe to remove the ritual pollution she caused. And if one of the children of the household cried, he would not pick it up unless it had just bathed and was undressed. Children and their clothes carry pollution. But even when she did transgress the old man's ritual codes, he was affectionate and "wouldn't scold."

She remembers her childhood as happy. Her mother and father were also affectionate. They all talked freely with each other, and although they were orthodox, she says everyone was relaxed with the children. She went to an English convent school, took music lessons, and in her own words was very innocent and inexperienced, without any real friends outside her own large household. When she did marry at nineteen, marriage brought about a complete change in her life. She says she was totally unprepared. "The sudden change was terrible."

She moved from Cuddalore to Madras City, where in her new status as daughter-in-law she joined the large extended family of her husband. He was the eldest of eight children (six sons, two daughters) and assistant to his father. Like her father, her husband and father-in-law were lawyers, but with that most likenesses stopped. She describes the atmosphere at her in-laws' as very different from that of her childhood.

Her husband, she says, is a quiet person who keeps everything to himself, even his sorrows. "It is hard to find out his opinion on things." Silence was his way of managing life in the extended household. "If he remarked on everything, it would have resulted in conflict." Lakshmi says her father-in-law was a stern old man who kept tight control over all household finances, including all of her husband's earnings. He was strict about money and did not allow indulgences. Lakshmi says that even after she had her children (two daughters and a son), she was afraid to ask her father-in-law for things, even for her children.

For Lakshmi her years in the joint family were years of misery. She says that her father-in-law's house was like a hotel. People were constantly coming and going. Relatives, out-of-town clients, and their wives all came and stayed. "We [the women of the household] looked after their comfort. They came and went as they wanted. Now, no one lives like this."

She says that she had been brought up to be the ideal dutiful daughter-in-law and she tried to be. She believed that if she was a good daughter-in-law, then things would work out well for her. But she was very unhappy. In contrast to her indulged childhood, as daughter-in-law she had time only for household work and was so busy, she says, she did not even have time to think about herself. "I had not even minimum comforts there. My children were sent to schools that were not good." She says her children were given neither proper dress, nor food, nor good medical treatment. When they were sick, she was not even allowed to buy them fruit.

"When I was pregnant, I was sent home only ten days before the birth [rather than at the seventh month, as is normal in Tamil society] and was wanted back by the end of the month because I was hardworking—so I could not give attention to my children." Her eldest daughter was sickly until she was about seven, "but they wouldn't let her go to a doctor. They starved her by putting too much water in her milk. She had a bloated stomach." Her son caught smallpox, but was given no medicine. But then proudly she states, "By the strength of their [her children's] constitutions they survived. I knew better, but couldn't get father-in-law to do anything."

It pleases her that, despite her children's hardships and the poor grammar schools they attended, they proved exceptionally intelligent and subsequently achieved top ranks in their classes at university. She says that before her father's death in 1958 she used to send her children to stay with him. "He looked after them and bought them things." It was her way of circumventing her father-in-law's austerity. "Father-in-law didn't mind because [while they were away] he didn't have financial responsibility [for them]."

When she was twenty-nine Lakshmi set herself the goal of getting a degree in Hindi through correspondence courses. In a household that gave little recognition to how she felt, she was looking for a way of doing something for herself. Her father liked the idea, but her parents-in-law were opposed to educated women and did not allow her to study. If she had earned her degree, she says, she could have found a job later, when she and her husband were on their own. That, she says, would have helped them get through the difficult financial times they had when, ten years later, the father-in-law expelled them from the house.

At thirty-one, her sense of being thwarted in her efforts to pursue something of her own direction in life was still strong. At this point, her father died. This, she says, was "the hardest thing that had happened in my life. I was depending so much on him. For the next year I was a nervous wreck. It was only his death that made me realize how much he helped." Following his death, she describes how she found that she was unable to walk without gasping for air. Her in-laws feared that she might have tuberculosis. They sent her to a doctor who found nothing physically wrong with her. It was her despair that caused her to gasp. They gave her some sleeping pills and sent her home to stay with her mother for six months. After that, she says, she was all right again.

In the year following the death, Lakshmi came to realize that her father's help and affection had enabled her to cope with the feeling that at her father-in-law's no one was interested in her or in how she felt about things. No one cared about her life or about what she wanted for her children. She described several times in the course of the interview her frustration at having been unable to buy her children fruit or send them to the schools she wanted, and how her father-in-law had denied them proper medical attention. His strict control of the household and, she was beginning to realize, her own efforts to be dutiful, were denying her control over her life, her basic interests, and her individuality. Her fusion within the family was psychologically suffocating her. "But for father, everything would have been much worse."

Lakshmi describes that horrible year as the turning point in her life. During it, she came to realize that no one could really help her. She had to be responsible for herself. Yet it was another seven years before she finally managed to get out of the household she disliked so much. Looking back, she considers those twenty years of joint family life the worst of her life.

She and her husband's departure from the joint family was very stressful. The father-in-law had begun to speculate and borrow money, requiring Lakshmi's husband to cosign his loans. Lakshmi feared that the father-in-law was building up such large debts that when he died, debt alone would be all that was left them. How were they going to take care of their own family, educate their children, and arrange their children's marriages? Her husband had complete faith in his father, saying that he would look after them. But by now Lakshmi was certain that her husband's assumption was, as she says, "a miscalculation." She knew this with a certainty that derived from her realization that she alone was responsible for the course of her life.

When at last she persuaded her husband to stop cosigning loans, the father-in-law reacted by abruptly telling his son that he no longer wanted to support him and his family. He told them to move out of the house. Lakshmi's husband, who had always believed in his father, was shattered. "He got the consequences of being too self-sacrificing. He helped his father raise and marry all his children [her husband's younger siblings], and then his father kicked him out."

Lakshmi was thirty-nine. Her husband was forty-one. Financially it was a very difficult time. Her husband could no longer work with his father, and now chose to give up law rather than practice separately. As a lawyer, he would still have had to face his father in court. In fact, he had never really liked law, which had been his father's choice for him. He had a variety of connections from his years as a lawyer and soon found a job with India Cements that paid Rs. 400 per month, a small income for a family. He never again talked to his father or visited his home until his father lay on his death bed. Lakshmi's husband was permanently scarred by his father's rejection. He had expected the old man to care for him in return for his own compliance and assistance. Instead, his father's rejection made his own years of sacrifice meaningless. In contrast, Lakshmi was ready for the move and grew stronger because of it. The whole process was part of her gaining responsibility for herself.

The first few years after their expulsion were hard, but her husband was capable and hardworking and was promoted rapidly. They borrowed to educate their children and to arrange the marriage of their first daughter. They also managed to buy a house with the assistance of a company loan. When her first grandchild, a boy, was born four years later, she says, it was the happiest moment of her life. She loves and is proud of her children and grandchildren. They are the source of her happiness in life now. Looking back to when they separated from her in-laws, she says, "I didn't even dream of such a good lifestyle as I now have."

Lakshmi clearly sees herself as responsible for making her new life. After all, it was she who came to terms with her own responsibility for herself after her father's death; it was she who saw clearly that she and her husband were sacrificing their children's lives as well as their own to their father-in-law; and it was she who persuaded her husband to stop cosigning his father's loans. Her sense of responsibility is now a basic precept in her view of life. "My policy is don't blame others. We are at fault for letting ourselves be cheated. He [her husband] should have protested that he had his own family to look after. . . . If I had had the guts to get out when I was young, I would have gotten out." Lakshmi feels that her experiences have strengthened her. However, she does regret not having acted sooner in life. If she had, she feels the loans they took to educate and marry their children might not have been necessary and much suffering would have been prevented. Her goal now is to enter retirement free of debt.

At fifty-two, when I first interviewed her, she described herself as leading a contented life. She did not want to put her children in the position of taking care of her and her husband. She told me, "Our son is earning well, but we refused his offer of money because we don't want to spoil his life like father-in-law spoiled ours. My pleasure is helping our children when they need it. We eat well and live simply."

I asked Lakshmi if her experiences were tied to an older way of life, one that a young woman of today would be unlikely to experience. In reply, she told me that one of her daughters lives in a joint family, and is very unhappy with her situation.

Had she given her daughter any advice? She answered that she doesn't stick her nose into her children's business because she knows that it would cause resentment. Each must learn for himself or herself what she has learned. It takes time and is part of life. They must learn it themselves.

Meeting Lakshmi at fifty-nine in 1986, it is easy to see the psychological strength and satisfaction that she has achieved. Her life began to improve when she finally recognized that, if she was to survive, she had to have the bravery to act on her realization that she alone was responsible for herself. Several other of my life history interviewees expressed very similar views. It is my sense that Lakshmi believes this to be true to a much greater extent than do most Westerners. The strength of this conviction may be partly because Tamil culture emphasizes compliance rather than independence. Consequently, she has had to forge on her own the separation she has needed, a process that has given her a sense of her own strength. It may be also partly due to the belief that how a person acts determines what will happen to him or her in life, for every action has its consequences. In this sense, we are all responsible for what happens to us in life.

When Lakshmi says "[I want] to be in charge of my life without others interfering," she expresses much the same sense of a need for control in life as an American does when speaking of "autonomy." "Being in charge," "having control," and "responsibility" (poruppu) all convey similar notions of agency and individuality, expressing a desire to control decisions affecting one's life. But there are also subtle differences between the Indian and American notions of control that reflect contrasting perspectives and social orders. For Lakshmi, responsibility for herself involves being in charge not just of herself, but also of how she relates to others, especially her children, grandchildren, and husband. Her father-in-law had prevented her from acting toward her children in the manner that she would have liked. For the American, however, "autonomy" conveys both a sense of "being in charge" and "freedom," stressing more the idea of being independent or separate from others. Indian individuality, therefore, emphasizes being responsible for who one is and what one does within the context of relationships, and thus Lakshmi's individuality is in part defined by her relationships and responsibilities for others. Finally, for the Indian, being in charge implies achieving the status and power to take responsibility for oneself and one's relationships. The individual replaces the authority of seniors with his or her own authority. In Lakshmi's case, taking responsibility pitted her against her father-in-law's control and his responsibility for the household as a whole. Expression of individuality and the adult process of individuation, therefore, are constrained by the authority structure of household relationships.

Although Lakshmi may have wished she had been brave enough to take charge earlier in her life, if she had, she might have not only isolated herself from her in-laws but also reflected badly on her parents. All would have criticized her for failing to be a dutiful daughter-in-law. After all, within a joint family everyone is expected to put collective interests before self-interests. Further, as noted before, Indians calculate the "costs" of fission. If she had isolated herself from the joint family too early in life, she might well have had to face alone whatever unexpected contingencies life dealt her, widowhood, for example. When she did force the split, it was at a point in her life when the disadvantages of her father-in-law's debts outweighed the advantages of joint family security. Separation made sense.

C. VISWANATHAN

Compared to Lakshmi, C. Viswanathan's younger adulthood went smoothly. The most difficult period in his life came much later when he went bankrupt at the age of forty-five. He was still working his way back to financial success when I interviewed him nine years later, in 1979. Before the age of forty-five, Viswanathan's life had been a steady climb to local eminence. During the two years before his bankruptcy, from 1968 to 1970, he was the de facto head of his caste within his village. He was the *kaariyakaarar*, "the man who got things done." He says that he had not wanted the title because a *kaariyakaarar* no longer commanded the respect that he once did. In his father's and grandfather's days, when a villager passed the *kaariyakaarar's* house, he would tie his head cloth or shoulder towel around his waist to show respect. Today, elected officials command the greater respect.

A member of the ancient Tamil weaving caste, the Kaikkoolar or Sengunthar Mudaliyar, Viswanathan lives in Akkamapettai, a small village of weavers, located a mile from Sankaridrug Town and about 8 miles from the inland city of Erode, a major wholesale textile center and railroad junction about 250 miles south of Madras City. When I first visited Akkamapettai in 1967, the clacking of handlooms was a constant background sound. Years later, when I recorded Viswanathan's life history, the roar of small power looms had replaced the rhythmic sound of handlooms. By that time he was operating ten power looms himself and was close to regaining the prosperity he had lost.

Viswanathan was fifty-four when I interviewed him in 1979. Educated to the eighth standard, he had been married thirty-two years and had ten children, five sons and five daughters. All but his three youngest daughters were married and living separately.

At the time of the interview Viswanathan was working for hire, as he said, "for coolie." Master weavers were supplying him with yarn and designs and paying him a piece rate for the textiles they contracted with him to produce. His master weavers collected and sold wholesale his production in Erode's weekly textile market.

By village standards Viswanathan is once again a reasonably wealthy man, although he is by no means the wealthiest and still lacks the resources to finance his own weaving. His immediate business goal is to be his own master weaver. He believes that his profits would be substantially higher if he were. However, that would take more than Rs. 20,000 a week, he says, and since wholesaling is largely done on account, he feels himself still significantly short of the cash reserves he would need to operate successfully as a master weaver. Viswanathan's ultimate goal at this point in his life is to complete his daughters' marriages and build his business to the point where it will provide his sons with a better life than the wage work they are doing. With three dowries to provide and still faced with debts stemming from his bankruptcy, he feels insecure about his future.

Viswanathan has been involved in the textile trade since his youth. He first learned the textile business from his father, who had operated a small retail enterprise, selling saris in the weekly markets of surrounding towns and villages. All his adult life his father had followed a weekly cycle, travelling each day to a different bazaar with his bundles of saris. On Sundays he sold in the weekly bazaar at Sankaridrug. On Mondays he was in Sengammamuniyappan Koyil Village, then on Tuesdays in Trichengode, and so on throughout the week. Friday was his day off. On the side, his father also did a bit of handloom weaving, involving all the members of his household.

In 1945, Viswanathan's father formed a partnership with two men from Trichengode and opened a permanent shop in Sankaridrug. For two years Viswanathan assisted his father in the shop. But his father and partners were restless for the daily variety of their former bazaar businesses, and in 1947 his father bought out his partners and returned to his old way of doing business, leaving Viswanathan to run the shop. Viswanathan was twenty-two years old, the age at which he also married.

I asked Viswanathan what he remembered as his first goal in life. He said he really had two. One was to visit a foreign country, a goal he accomplished when he toured Sri Lanka in 1966, following his father's death. He said his other aim was "to be generous to others, without quarrel."

Stating this last sentiment, Viswanathan expresses not only an ancient value in Tamil culture and one of the defining characteristics of a good leader, but also the central precept by which he himself has attempted to lead his life. He has tried to make generosity his public hallmark, and he is known to his supporters in the village and surrounding countryside as a generous man. Less successfully, he has also attempted to project the image of a leader who is above petty factionalism—as he says, a man "without quarrel." But public eminence attracts contention.

Like most successful men, he has his enemies. Viswanathan's bitter rival is a lineage (*pangali*) mate, a man who has been in competition with him since his youth. Today, this man has succeeded Viswanathan in several of the public offices that he himself once held. Even so, Viswanathan is seen by his supporters as by far the cleverer man.

Not many years ago his rival learned that Viswanathan had made an offer on a piece of land adjacent to Viswanathan's mother's house. The rival decided to spoil whatever plans Viswanathan had for the land by buying it for himself and building his house on it. He countered Viswanathan's offer with a substantially higher bid. Surprised, Viswanathan upped his offer and was again countered by his rival's even higher bid. Viswanathan knew this piece of land well and was aware that it flooded during heavy rains. He also understood that his rival was looking for a piece of land on which to build his new house. The price was now higher than Viswanathan felt the land was worth, so he withdrew his offer and left his rival to pay the inflated price. The rival, thinking himself the victor, gleefully built his house, but to his horror found himself flooded during the next heavy rains. Being made to look the fool and imagining Viswanathan's delight at outwitting him, the rival's enmity proved enormous. When rains flooded his house in 1978, he attacked and nearly killed Viswanathan with a hoe. Viswanathan responded with a lawsuit for damages.

From 1947 until 1958 Viswanathan managed the cloth shop in Sankaridrug. It was an easy time of life for him. His business grew, and because he was a generous man and a man of his word, his public reputation also grew. During those years, "I was shown much respect. My signature was a trusted one. If I sent a stranger to collect money with my signature, then the money was given without question. I commanded great respect."

Listening to him, his youngest brother comments to me that people still speak highly of him and characterize him as a generous man. However, Viswanathan marks 1958, when, he says, he entered the height of his power, as the beginning of his downfall. It was in that year that he was first elected to public office. Running against his rival, he was elected a member of the town Panchayat, the local governing committee. He believes his political success gradually led him to miscalculate his business affairs. Believing that his popularity was in part a result of his generosity, he slowly increased the shop sales he made on credit.

In 1962–63, he was made director of the Sankaridrug Cooperative Bank. And in 1962, he was secretary to the House Buildings Society, the local housing board. Then in 1964, he was re-elected to a second five-year term on the town Panchayat, again defeating his rival.

During his tenure in office, Viswanathan says he was responsible for a number of village improvements. He brought electricity to the village, installed street lights, dug street gutters and a public well, and built for the village community a temple dedicated to Subramaniyam. He also built a housing colony in the village, "fighting," he says, "with the landowners until they sold land . . . V. V. Giri, [at that time] President of India, came for the putting of the foundation." Demand for housing was increasing because of a new cement factory that had been located near the village. It was this factory that had drawn President Giri to the locality, enabling Viswanathan to arrange for him to attend his ceremony.

Finally, Viswanathan also served on the High School Committee for Sankaridrug, collecting money for the high school's expansion. And, as noted, from 1968 to 1970 his caste designated him their big-man, or *kaariyakaarar*.

Viswanathan himself was a member of the Dravida Munnetra Karagam Party (DMK), the ruling regional party in Tamil Nadu in the late 1960s, and had good ties with one of the party leaders, a state-level minister. In 1968, Viswanathan used his caste and locality ties with the minister to get his youngest brother a government post. Viswanathan reminisces that this was the "happiest time [of my life]. Because of good business I was respected and was powerful with people."

But although he had been generous with his shop customers, they had not been paying him back. Intensely involved in politics, he had let his attention wander from his business finances. One morning in 1970, perhaps with the connivance of his rival, the textile wholesalers from whom he bought cloth for his shop arrived at his house with policemen to arrest him. They had brought a case against him for failure to pay his debts. Viswanathan owed a substantial sum.

"They said that if I paid something against my account, they would drop the case. But at that time I had no money. So I went to a nearby village, to another caste man, a Konar [dairyman], and pledged a [gold] chain of four sovereigns weight for Rs. 500. I gave that to the wholesale merchants, but they wanted me to pledge the house to them [as a guarantee, which he did]. Then, within the year, the wholesale merchants were bankrupt. Six months ago [January 1979], they were back, still asking for money." Viswanathan still owes his creditors and says he has promised to pay them back when his business improves.

At forty-five, Viswanathan was forced to close his shop. "I just had the stands from the shop. All textiles were given for credit. I was ashamed to come out of my house and thought of suicide." He says he was without work for three months. His failure had hit him unexpectedly, and he felt his reputation and honor were completely destroyed. As a respected leader in the locality, he had thought that his successes and eminence were unassailable, the rewards of his generosity and integrity. He had misjudged, and it was his own fault.

He considers himself alone responsible for his own actions. "I don't take advice from others—my wife, friends, or others. If I think something is good, I do it and take the consequences." He recounts how both times he was elected to the town Panchayat, he had been offered bribes of Rs. 10,000, plus contracts and other benefits, to support a particular council member for president of the Panchayat. Both times he says he refused and voted for his own candidate. "In this way I developed my reputation for honesty. I didn't misuse my position."

But Viswanathan does feel he miscalculated the nature of life. In 1970, he was again asked to stand for the Panchayat elections, but this time he refused because of his losses. His rival won his seat and has since remained in office. When I interviewed Viswanathan, he was still traumatized by the sudden collapse of his life. His bankruptcy destroyed a fundamental sense of confidence he had had in the relationship between action and consequence. The Tamil world view is that good actions generate a good life; Viswanathan's life had always seemed good to him and he had thought that because he was a generous and trustworthy man, it would go on being good. Now, still clearly anxious about what the future may hold, he believes he was mesmerized by public service and the eminence it provided him when he should have put his business and family first. He is attempting to regain the sense of security that he once took for granted by limiting his affairs only to those of family and business. For Viswanathan the connections that joined his ethic, actions, and success, which once seemed self-evident, now no longer seem to match the uncertainties of reality. He is anxiously trying to look out for himself.

In 1967, Viswanathan applied for an electrical permit to install power looms. The permits were granted in 1970, and three months after his traumatic bankruptcy, he again mortgaged his house for Rs. 2,000 and bought his first power loom. "All the family worked hard on that loom, and then I bought a second loom, after one year . . . [At the end of] the second year, I bought two more looms through further borrowing and from earnings. In the fourth year I also bought two. Fifteen months ago I got a State Bank loan and bought two more looms. Then, borrowing on those looms, I bought two more." Viswanathan has trained and now employs three loom operators to assist him.

At best, weaving is a seasonal business with wide swings between boom and bust. Throughout the interview Viswanathan describes rough cost estimates of his goals, like a man reassuring himself that he will have the resources to meet his expenses. He says that about six months out of the year he has enough work to operate only two or three of his looms. If he were his own master weaver, he calculates he could vary his profit margin to fit the market and would then be able to work year around. He figures he will require about Rs. 10,000 in order to marry each of his unmarried daughters in the manner he wishes. This is a small sum for a man of his stature and is indicative of Viswanathan's financial anxiety. It is unlikely his daughters will be able to marry as well as they might have, if he had been willing to provide larger dowries and more expensive weddings. And he is sacrificing his own prestige as well. He is anxious about his debts and concerned that he be able to leave his sons with a good business. Although he no longer is as powerful and influential as he once was, he again commands the respect of his supporters. It is his public eminence that is no longer what it was. He has traded that for the goal of a more secure financial future. Nevertheless, his youngest brother and ally tells me that Viswanathan is a lot richer than he acts.

If Viswanathan is an example of a man who first achieved public eminence because of his reputation for integrity and generosity, he is also an example of a man who has held to his ethic of generosity throughout the ordeal of public shame and the rebuilding of his economic fortune. It is a Tamil belief that generosity helps nurture a man's wealth, while stinginess destroys it. Reflecting this view, his brother once told me that I should never directly refuse a request for alms because if I did, then I would suffer the loss of my own wealth.

Making clear the responsibility of the actor for his own fortune, the ancient Tamil poet-philosopher Tiruvalluvar writes of such men:

> Who lose the flower of wealth, when seasons change, again may bloom; Who lose "benevolence," lose all; nothing can change their doom.—chap. 25, verse 248, *The "Sacred" Kurral of Tiruvalluvar* (Pope 1980:35)

Despite the vicissitudes of his life, Viswanathan continues to embrace this Tamil ethic as his guide for social action.

In both public and private life individuals are known for what they accomplish. When success, as a feature of individuality, is recognized, individuality is recognized. In Tamil culture, eminent people are not merely distinguished as economically and politically successful within their communities, they are also identified as people who embrace responsibilities for the good of others. Indeed, they achieve eminence in proportion to their responsibilities within their communities. The offices a successful person holds in institutions designed to serve public interests are expressions of public-mindedness. So too is an individual's reputation for generosity. Generosity, responsibility, and eminence all define one's individuality within one's civic community.

M. TANGAVELU

At twenty-nine when I interviewed him, M. Tangavelu is one of my younger life history informants. He is an enormously energetic man, a junior officer in a Madras branch of the State Bank of India, and a man who has devoted much of his early adulthood to helping the disadvantaged. Service to others is an ideal for action that fits well the highly personalized nature of Indian communities within which, paradoxically, men and women are honored as individuals in proportion to their altruism.

However, just as Viswanathan found that eminence was no protection against financial disaster, Tangavelu is beginning to realize that his public-mindedness conflicts with the bureaucratic nature of banking and is no shield against the resentment of rivals and less hardworking or able coworkers, whose complacency and seniority he threatens. Just as a "big-man" would, Tangavelu sees his role in banking not as a bureaucrat but as a facilitator; he tries to use his institution to serve a clientele. Banking, he believes, offers opportunities for helping people. Indeed, it was the success of his first bank projects in Erode that earned early promotions for both himself and his bank manager. But reception of his ideas in Madras has been quite different. Rather than expressing approval, his colleagues have criticized him for what they see as at best wasted effort and at worst the misuse of bank funds. Chagrined, he observes, "Somehow people are always trying to pull me down, but I am indefatigable."

He wonders now, at age twenty-nine, whether he is being professionally wise. Should he give up his public-spiritedness because of the

trouble it seems to be causing him? "My colleagues are saying it is fool-
ish to give money on loan to the poor, or to help people in need. . . . But
I don't want to stop. I'll keep doing [such things]. Many of the things I
do are what government policies are for and I have the power to grant."
He wonders why he should be admonished if the banking policies are
there precisely to assist the poor. But what Tangavelu still fails to realize is that his implementation of such policies makes him look danger-
ous to his seniors, who wish to keep their futures secure by avoiding
risks—in effect, by sticking to the normal rules of banking. Although
surprised by his seniors' chastisement, he is nonetheless beginning to
strategize about how best to protect his own banking career from at-
tacks. He says his ambition is to become a bank executive, so that he
will be in a position to influence bank policies in all branches.

Born and reared in Erode in modest circumstances, Tangavelu belongs
to the Pandaram caste, a small non-Brahman priestly caste, known officially in government lists as the Jangamars. Traditionally, the men of his
family have served as priests at the temples of Maariyamman, a fierce
village goddess. His paternal grandfather was a Maariyamman priest,
but his maternal grandfather was a teacher. Tangavelu's father and
mother are also teachers in Erode, his mother having completed eighth
standard and his father his SSLC, a diploma similar to an American high
school diploma. Although he comes from a very poor family, Tangavelu
says his father "struggled to come up in life." Today he is founder and
headmaster of his own small school.

Among the traits that make Tangavelu unusual is that he is one of the
few Pandarams with a university education, a B.Sc. degree in math,
awarded when he was twenty. His sister also has a university education.
After completing his degree, Tangavelu immediately applied for a job
with the State Bank of India. He stood for the bank exam, was interviewed, and hired on merit. His first bank posting was in Erode. Although, he says, it usually takes seven to eight years to become a bank
officer, he was promoted after five years and, after a second assignment,
was posted to Madras in a junior officer position, an assignment he considers a plum. At the time of the interview, he had rented a room and
was living a somewhat lonely existence separated for the first time in his
life from his family, mentors, and hometown friends. He said that his
situation would improve if he were to marry, and he had recently con-
sented to his parents' wish to begin searching for a bride.

Over the last two years Tangavelu has begun to assume the role
of head of his joint family. Although his father is living and still active,

Tangavelu had successfully arranged the marriage of his sister the previous year. He says he took over the task from his parents after they twice selected potential grooms whom he thought unsuitable. He wanted his sister's husband to have a good education and "way of living" that would match her own. It took over a year for him to find the alliance he wanted for her. The search, he says, worried him a great deal. He was living alone in Madras City with "no one to share the troubled times with. I went home every week. The whole year was difficult." He felt heavily the responsibility of arranging his sister's life and knew that if he failed, she would be the one to suffer. He worried also because there were few educated men in his caste and, as the months passed without finding a groom to his liking, he was frightened that he might have made a mistake holding out for a university educated groom. "But then a suitable boy turned up, and they were married six months back. . . . At first they lived in Rajasthan. But now they have been transferred to Madras."

Having gone through what was for him a long period of self-doubt and then having succeeded with his sister's marriage, he reflects, "I feel that if you are sincere and work, then things work out. There may be problems at first, but then things tend to work out." This view has become Tangavelu's philosophy for action.

He says that so far the best period in his life has been from 1970 to 1977, when he was working in Erode. It was during those years that he was first hired and then promoted by his bank. It was also during those years that his brother found a job, and that he successfully arranged the advantageous marriage of his sister. At the Erode bank he found that his manager encouraged his predisposition toward social service. He gave Tangavelu opportunities to develop his own banking projects and considerable freedom to carry them out. The bank also provided opportunities for travel. Together, the travel and successes at the bank, he says, gave him considerable job satisfaction. These were heady years for a young man of very modest background who was a mere bank clerk.

Working for the bank, he says, it is easy to implement projects. "We [bankers] can serve the poor. Take a social worker: he lacks finance. But if you are in a bank and interested in social work, then you also have the funds to achieve your goals. . . . [Working for the bank] gives me job satisfaction because I see the happiness my work gives people." As an illustration, he describes how he arranged loans in five Harijan colonies for a milk project. The loans were used to buy buffaloes. "The project," he concludes, "was very successful."

While at the Erode bank, Tangavelu's greatest success was implementing a "village adoptions" project. "Village adoptions affect people of all walks of life. Villages lack finance, modern technology, and leadership. . . . Small farmers must borrow money to plant. The interest they pay may be 30 to 40 percent, so income is low for farmers. Because of debt the poor are like slaves. The rich [farmers] live in cities."

To counter this cycle of debt, Tangavelu says, the idea is for a bank to adopt a village. With local men the bank forms an administrative committee composed of the village headmaster, a few farmers, some village businessmen, plus a few officers from the bank. The committee surveys the economic potential of the village, interviews people from different walks of life to assess needs, forms a cooperative society for the farmers, and makes long-term loans at very low government sponsored rates, about 4 percent for the poor. The idea, he continues, is to help people escape the control of the rich and to enable them to take charge of their own finances. "Often this is all they need to get ahead." Once started, the adoption project is self-administering. The village committee that interviews the borrowers "takes the responsibility to see that the villagers pay their loans back. [They] use social pressure."

At Tangavelu's initiative the bank also helped fund "Agro Service Centres," which teach about tractor uses, and provided loans for school building and "for teachers to buy books for their higher studies." Tangavelu says the bank gave out Rs. 25 lakhs (2,500,000) in agricultural loans alone to its adopted village. The committee decided that sugar cane would be a good cash crop for its village farmers, and the bank lent the money that enabled the villagers to make the crop shift. As a result, Tangavelu says, the farmers were able to greatly increase their profits. "Now the adoption project is so successful that the villagers have had the bank open a branch there." Tangavelu says he also managed to involve the Rotary Club in his schemes, arranging for them to conduct village medical and dental camps.

When he was in high school, Tangavelu says, his desire was to "visit many countries, meet many people, and serve many people." It all started, he says, when he was in school in the fourth standard and became interested in collecting foreign stamps. He wrote to foreign consulates in Madras and, when he had a little money, would order stamps. Over the next several years he had nearly twenty foreign "pen pals." It was during this time that he became interested in service to others. It started with a friend.

"When we saw small boys—many people—unconscious in the street
. . . . we used to help these boys, me and my friend. [We would] get them
some money and help them to get home. They were boys who had come
to Erode to find jobs. I spent my money on stamps and pen pals. But I
had a friend, now dead, who was from a rich family. He gave money to
help these starved boys. So this was also a goal which I had during my
school days."

He marks joining the bank as the next turning point in his life. In that
year he also attempted to join the Rotary Club, "to get pen pals," he
says. In south India, both the Rotary and Lions Clubs are elite service-
oriented organizations whose members are businessmen and professionals. When Tangavelu approached the Erode Rotary, they suggested
that he organize Rotaract, an affiliated club for young men. The idea appealed to Tangavelu because he thought it would fulfill several of his interests. Through the club he would meet new people and, he hoped, have
contact with foreigners. Also Rotaract, like Rotary, is a service-oriented
club. Finally, organizing Rotaract would put him under the wing of older
influential members of the parent Rotary Club. Besides, he adds, "my
bank needs these kinds of activities [in order] to [contact] . . . more people and to draw [their accounts] into the bank. Rotaract helped me and
the bank. I met lots of important people, and they brought their accounts
to the bank. I linked the bank and Rotary. I got promoted for this."

The relationship between Rotary and the bank was a symbiotic one.
Rotary used the bank to fund its service projects, and the bank used the
Rotary Club for the community links it provided. Inspired by Tangavelu,
his manager and mentor joined Rotary.

After founding the Erode Rotaract, Tangavelu was elected its president for two consecutive terms. During his second term, he organized
and became the first governor of Rotaract District 320, covering Tamil
Nadu, Kerala, and Pondicherry.

Tangavelu was just a bank clerk, but, he says, his contacts were so
extensive that people were always coming to the bank and asking for
him. So his manager put him in the manager's box. "I was very lucky,
because my managers were very supportive and allowed me to make decisions that were beyond my status. The 'village adoptions' [scheme] was
all my idea."

Erode was a quiet town with few entertainments. Tangavelu decided
he could enliven things. He says as district governor of Rotaract he was
in the position to invite attachés of foreign consulates as well as visiting

Rotarians from different countries to Erode. He organized an international exhibition of foreign handicrafts and coins, arranged a visit of young Rotarians from Australia, and "screened foreign documentary films in Erode. This was all new in Erode, and because of my interest in foreign countries."

Through Rotaract, he says, he also did service projects. In Madras, he contacted CARE, which wanted to distribute bread to the poor. "I linked the project to Rotaract. Rotaract received bread and formed centers in slum areas. They distributed bread to 1,800 children. A very laborious job. They did it for four years. [We] needed six people for this. But many days people would fail [to show], so I would have to go. You could see the eradication of malnutrition. Before they had bad eyes. [I] saw lots of improvement in health. [But] now the project is discontinued."

Another of Tangavelu's successful projects involved selecting a group of handicapped persons and helping them to establish egg stalls. The stalls were also made egg-shaped. The bank made the loans the handicapped needed to build the stalls, buy chicks, and raise the poultry that supplied the eggs to the booths. The handicapped sold the eggs, earning Rs. 300 or so per month, he says, once they were started.

Reflecting on the criticism he has received in Madras, Tangavelu says the last two years away from Erode have been difficult. He says he has had lots of problems, that he has not been able to find a suitable place to live, and that Madras banking is different. "People are not sincere or encouraging and [so for me] the atmosphere [at the bank] is not good."

Tangavelu sees himself as at another turning point in his life. His family thinks that it is time for him to marry and are urging him to do so quickly. They think it is getting late for him to marry because the age difference between him and potential brides will appear too great to their families. He says that he also feels ready to marry.

"It is time to get married. Living alone is a big problem for me—food, housing, and feeling lonely. Getting married I can settle my life and solve these problems. . . . But I am not keen to marry just to get married. I must find a suitable girl. I would not like getting married unless I find a girl that I like. I would rather remain a bachelor." The problem, he thinks, will be in finding a woman who shares his interests. "Here, girls are interested in movies and a gay life."

Tangavelu is very much aware that his goals in life have been changing. "My travel ambition is still there. But now I have new goals. I never thought I would become a banker. Now I want to rise in banking so that

I can do more for people. Another goal is to become a Rotary governor in the later part of my life. [I also want] to have the opportunity to do much more for the untouchables and downtrodden and the destitute children. Also my spirituality—[I want] to develop my mind to understand God and to feel the spiritual things."

Tangavelu recognizes the predicament of his life:

"Every day I am doing something unusual. Every day! Most people don't do these kinds of things. They get up, work, go home, read a magazine, and sleep. I create projects to back. I go out and get people to deposit. I represent people to [bank] officers to get loans [for them]. I get people coming every day for help. . . . But people [his colleagues at the bank] often resent these things. I am always helping people in need."

By Tamil standards an unmarried twenty-nine year old man such as Tangavelu is still a boy. Marriage and fatherhood remain important tasks he must complete on his way to full adulthood. His sense of being ready for marriage parallels his maturing awareness that it will not be easy to achieve the goals that he has set for himself. Until now praised and encouraged by elders for his ideals, he has considered his successes merely the rewards of hard work and following the ideals of benevolence that Tamil culture embraces. He has had a childlike sense of being rewarded for behaving in an ideal manner. His experiences in Madras have made him realize that his career ambitions pit him against less idealistic competitors and that his career could easily be destroyed by a naive pursuit of service to others. He intends to calculate his career course with care, believing that if he succeeds in banking, he will be in a better position to serve the less fortunate.

THEMES OF INDIVIDUALITY IN FOUR LIVES

In electing to tell the lives of Sivakumar, Lakshmi, Viswanathan, and Tangavelu, I have made no attempt to represent what in some artificial sense might be considered average persons. All four tell unique stories and in different ways are successful individuals, even when they also describe failures and setbacks. Yet in another sense, the stories that these four tell raise issues and involve relationships, aspirations, and attitudes that are widely familiar to south Indians. Their lives as they tell them—their difficulties, their goals, how they have dealt with events, how they have evolved toward the turning points of their lives, and how they have achieved what they have—are quintessential to contemporary south Indian social experience.

Thus, despite the uniqueness of each individual's story, the reader will recognize that each thinks of his or her public face in terms of widely shared Tamil notions of behavior and status, and that each has a sense of his or her private voice that is closely linked to these public notions. What distinguishes these two senses of individuality—a private, internal sense and a public, civic sense—is that the internal sense involves a psychological awareness and evaluation of self and of the need to achieve some control in life. Lakshmi realized she alone was responsible for how her life turned out, for example. By contrast, civic individuality is what is manifest to others, features of identity and character that distinguish the person in the public's eye.

The eminence and respect that Viswanathan once had are thus characterizing attributes of leaders and of leadership organization in both village and urban south India, even while eminence and respect are also central concerns of Viswanathan's sense of himself. That is why, when he thought he had lost his public honor, he contemplated suicide. A central aspect of his sense of self had been destroyed. So too, Tangavelu's altruism, which is so important to his sense of self, is representative of a social ideal, and Lakshmi's and Sivakumar's shared sense of responsibility and the dilemmas that surround responsibility reflect a south Indian view of causation, agency, and social order that applies to both the private self and public life. Therefore, although the life of each is unique, each is also typical of his or her culture, and each interprets himself or herself in terms of shared cultural ideas.

Three cultural themes, which are central to my informants' telling of their lives, reveal how Tamils in general express and value individuality. These are the themes of responsibility, eminence, and generosity. These three themes compose an ethos of individuality common to Tamils that is associated with a perception of action and causation that assumes that the individual is both the primary architect of his or her own life and the fundamental agent in society. Recognition and appreciation of achievement are central to this view of individual agency.

Let me here also add, as should be obvious, that these three themes by no means characterize all that can be said about the individuality of these four life storytellers. The story of each is much bigger than these themes encompass. For example, there is Lakshmi's heroism and Viswanathan's anxiety, just as there is also Sivakumar's desperation and Tangavelu's activism. Indeed, the tellers describe a rich and complex sense of their own individuality and a clear recognition of their own conscious individuation.

But what is uniquely individual is not my focus here. My concern is with what all Tamils recognize as valued expressions of individuality, aspects of being by which a person is judged and, being judged, singled out. Each of the tellers incorporates their sense of these themes in their description of who they and others are. The individual interprets his or her own individuality, therefore, in terms of a cultural point of view that encompasses these three themes.

THE THEME OF RESPONSIBILITY

In my informants' stories, achievement of responsibility distinguishes individuality both in public life and in self-awareness. A Tamil's sense of responsibility encompasses three related notions: (1) *agency*: the individual is an actor responsible for his or her actions; (2) *causation*: actions have consequences so that the decisions one makes and the actions one takes are believed in a very direct way the cause of how one's life turns out; and (3) *social order*: the more senior (and less subordinate) one is, the more control one has over one's own life and the lives of others. When informants describe taking responsibility for their lives, they describe their individuation. A sense of being responsible for who one is and for how one's life turns out is the fundamental theme of a Tamil's understanding of self as separate from others. In civic life, too, responsibility distinguishes a person, and as in the case of the individual's sense of self, responsibility in civic life involves a recognition of the individual as an agent.

Although Tamils express a strong sense of responsibility for their lives, they do not deny unexpected occurrences a role. A person may fall ill or die without warning—run down by a bus, for example—or may have the course of his or her life change from a chance meeting with someone on a train. One of my informants described meeting in this serendipitous manner a man who became his guru. My informant, who was at the time working for a Kerala textile mill, said that he had been thinking about starting his own handloom textile design business and that his chance discussion with the guru, whom he had never met before, was what convinced him to proceed. Within a few years he was operating a highly profitable enterprise.

When events like these occur, Tamils will sometimes say in essence that the event was fated. "It was written on his [fore]head (*talai eṟuttu*)," or they may say he was born under a particular star that determined his fate. Generally, however, it has been my experience that Tamils speak of fate more when they are referring to others than to themselves, the person run down by the bus, for example. If they are the one run down and they survive, they are likely to blame the accident on the bus driver's wild driving or on themselves for not being more alert. Tamils may even combine the two kinds of explanation saying the person's death was fated, "written on his forehead," but that it was also the bus driver's fault. As anyone who has lived in India knows, the reaction of the crowd to the accident will be to blame the driver, and, fearing a beating, drivers run for their lives after such misfortunes. Tamils, therefore, do not obliterate their sense of responsibility for their lives with their sense of fate. Things can be fated, but individuals are still responsible for their actions.

Consider as a final example the brother of one of my assistants. This man was born with a birthmark, indicating that he embodied a malevolent force (*drishti*) that would cause his parents-in-law's death when he married. Responding to what was beyond their control, his family made it their responsibility to marry him to an orphaned woman.

Tamils also sense that their lives are affected by the current of events. Older informants will reflect that their lives have "flowed from circumstance," meaning that the direction of their lives has been dictated by events that were beyond their control. However, they do not mean by this that they lack responsibility for how their lives have turned out.

Agency   Although it is especially apparent in Sivakumar's and Lakshmi's telling of their lives, each of this chapter's four main informants describes a strong sense of responsibility for who he or she is and the course his or her life has taken. For example, Viswanathan states that he does not take advice from others. He says that he decides upon what he thinks is a good choice and takes the consequences. In effect, he asserts that the results of his actions are his own responsibility. Tangavelu claims responsibility for who he is and what he does by saying that he is different from others, that he is always doing things, going out and getting people to come to him for help. Doing so, he describes himself as an instrumental figure, a man who gets things done, a viewpoint he shares with Viswanathan. He also expresses his sense of responsibility, qua "agency," when he describes the things that he wants to achieve, the targets of his energy. And finally, he sees himself as responsible for others, his sister, for example, and he is very aware that his responsibilities have consequences for both himself and them. Yet again, Lakshmi sums up her sense of responsibility for herself by saying that each individual alone is responsible for what happens to him or her in life. Of the four, only Sivakumar describes his disappointment in life, but he does so blaming himself, acknowledging that he is too diffident. Failing to take responsibility for key decisions in his life, he says, life has not at all been what he had anticipated in his youth.

Each of these four, in speaking of responsibility for him or herself, describes a perception of individual agency that would seem to contradict the well-known view that Indian society stresses compliance, that individuals act not as their own agents, but as the agents of groups within which they are subordinate. Lakshmi and Sivakumar, in deferring to their family elders, might be taken as examples of this latter view. But the four life histories reveal that such a characterization represents only half of the picture. In fact, typically a tension exists between group and self; it is an expression of the ubiquitous fusion/separation psychological polarity that Kakar (1981:34) considers characteristic of Indian social life. Thus, rather than mere compliance, the central issue of both Sivakumar's and Lakshmi's lives concerns precisely this tension. Both life histories suggest that assuming responsibility for oneself involves some resolution of the fusion/separation polarity in favor of a sense of control. Blaming his diffidence, even Sivakumar sees himself as the primary agent of his unhappy life.

Causation   When Indians speak of their responsibility for themselves, they assert not only their responsibility for their actions, but also for the consequences. Each of my older life history informants claims responsibility for what has happened to him or her in life. They see their goals, the decisions they have made or avoided, and their consequent actions as the direct causes of their life course, whether those decisions are seen as flowing from circumstances or the result of setting goals. Viswanathan, for example, clearly links his view of causation to his own choice of action: "If I think something is good, I do it and take the consequences." He considers his bankruptcy the product of his own miscalculation. He put public service before business because he thought his eminence made him invulnerable to misfortune, a misjudgment for which he "took the consequences." Lakshmi states it just as bluntly when she admonishes, "My policy is don't blame others. We are at fault for letting ourselves be cheated." Still a young adult, Tangavelu's sense of causation and life direction is at a formative stage, but he too senses his responsibility for what happens in life when, following his sister's marriage, he states, "I feel that if you are sincere and work, then things work out. There may be problems at first, but then things tend to work out." And when comparing himself to others, he observes that he makes things happen: "Every day I am doing something unusual. Every day! . . . I create projects to back . . ." Finally, even Sivakumar recognizes that his diffidence and failure to stick up for himself are the causes of his disappointing life.

Social Order   As previously noted, whereas an American might speak of "autonomy" and "freedom" as expressions of agency and individuality, Tamils speak of "responsibility." Thus, Lakshmi sees having responsibility for herself as having control over her life without the interference of others, much as an American might speak of autonomy and freedom. But Lakshmi's sense of control is also distinct from these American perceptions. For the American, autonomy and freedom also imply a sense of equality and separation from others, independence, and the expectation that one has the right to go one's own way. Because relationships limit autonomy and freedom, the American must compromise individuality to establish social relations—for example, to be a wife or husband, father or mother, employee, or friend.

For the Indian, by contrast, responsibility implies not only autonomy in the sense of control over decisions affecting one's life, but also the responsibility the person assumes or seeks to have *for* others, as Lakshmi suggests when she speaks of her desire to control her relationship with her children without outside interference. The difference here between an American's sense of "autonomy" and a Tamil's sense of "responsibility" is that the Tamil thinks of the self in relation to others, while the American thinks of autonomy as separating self from others. The Indian idea of control assumes a hierarchical social order within which persons take on responsibilities for others as they achieve control over their own lives. Within this order, according to their interests, seniors control the relations of juniors; they have power over them. When Tangavelu speaks of trying to arrange his sister's marriage, he describes his responsibility for her. Doing so, he refers not only to his duty, but also to his power to act on her behalf and so to affect her life for better or worse. The responsibility weighed heavily on him. So too, Viswanathan speaks of his responsibilities for his sons and daughters.

Indians are finely tuned to this hierarchical power structure and acutely aware that their lives are framed by it. They recognize that in order to have control over their own lives, they must be in control of others. They must either achieve positions of relative seniority, for example, by becoming a head of household, or be granted some control over decisions, as, for example, the management responsibility Viswanathan received when his father left him in charge of the shop. Given circumstances and cultural norms, Indians continuously weigh the costs and benefits of complying with seniors against those of self-direction, much as Lakshmi and Sivakumar have done. Acquiring control over their lives, individuals recreate the hierarchical social order with themselves as seniors, since by their seniority they achieve the power to control their relationships and make their own decisions.

THE THEME OF EMINENCE

If in private life individuality is expressed as responsibility for who one is and how one's life turns out, then in public life the individuality of a person is valued when he or she is distinguished by eminence and public responsibilities. As previous chapters have amply demonstrated, eminent persons are considered key instrumental figures in society. They act as agents on behalf of their communities, and they head, and sometimes found, institutions that are designed to serve the public good, or at least the good of those who support them. Eminence also has its smaller aspects. For example, the female and male heads of household are preeminent within its domain, and their headships will be known and their civic identity distinguished by this eminence-on-a-small-scale. The challenge for each person, therefore, is to achieve some degree of eminence and with it the right to make decisions. In civic life, as in the family, hierarchy is a feature of individuality, and when a person's eminence is stressed, his or her individuality is stressed.

Tangavelu is not yet publicly eminent, but if he continues to succeed in banking and his community projects, it is likely he will achieve public eminence one day. Among his kin and caste fellows, however, Tangavelu has already achieved some eminence based on his education and employment. In recognition, his father allowed him to arrange his sister's marriage. Viswanathan achieved local eminence for a time, and at the peak of his prominence held public office, was a member of the managing boards of a number of important public institutions, and was designated the village *kaariyakaarar*, literally the "agent" of his caste. Within the context of her kin circle, Lakshmi, too, has achieved some degree of eminence and with it control over her life. This she has achieved by becoming the head of her own household and through the accomplishments of her children. In her life story, Lakshmi's children's achievements are more important to her sense of pride than are her husband's, but it is also clear that her status is dependent in part on her husband, on who he is, and what he has done. Only Sivakumar still lives under the control of a senior kinsperson, his mother, although he has achieved a position of importance and influence in his work. However, without control over his personal life, Sivakumar's achievements are dust in his mouth. Sivakumar recognizes his self-interests but has allowed his mother to choose the course of his life. Subordinating himself, he has never fully individuated.

THE THEME OF GENEROSITY

Generosity is perceived as an individual act and is a source of eminence and goodwill. When Indians appreciate successful persons, even moderately successful persons, they value them for their generosity, graciousness, and simplicity of life. These are traits that demonstrate that a person values others and does not act merely out of his or her own self-interest. Viswanathan and Tangavelu both seek to be known as generous men. Lakshmi, too, in middle age and as the ranking woman of her family, describes her generosity—she allows her son to keep his salary for himself—while she condemns her father-in-law as being tight-fisted. A generous person is someone who is interested in serving others, and his or her reputation for these traits—service to others, graciousness, generosity—authenticates his or her concern for others. A man builds a following by the benefits he provides, and a woman builds the affectionate relationships on which she depends and that give meaning to her life. A generous individual is also a person open to appeal who is seen as willing to represent the interests of others.

Indian communities always reflect the presence of generous individuals. These are the ones who manage and found the small local libraries, the scholarship funds, charitable organizations such as medical dispensaries, the school building funds, the cooperative societies, the cultural associations such as music societies, the Rotary and Lions Club charitable ventures, and the temple building and renovation societies. Tangavelu's concern for the poor is motivated by this ethos, and Viswanathan bases his claim to prominence on it. When a man acts generously his reputation as a leader grows, and he gradually achieves public eminence and fame (*puhaṛ*). Like an eminent man, a generous man, therefore, is defined by a public recognition of individuality and instrumentality that is circumscribed by values that subordinate his liberty to the common good.

In general, generosity appears to be more a theme of men's civic individuality, while for women more commonly it is a feature of their private lives. This is because men's lives are more public, and they control more resources than women. But as I have described in chapter 3, women, too, may acquire a reputation for generosity in the public sphere. Widowed women of means, for example, sometimes are philanthropists, and I know of a few such women among the Beeri Chettiars of George Town. One woman donated a house for a free medical dispensary, and in the past, others gave endowments to the Kandasami temple. These women are praised for being good women, and they have local fame. But as we have seen, among men a reputation for generosity legitimatizes and increases his influence. It is an essential feature of his claim to lead. Outside George Town, there are leading Tamil women, and for them, too, generosity is central to their leadership. But within the Town, the generosity of women lacks this political purpose. In the Town, at least until now, there have been no political women, nor has any built a political constituency in the pattern of men. But the reader should know that as I write this, the chief minister—the highest elected officer—of Tamil Nadu State is a woman, Jayalalita, a former actress, the protégée of the previous chief minister.

Graciousness and simplicity are valued traits that are related to generosity. When individuals act and speak graciously toward others, Tamils believe that these individuals respect their humanity. They demonstrate their commonality with others, which expresses a form of selflessness, even though they may be powerful persons. Finally, by living simply, generous individuals demonstrate that they are not self-indulgent. Their simplicity of style makes their altruism credible.

Eminence based on generosity, graciousness, and simplicity is an ideal, of course. Indians are cynical about the altruism of leaders and others in the day-to-day world. They will say that many pretend to these things, but few are genuinely altruistic. Rather, Tamils presume that public figures are out to gain benefits for themselves. I have often heard wealthy individuals criticized for trying to buy eminence, for example, when they found a charitable society out of the blue. There is, therefore, a paradox built into a valuing of altruism of this sort: it is in the self-interest of individuals who wish to achieve eminence to act altruistically. Reflecting this, the more eminent a person becomes, the more people doubt his altruism. How can someone be selfless who has amassed great influence and achieved a status of increasingly important individuality?

I suspect that some of the criticism that Tangavelu has experienced in Madras is of this sort. After all, he has earned unusually rapid promotion through his charitable activities, and it is only natural that men who see themselves threatened or in competition with him would try to deny him this avenue for promotion. Similarly, walking down the road after interviewing Viswanathan, my assistant commented skeptically that if what Viswanathan said about never abusing his office were true, he must be the *only* member of his political party who did not. A believable reputation for altruism takes years to achieve, and it is a fragile reputation to maintain.

For all their worldly skepticism, Tamils do nonetheless value generosity highly and see true examples of it as expressions of great moral worth. Generosity is often considered an attribute of small town and village life where Tamil social values, it is believed, still guide behavior. Tangavelu and Viswanathan both come from such places. And, of course, according to karmic beliefs, generosity ultimately generates rewards for its agents. Over the years, I have learned of a number of cases of extraordinary generosity, some told to me by beneficiaries and some by benefactors. The gift of Rs. 60,000 mentioned in chapter 1 is one example. Tangavelu's unusual efforts represent a second. And the fame of the Kandasami temple, which I have described in previous chapters, is founded on the generosity of individuals, so much so that generosity has become their legend.

CHAPTER EIGHT

Locating Individuality within the Collective Context

A story is told in India that once there was a man who, hearing from his guru that God was present in everything, went for a stroll in the jungle.[1] Suddenly, a huge bull elephant emerged from the undergrowth followed closely by his trainer. The trainer was shouting, "The elephant is mad! Run for your life!" But knowing that God was present in the elephant, the man continued on his path, paying scant heed. The elephant trumpeted and charged. Alarmed, the man reminded himself, "God is present in the elephant." But the elephant kept coming, huge in his vision—blotting out the background. At the last second, the man leapt aside. A narrow escape. The elephant charged on into the jungle. Shaken, the man returned to his guru for an explanation. "I could have been killed on the spot! Was not God in the elephant?" The guru replied, "Yes. But why didn't you think that God was also present in the trainer?"

In this world, life requires that one be able to act on the basis of one's own judgment and initiative, even if, as the story says, God is present in everything.

The lesson of the parable can also be applied to the individual in the context of caste and family, two arenas wherein both social science lore and Indian social values have it that groups control individual behavior. As in the parable, even if caste and family form a part of every Tamil's identity, each must think and act for himself or herself. The private voices of Sivakumar, Lakshmi, Viswanathan, and Tangavelu reveal as much. Each of these persons described a process of individuation set in the context of compelling, if quite ordinary, events. Each told of a struggle to mediate between their responsibility for their own well being, and Tamil values that told them that if they were selfless, then all would work out well for them. As a result of the struggle, each told of developing a strong sense of self separate from others.

When South Asianists have stressed collective identities, they have paid attention to group identities, but they have overlooked the significance of the struggle that occurs between the person's private interior self and the collective pressures of caste and family life. The struggle is a tip-off that the marriage of group and individual is imperfect, that the relationship between the private self and social order must be mediated. As Sivakumar's and Lakshmi's narratives show, the family is often an important context within which this conflict is played out. Here in this chapter, I examine how the private self is expressed and interacts with collective interests in the context of family and society.

INDIVIDUALITY AND GROUP IDENTITY

In Tamil society, individuality finds expression in the context of others, notably among kin. Consider the balance that exists between a person as an individual and his or her identity as a kinsman. Thinking and acting for oneself requires thinking of others, taking them into account; as we have seen, the person depends on kin, just as they depend on the person. For example, while social trust begins with the individual and depends on one's actions, as the story of Viswanathan shows, social trust also is based on the reputation of one's kin. Tamils refer to such trust as one's family honor or name. It is here among kin that an important crossover point between private individuality and the collective interests that circumscribe civic individuality is made manifest. When individuals through the exercise of their own initiative earn honor and respect, they simultaneously contribute to the family name, and in fact their name (and so their reputation or honor) may become the name by which others related to them identify themselves. Taking a prominent relative's reputation as part of their own, lesser-ranking relatives can use this person's honor to benefit themselves. Recall Bala's admonition that I be careful to whom I showed his genealogy, lest someone use knowledge of it to falsely claim a connection with him.

Interestingly enough, in this patrilineal society a man will often use a family name that refers to persons to whom he is related through women rather than men. When it comes to fame and negotiating advantage, Tamils feel no compulsion to stick to the male line in order to trace their connections. One's kin are all one's kin, traced through both males and females, through ties of marriage and lines of descent. Bala's ally, K. Sundaram, the retired postal employee whom I describe in chapter 6, was repeatedly mentioned to me with a reference to his maternal grandfather, O. Tanikacalam, the lawyer, judge, and Justice Party leader. This was the man who gave Sundaram his family name. Similarly, Bala's wife's kin group is known as the "Kaḷi Raṭṭina group" after Kaḷi Raṭṭina Chettiar, the man who in 1901 gave the cup of diamonds. Although Bala counts among his kin many prominent figures, it is the reputation of Kaḷi Raṭṭina that lends a special aura to Bala's name.

When a family is respected and judged honorable by those who know it, then the interests of individuals within the family are facilitated because people know that the family will want to protect its name. Family members restrain the behavior of their members because it is in the interest of each to do so. Each benefits from the family's good name. (But beware of strangers because their family and reliability are unknown—unless a big-man or woman with whom you have a lasting relationship recommends them.) Individuality, therefore, finds expression within the context of social groups, including the family, and identity and reputation involve an interaction between the person as a separate individual, responsible for his or her identity and actions, and the identity and reputation of groups, such as the family, which support and benefit its individual members.

By contrast, an individual who behaves in a way that Tamils would describe as "without honor" or that detracts from the family name, is in real danger of being ostracized by kin. Without kin, a person is isolated and vulnerable. Take the case of Saroja, a headstrong woman. Although Saroja thinks for herself, she puts her interests before those of her own family. A neighbor described her to me as a woman without honor, a woman of bad character. I present her story to represent a case that falls at the separation end of the fusion/separation polarity. The isolation she anticipates is the antithesis of the psychological suffocation that Sivakumar describes in his life story. Tamils disparage a life lived only for the self. Hope, they believe, flies from such persons.

Saroja, forty years of age and living in a small ill-kept brick and cement house on the edge of a poor Madras neighborhood, has an overriding fear at the time of our interview that she will be abandoned by her immediate family because of the way she has behaved in the past. She has one son and two daughters. The eldest daughter is engaged, while the other two are approaching marriageable age. When her daughters marry, they will go to live with their husbands. Her son will soon get a job, but, she feels, he will not take care of her. My assistant, who knows Saroja, whispers to me that Saroja's son is a petty thief. She says that people believe he steals in order to shame his mother because of her behavior.

Saroja tells me that she fears her husband may abandon her because of all the trouble she has caused him, and because when she was thirty she had taken a lover, the executive officer of a nearby temple, who had helped her to arrange the building of her house on temple land. Her husband, she says, is often angry with her and sometimes beats her. He works as an electrical fitter at the Madras Integral Coach Factory, which specializes in the manufacture of railroad cars. She thinks he will take a job in Dubai—he has been talking about it—and that will be the last she will hear of him. She feels particularly vulnerable because she believes there is something wrong with her liver and because her eyesight is failing. She has already had an operation on one eye and has what she describes as a growth on the other. She believes she is going blind and is afraid that it will make her totally dependent. Yet she has no one to depend on because she has antagonized or alienated all who normally would be close to her. Her greatest fear is that, if her husband leaves or forces her to leave, she will have no option but to live the life of a beggar.

Saroja describes herself as rebellious from a young age. She grew up in a village near Salem and claims her father, who is still living, was a prosperous farmer. As per custom, at marriage Saroja went to live with her husband's family, which was at that time a large joint family of thirty members. Like her father, Saroja's in-laws were well-off farmers. She says she had three mothers-in-law, the wives of her father-in-law and his brothers. She recalls bitterly that she was treated like a slave, a status she felt was exacerbated because her husband had a low standing within the family. He is one of two sons by his father's first wife, a woman who had died young. The father had then remarried and had seven children by his second wife. The second wife favored her own children and had seen to it that they were well educated and given primacy in the family arena, while she denied similar opportunities to Saroja's husband. As a result, Saroja says, her husband is uneducated, while one of his stepbrothers is a university graduate with a B.Sc. degree. Saroja herself feels she married the lesser man, although she is proud that he neither drinks nor smokes. Nonetheless, she thinks he is a weak, ineffectual person, and she demands that he give her his salary. She is the dominant spouse. She does all the calculating and strategic planning, including arranging her children's weddings, what her daughters' dowries will be, and she attempts to maintain primary control over what little she and her husband own, her plan being that, should she be abandoned, she would control enough assets to avoid being pauperized.

Saroja says proudly that she bore her son within the first year of her marriage, and by doing so fulfilled one of the functions most desired of a wife. But she says she fought constantly with her in-laws over food, soap, tasks, and her own behavior, which her in-laws felt was grossly inappropriate. Saroja says angrily that they treated her like a village hick, telling her to wash when her legs were muddy, not to stand by the window when she was combing out her hair, and not to sit with her legs and feet sticking straight out before her when pouring milk for her child, all requests for behaviors that are common etiquette. But it is clear from her description of the issues about which she and her in-laws fought that she was both defiant and rude in her behavior. By the end of the first year, her mother-in-law took Saroja back to her family, complained of her behavior, and left her, apparently for so long as it took for her to shape up. Having a daughter returned in this manner disgraces a family. Who would want to arrange marriages with a family where the daughters behaved like Saroja?

In defiance, Saroja wrote her husband that she would never return to her in-laws'. She says she wrote that when he had the courage to establish his own house, she would go with him and would mortgage her jewelry to help them. Fifteen days later, her husband came and got her and they moved to Madras.

In Madras, life was difficult. They lived in rented quarters, but slowly saved money so that over time Saroja was able to buy three cows. Today, she uses the milk they produce in part to meet family needs, but primarily she sells it to her neighbors. But here again neighbors complain that she overcharges them and dilutes the milk excessively with water—beyond, they say, what is considered normal for milk sellers to do. As a result, Saroja's milk business is not doing well. Add her business practices to her son's reputation as a thief, which others take as a mark of her own failure as a mother, and add these to the scandal of her ongoing adulterous love affair, and it is easy to understand the disapproval of nearly all who know her. She is a woman who has isolated herself by her actions.

When my interview with Saroja was nearly over, I asked her whether, looking back on her life, there was anything that she would change.

"Yes," she said. "I would ask not to be born female. Women are treated like slaves, scolded by everyone. If I had been a man, then I could have done everything that I have, and no one would say anything."

As an ethnographer, I have often thought about the simple poignancy of her statement and wondered whether it was true. A male Tamil friend, to whom I related her story, told me that there was truth to what she said. Certainly, her judgment fits some of what I have seen. I have known many men who have taken lovers, for example, without any loss of status. In George Town today, Tamils distinguish between a man's "big house" (*periya viiḍu*), his marriage-centered household, and his "small house" (*cinna viiḍu*), his concubine-centered household, with only mild embarrassment. It is not unusual for wealthy and powerful men to have concubines. But there is more to Saroja's isolation than just a double standard. What comes across from Saroja's telling of her life story is that she is self-centered and puts herself before everyone, traits that would isolate a man as well.

FEATURES AND THEMES OF INDIVIDUATION

Socially successful Tamils are not those who think only of themselves, nurturing no one, like Saroja, nor those who submit completely to the dictates of others, like Sivakumar. Among the Tamils I interviewed, the majority fell between the extremes these two represent. Tamils were clearly aware of their individual interests and desires and sought to fulfill at least some of these, but they were also aware of their responsibility for their relationships, and, while they chose actions that sometimes ended close ties, they were fully aware that their own honor and success depended on their relationships with others. Their kin and social connections were important to them, brought them happiness as well as grief, and were integral to their sense of who they were, and their ability to negotiate life.

In Tamil society, individuals need their relationships in order to accomplish their own private ends. This requires them to nurture relationships that they consider important to their private interests. For example, while a woman might want to live separately from her in-laws with her husband and children, nonetheless, she also weighs the importance of the joint family to her needs and goals as wife and mother and judges what the cost to her might be of splitting the family. Self-interest, therefore, involves living, working, and identifying with others, and Tamil individuality necessarily finds expression within the context of such groupings. Individuals end relationships and break away from groups with which they have been closely identified, knowing that they must avoid isolating themselves. Among my informants, in every generation, families partition because it is in the interest of individuals to do so. All it takes is for one of the male coparceners to feel that his advantage lies elsewhere. And, as we have seen in Lakshmi's case, women often play a critical role deciding when that might be.

A distinction needs to be made here between the joint family and the joint household. Today, most Tamils do not live in joint households, a household of economic co-sharers and their wives and children.[2] Many do, however, continue as members of a "joint family," a property-owning economic unit formed by ties of joint ownership among male co-sharers who live separately. Lakshmi's son, for example, lives in Bombay. She and her husband feel it is their prerogative to control his salary and, with this prerogative in mind, have given him permission to keep all his salary, although he himself has offered to remit a portion home. Similarly, Lakshmi's eldest daughter lives with her husband in Madras in a house owned by her husband's coparceners, who live elsewhere. For all intents and purposes they live an independent home life, except that the house is jointly owned and her husband works in partnership with his father. When Tamils live in separate households within the joint (that is, co-property-owning) family, their struggle to achieve a sense of control in their lives is greatly reduced. Although few of my informants currently live in joint households, all of them have experienced such households at least for a time, for example, as a child, or during the early years of marriage, and in some instances for the greater part of their lives. Joint households feature prominently in their life stories when they describe their own struggles for individuation.

Knowing that private interests at some point run counter to collective interests, Tamils recognize the inevitability of partitioning, as do Indians everywhere. In many cases, dissolutions are friendly, but because property and loyalties are involved, often they are not. For example, one of my informants, Arumugam by name, told me that he and his brothers divided their businesses and filed for separation in 1942, but that it was not until 1979 after a long court battle that the final division was settled.

The motivations underlying family partitioning are, of course, related to issues of control. Comparing life stories, one of the common themes is a desire to have a sense of control over decisions affecting one's life. In the joint family, as in other social groups, control theoretically rests in the hands of its preeminent members: in the case of the family, its heads, the senior male and his wife. In point of fact, I observed that the most successful joint families (those that stayed together the longest) were headed by men and women who gave their sons and daughters-in-law control over important areas of their lives. Viswanathan's father, who left him in charge of the textile shop when he returned to his itinerant cloth trade, is a case in point. Tensions between father and sons are reduced by such abrogation and division of responsibilities. Another family head, Arumugam, the man mentioned above, who is also a textile merchant and manufacturer, worked out with his seven sons that they each contribute a specific amount to the joint household, but otherwise allowed them complete control over their own earnings and a free hand in the management of part of the family enterprises. They lived together with all their wives and children in a huge house when I interviewed Arumugam, then seventy-six years of age. The sons and their wives liked the system because they did not have to go to the family head when they wanted money for a purpose of their own. Compare their situation with the lack of control over even small details and personal desires in Saroja's and Lakshmi's descriptions of their joint family experiences. Yet, even in a house as liberally managed as Arumugam's, partitioning eventually occurs because individuals wish to control their own resources. In fact, Arumugam's eldest son had declared the Sunday previous to our interview that he wanted to move out of the big-house and separate. Now all of the sons will separate, for this is the pattern of household partitioning. Arumugam was saddened, saying that he wished he had not constructed the big-house, which he had built just four years previously in "hope that the family would not crack." He says he had sufficient land and wishes instead that he had built a number of separate houses in the same compound. The desire to control the decisions that occur within one's own living space is a compelling motivation behind partitioning, as Lakshmi's and Saroja's stories also show. So too is the desire to control other features of one's life. Arumugam empathizes with his son's wish to live separately. But he also blames the government for "sparking the breakup by giving the individual more legal importance than the family." His son's concern about income taxes are a factor in his decision to partition. Here we see the individual weighing his personal interests not as an isolated person but as a member of groups, the joint family and his own elemental family consisting of himself, his wife, and children.

As we have seen, Tamil individuals achieve control over their private lives when they acquire a role of responsibility within their household and over economic affairs. This may occur in a number of ways. For example, a dependent coparcener, usually a son or brother of the household head, may initiate the division, as in the case of Arumugam's son. Keeping in mind that jointly owned property will be divided and that cultural values emphasize the collective interests of the family over those of the individual, it is easy to understand that such an initiative is emotionally stressful, somewhat analogous to filing for divorce in the U.S. Once separated from the joint family, the partitioner himself becomes the head of his own elemental household. Preeminence gives the partitioner control over decisions affecting his life and responsibility for himself and his dependents.

Alternatively, responsibility may be acquired when a family head delegates responsibilities to his coparceners, sharing out his control and responsibility, as Viswanathan's father did with him and as Arumugam did with his sons. However, such solutions to problems arising from control are temporary because the control that a dependent has over his life is partial, leaving the person to stew over those features of his life that are controlled or affected by the behavior and decisions of his cosharers. In 1942, it was Arumugam himself who instigated the division among his co-sharers, his brothers, because he judged himself the best businessman among them and disliked the fact that not only did they benefit without effort from his business acumen, but also that he shared their losses, slowing down his own economic progress. Six years earlier, when he had been thirty-two years old, he had borrowed Rs. 250 from his mother-in-law to start his own small wholesale cloth business. It was then that his own personal success had begun to outstrip his brothers', and he saw his wholesale business as rightfully belonging separately to himself. Splitting the family made it possible for him to "go it alone."

Yet a third way a man acquires the status of head is when he has responsibility and control thrust suddenly upon him when his father dies and he realizes that now he is responsible for his household and in control of himself and his dependents. I have heard Tamils describe such a moment in their lives as the point when they became adult. For the first time they see themselves as responsible for their lives and their families.

The point to be made, therefore, is that the way both men and women acquire control over their private lives is by ascending to a position of preeminence within their household. This gives them control over their economic affairs and most decisions of daily life. But the road to preeminence within the family is often a rocky one because life histories indicate that Tamils must learn by trial and error that they are responsible for themselves. This idea of learning that one is responsible for oneself—indeed, that the individual is the sole agent responsible for his or her life—is a central theme of my informants' descriptions of individuation. Informants describe this realization first in their late twenties or early thirties. But it is among older informants where it finds its strongest expression.

When I interviewed Chinnamuttu, he was about to have his eighty-third birthday. He was a healthy, vital man, with a sharp mind, who lived on the veranda of a large house occupied by one of his sons in the T. Nagar section of Madras City. In old age, he no longer lived with his wife—she lived separately with another son. He had given up his possessions and the wealth and power that he had once earned for himself and now lived simply, with minimal possessions.

He told me that when he was young his only aim was to make a living. He was poor; his father operated a tiny grocery business, and so after marriage at eighteen, he went to work for his father-in-law, who had a small piece-goods textile business. He said that he really had no particular ambition, no vision of how he wanted his life to turn out. Rather, he developed his business goals gradually through contact with friends and in response to changes in his circumstances. He worked for his father-in-law until the latter's death in 1920 and then did his own piece-goods business, gradually developing it, acquiring powerlooms to supply his own needs, and moving into bigger markets, first into Erode, then Madurai, and finally Madras. He prospered during World War II and in 1946 purchased from a French owner a cloth mill in Pondicherry, 90 miles south of Madras City— "because of friends and circumstances only. . . . When you have more money," he said, "you need to find a place for it. Water flows, you can't stop it." Then, sometime later, he built a second mill, this one in Pudukottai, about 250 miles south of Madras.

Things went well until about 1965, when because of labor problems the central government stepped in to oversee his management and then took over total control in 1974. They took over the mills supposedly "to better them," he said, but "instead worsened them. They heaped up losses. The government has no interest in business. An appointed man is interested in helping himself, not the mills." Chinnamuttu was clearly angered by the injustice and by his inability to do anything about it. He told me, "You can't take the case to court because it's the government."

Assuming that the mill takeover was a period of major difficulty in his life, I asked Chinnamuttu how he dealt with what had happened. In reply, he told me his personal philosophy:

"I was the same with or without the mill, the same person, the same bent of mind. It made no difference in my career. . . . I never felt those years were hard times. It depends on the mind. If you have the right frame of mind, there are no hard times. No one can inflict harm on me. The wrong done to us is because of ourself. We place ourselves in such a position as to be harmed by other men. This is an idea that I didn't have when I was young, but gradually grew as I got older. How can you understand when young? This is a lesson learned from the world, [an attitude] which you get by moving with wise people."

I asked him whether he had had any mentors in life. "No," he said, "I'm self-found and self-made. I don't follow after anyone. No hero worship. No one can help us or harm us. It is in our hands." A while later, at the conclusion of our interview, he added a final comment: "Ignorance," he said, "is the cause of all misery. Remove ignorance and man is all right."

It is a tradition among sociologists and anthropologists to offer explanations of social history that depict impersonal social forces as the cause of events and circumstances affecting the course of peoples' lives. An economic downturn leads to a person being laid off from work, to household crisis, to divorce, for example. Chinnamuttu's explanation of himself was much more complex. I am struck by the multiple perspectives he employed to tell his story.[3] Describing his earlier years, Chinnamuttu depicted the events of his life as resulting less from his own efforts to achieve some ultimate goal or set of goals, than from what he considered "the flow of circumstance." Here he seems to mirror the sociological perspective, the individual caught up by events. But having told me that his life course was not all his own making, he also let me know he felt responsible for how he had responded to the events and circumstances that he encountered. From this second perspective, he views himself as an actor. Finally, Chinnamuttu's telling reveals a third perspective. He saw himself as a separate, autonomous individual who was solely responsible for the meaning of his life.

Chinnamuttu's concern was to explain to me his inner view of life, what I would describe as his private individuality as opposed to Bala's civic individuality or Kasi's description of his own public, civic identity, which I related in chapter 2. Look again at the multiple perspectives Chinnamuttu used to tell his story. Several themes, which compose his sense of his private self, are apparent: First is Chinnamuttu's sense of responsibility for who he was and how he had acted. He was as he said, "self-found and self-made." Then, as a responsible actor, he declared himself independently in charge of the decisions that had affected his life, and he explained the course of his life in terms of an interaction between himself as actor and shifting circumstances over which he lacked control. Finally, he saw himself as separate from others. He had no mentors and, as he said, "didn't follow after anyone." In other words, the outstanding thematic features of his own awareness of himself were his sense of responsibility, agency, independence, and ultimately, his separation from others. "No one," he says, "can help us or harm us. It [life and its meaning] is in our hands."

To summarize, private expressions of individuality, as these emerge in life stories, are closely associated with personal motivations and private interests, wishes, and goals, even while these expressions are always located in collective contexts—the family, the caste community, institutions, the society at large. When my informants describe their lives in terms of these goals and motivations, they focus on issues of control, responsibility, and causation, which, as we have seen in chapter 7, are expressions of a Tamil ethos of individuality. They speak of becoming aware that they are responsible for their own lives and of their struggle to act on that awareness. They describe conflicts, family splits, lawsuits, and the deaths of seniors by which they ascended to positions of preeminence within their households. As household heads, they describe achieving control over decisions affecting their lives, but also how preeminence means that they take responsibility for others, their dependents. And with increasing emphasis as they get older, they speak of their sense that each alone is the primary agent of his or her life. Reflecting a sense of life process, the Tamil's awareness of himself or herself is a developing, changing thing.

CHAPTER NINE

Conclusions

One day, while writing this book, I asked one of my Tamil friends in Santa Barbara to ask his father how important he thought individuality was in Tamil society. His father, an elderly businessman, lives in a small town near Madurai. The father wrote a few weeks later, stating that he thought individuality—he used the word *tanittuvam*—was basic. There is no more important thing. In his letter, my friend's father likened life to a building and the individual to its architect. Tamil society was itself the design of great men like Tiruvalluvar, he wrote, referring here to the fifth century author of the *Tirukkural*, a poetic Tamil text of aphorisms that has enjoyed and continues to enjoy great currency and respect in popular Tamil culture (Cutler 1992, n.d.). I found this reference to the *Tirukkural* interesting because central among Tiruvalluvar's topics are issues of reputation, judgment, responsibility, and action. Tiruvalluvar's perspective presumes the reality of the person as an effective agent of his or her own life.

Working as an ethnographer in Tamil Nadu, I have often sensed that the Tamil's world view perceives the person concretely, looking out at the world from the perspective of the self, posing two interconnected questions: "What is my social context? How shall I act?" It is a view that presumes the reality of society and of the person as the agent of who he or she is, and it is a view that recognizes the public and private self. This is certainly the way modern Tamils interpret the messages of the *Tirukkural*. Given birth and circumstances, as a person acts, so the person is, and so should he or she be judged. From an American perspective, this Tamil view of the contextualized individual lacks an abstract sense of all persons as fundamentally the same. As I have indicated in this book, abstract notions of the individual carry little meaning for Tamils. This creates something of a paradox for the Westerner: Tamils have a strong sense of individuality, but no abstract notion of the individual.

Consequently, despite what my friend's father had written, many Tamils, if asked whether or not the individual is important to a characterization of society, might answer no. The chances are such a response would be because Tamils have no overarching integrated conception of the individual as a skin-bounded indivisible entity, separate from others, of the sort that Marriott (1989) argues characterizes Western notions of the individual. Nor, outside of contemporary Indian constitutional law, do Tamils conceive of the individual as the basic unit of society, as Arumugam's criticism of laws that favor the individual over the family attests. So, too, Tamil values emphasize individual compliance with the interests of seniors, family, and caste, rather than individual freedom or equality, and they are critical of egoism. For a preeminent person, the ideal is to subordinate personal interests to those of community or other constituents.

But if our hypothetical Tamil were instead asked whether who a person is and what he does is important to an understanding of society, then he would answer as my friend's father did: obviously so. Elaborating, he might add that each person is distinct, an aggregate of manifest qualities and has his or her own nature. Each is an agent with his or her own responsibilities and roles, goals, achievements, and reputation; an agent who naturally interacts with and affects society in his or her particular manner.

Consider Bala, Lakshmi, Saroja, Sivakumar, or any of the persons described in this book. Bala is a social architect each of whose institutions is the "lengthened shadow"[1] of himself. Attracting his constituents to the institutions that he controls, he organizes a following, making himself the center of his community, even while he also attempts to recreate and maintain a sense of neighborhood cohesiveness among the George Town Beeri Chettiars. Lakshmi's sphere of influence is limited to her kin, but consider how her growing awareness of responsibility for herself affected relationships within her husband's joint household. Ultimately, she was instrumental in its restructuring and her design affected the lives of all concerned.

The manifested individuality of each person is observed and characterized by those who know him or her, and the distribution of those who know a person defines the spatial and social dimensions of the person's individuality. Knowing who a person is—whether he or she is trust-worthy, for example, or is in a position to help when one needs assis-tance—is critical to how one interacts with that individual. Tamils base their decisions and interactions with others on their assessment of who each person is, not just on one's character but also on other attributes such as gender, caste, family, education, and positions in life, including eminence, occupation, offices, influence, relationships, and status within one's family.

Given the personalized nature of Tamil society, it is not surprising that institutions are characterized in terms of their leaders, and each is valued or disregarded according to how its leaders act and what access they provide to benefits. The Beeri Chettiars characterize themselves as a caste community in terms of their past and present leaders. Leaders, not caste, are the determinants of social organization; caste itself is con-ceived as a highly personalized configuration of relationships, created by its leaders. What gives a caste its corporate form are its big-men and their overlapping institutional constituencies.

In this manner, Beeri Chettiar leaders have created in George Town a caste community for themselves, and in their pursuit of wealth, power, and prestige, they have founded the institutions that form the framework for the leadership of the caste. It should be understood that Tamil pub-lic individuality is recognized within particular social contexts and is de-fined spatially by the localities within which a person is known. In the case of a big-man, the distribution of his institutions of leadership and the location of his constituents are spatial expressions of his individual-ity. Only a man of relatively great importance is known beyond his con-stituency circles.

In the nineteenth century, Beeri Chettiar leaders organized their iden-tities and caste community around a mandala of religious institutions with overlapping constituencies. This type of highly personal organiza-tion was well suited to the levels of social trust that facilitated business at that time. But circumstances change. By the end of the nineteenth cen-tury, Beeri Chettiars, demanding more relaxed behavior codes, rebelled against the dictates of caste headmen, seeking to replace personalized trust relationships with bureaucratic standards and regulations. In the twentieth century, this movement away from personalized trust has con-tinued and, as it has, the institutions of leadership that once organized the George Town Beeri Chettiars as a caste community have weakened.

Yet personalized social trust continues to have its place in Madras soci-ety and leaders still found or manage institutions to create constituencies and to establish their reputations. In fact, among the Beeri Chettiars the main locus of community assets used for the benefit of the caste are still housed within caste institutions, the Kandasami temple and the myriad of organizations founded by community leaders such as the Vasantha Maṇḍabam, schools, medical dispensaries, libraries, numerous endowments, lending societies, the caste *maḍam*, the Abanatha Dharma Siva Acharya Maḍam, and the caste funeral shrine and tank.

Nevertheless, it is clear that personalized social trust is not nearly as important to Beeri Chettiars today as it once was. And the changes that the George Town community have experienced over the last one hundred years reflect this trend. Beeri Chettiars have been moving away from George Town, and there is a diminished need for those who still live among their caste fellows to do so. The transition the Beeri Chettiars are acting out is common to contemporary urban life. People have a new freedom, but this freedom has a cost: urban anonymity. In the new city neighborhoods, people lack knowledge of their neighbors. Even in George Town, this trend is evident as new people replace old residents who move away. One consequence of anonymity is rising crime rates. Another is increasing personal autonomy. And yet another is the growing acceptance of intercaste marriages initiated by couples who have met in their workplace or while in school. Rising crime rates and intercaste marriage suggest that urban Madras is becoming a very different kind of city. As bureaucratic means of enforcing reliability have increased, the need to maintain a tightly knit caste and neighborhood community has diminished and the day-to-day importance of keeping tabs on large numbers of people—on individuality (as opposed to an abstract notion of the individual)—is less.

Increasing anonymity and autonomy represent an undermining of the importance of being known for who you are—of individuality—and of the way in which the city is organized. The organization of the city is becoming impersonal. Paradoxically, despite increased autonomy, the importance of individuality is decreasing as personalized relationships and the caste community become less important. *Individualism* may be on the rise, but the importance of *individuality* to social life is on the decline. Yet it is easy to exaggerate this trend. Madras City is still a highly personalized society, individuality is still important, and you need to know the right people to get things done. Despite the size of Madras, relationships still seem intimate to me and fear of violent crime almost nonexistent when I compare Madras rates with those of my own university district in California. But the trend is clear. The future will bring more anonymity and with it less trust, but Madras will also be a more open society than it was.

The implications of the depersonalizing transition for the Madras City of the near future are profound. What some might label the consequences of "modernity" are unravelling the weave of the old personalized order. The new order is impersonal, and its norms are set not locally, but in the arena of law and politics, where standards are still superficial, fluid, and much contested. According to Giddens (1991:2) "modernity" is a global phenomenon

> characterised by profound processes of the reorganisation of time and space, coupled to the expansion of disembedding mechanisms—mechanisms which prise social relations free from the hold of specific locales, recombining them across wide time-space distances. The reorganization of time and space, plus the dis-embedding mechanisms, radicalise and globalise pre-established institutional traits of modernity; and they act to transform the content and nature of day-to-day social life.

The pervasiveness of doubt (Giddens 1991:2–3)—of anxiety about society's organization and one's fit in society—is an important expression of this transformation of daily life. In India, if identity specific to localized social relations is taken as characteristic of the old personalized order based on trust, then uncertainty of relations is characteristic of the new order in which standards are highly contested. It remains to be seen how this metamorphosis will be played out in Madras City, but the sense of growing uncertainty is present. The assassination of Rajiv Gandhi just outside of Madras City and the machine-gun-carrying bodyguards of Tamil Nadu's chief minister express as much.

What I have attempted to do in this book is expose the importance of individuality in all its many features in Tamil society up to the present day. The attempt has been to reveal the dimensions of individuality and its role in Tamil society, to describe how it is valued and expressed. This effort stands in direct opposition to the conceptualization of Indian society proposed by Louis Dumont and in partial opposition to that of McKim Marriott.

As we have seen, these two theorists, for quite different reasons, argue that any approach to understanding Indian society that emphasizes the individual is misconceived. Emphasizing the divisible nature of Indian personhood, Marriott focuses primarily on Hindu textual interpretations of the physical dimension of who a person is and explains motivations in terms of strategies designed to maintain or improve personal substance. Certainly, interpretations of personal substance and concerns for keeping it in balance and improving it are aspects of how Indians think about personhood. Some Americans also find this Indian way of thinking fascinating. But what of other features of personhood, including the stress Tamils place on individual achievement, personal reputation, eminence, and individuation? Marriott's (1976) conception of the dividual disregards these, and his explanation of motivation is consequently distorted.[2] Why not add to Marriott's dividualist conception Tamil ways of assessing and valuing individuality, which also view the person as an aggregate? This generates a more complex and complete image of Tamil personhood, as well as a better sense of the concerns and roles of individuals as agents of their own destinies. Such a view has the added advantage of recognizing the role that individuals play in history.

Take, for example, Saroja's story, which I described in chapter 8. In my interview with her, Saroja came across as an unpleasant person: selfish, crude, harsh. But her life breaks the smooth fabric of convention and reveals the tensions that lie beneath because she goes far beyond what Tamils think is appropriate behavior for a woman. She is offensive, but there is also something about her that I admire. She is brave, realistic about how people judge her, and self-reliant. And sometimes it is someone who is judged a bad character who inspires the anthropologist's best insights. Deviance and personal conflict draw attention to what defines the ordinary dimensions that compose a person's individuality.

Saroja's telling of her story reveals a complex sense of self: First she identified herself as a member of a caste and as a native of her father's village, her own village—her *sonda uur*.[3] She said she was a Kaikkoolar or weaver, referring here to her caste, who came from a village near Salem. She told me that it was the custom of her caste to tattoo the tip of a woman's tongue with a blue dot when she married. She stuck out her tongue to show me. "They remove the dot of widows," she said, merely smiling when I asked her how they did that. Second, Saroja identified closely with the land of her native village, and she was very proud that she owned two acres of land in her own name given to her by her father.

A third dimension of Saroja's sense of herself was her gender. Saroja believed that her rebelliousness was thought the worse because she was a woman, and she resented the greater autonomy that men enjoyed. In the context of Tamil culture, Saroja's gender made her a dependent. She needed men—her father, her husband, her son—to take care of her. Her efforts at independence, such as taking a lover and running a milk business, were only partially successful as ways of controlling her life because these actions hurt others and attracted criticisms from those who knew her. Nonetheless, very aware of her dependence, Saroja thought that if she were a man, she could do as she liked. Yet, almost in the same breath, she projected pride in her womanhood. She was clearly pleased with herself when she gave birth to a son. It was also apparent to me, when I asked her how she would have changed her life if she could, that the idea of being a man—she said, "I would ask not to be born female," rather than "I would be born a man"—did not altogether suit her. She was angry with men. She felt men mistreated women and she seemed angry to be dependent on them.

Curiously, Saroja did not mention her mother in her life story. Nor, it will be recalled, did Lakshmi mention her mother in her life-telling, and I would hypothesize that this is common to women's life stories. My sense is that there are complex reasons for this. Primary among these is that in talking about the direction of their lives women are concerned with the life adjustments that they have been forced to make. At marriage, the burden of adjustment falls on women, not men. This is why in India, as Ramanujan (1991) has characterized them, women-centered folktales begin with marriage and then proceed to tell the story of a woman's undeserved tribulations before final achievement of a desired life. As Lakshmi made clear, a mother can do little to prevent or affect the trial of adjustment that a daughter must make as a wife and daughter-in-law. To control her own life, a woman must have the allegiance of her husband and sons; she must have their loyalty. A mother, then, can play a major role in a son's life, but in adulthood mothers have a much less important role in a daughter's.

A fourth dimension of Saroja's individuality is age. At eighteen she married and became the mother of a son. At thirty she took a lover. This was an act of defiance, but also a deal Saroja struck with the executive officer of the little temple in exchange for helping her build a house on temple land. At that age, Saroja described herself as defiant and unafraid. But as an act of independence the deal had its drawbacks. Saroja felt she had to maintain the relationship to keep her house; she was merely trading among different kinds of dependence. At forty, her health deteriorating, Saroja was afraid. She understood her dependence and feared abandonment. Clearly, age affected Saroja's sense of who she was, and who she was and the kinds of concerns she had were different at different ages. Saroja's individuality reveals itself as a changing, evolving thing.

A fifth determinant of Saroja's selfhood involved the balance she had struck between self-interest and her need for others. Saroja was strikingly independent and placed her interests before those of others. She separated herself from others, defied them, ran from them. She set herself in opposition to others. But interestingly, she was never without relationships, and she described herself in terms of a series of relationships as wife, mother, lover, and dependent. In fact, a key feature of how she saw herself was in terms of men—her father, husband, lover, and son. Elsewhere, and at other times, when I interviewed Tamil women, they always described themselves in relationship to men, especially husbands, fathers, and fathers-in-law. But by contrast, when I interviewed men, they rarely described themselves in relationship to a wife. More often a man described his mother, but in many cases women simply played smaller roles in Tamil men's senses of who they were.

A sixth dimension of Saroja's individuality concerns issues of power and control. Who has the power to define who a person is? In society, people use a variety of conventions, values, and statuses to impose definitions on a person, to control and constrain what happens to him or her and what he or she does. The individual must mediate between these dictates of others—his or her society—and those of the self. As I have argued in this book (cf. Kakar 1981), if others have too much control over who a person is, so that the person's sense of agency is tightly constrained, the person suffocates psychologically. But with too much independence, the person suffers isolation.

This psychological polarity was Saroja's dilemma. Her solution was to court isolation rather than suffer suffocation. In her ongoing fight to escape control, we see her making her husband move out of his father's house, hawking her jewelry to pay for a new apartment in Madras, taking a lover, starting her milk business, cheating, and controlling her husband and his paycheck. All of this so that she could control her life. But she went too far. She hurt those who might otherwise have cared for her when she no longer would be able to care for herself. Listening to her, I admired her bravery, but did not envy the fate she had made for herself.

Finally, there is a seventh dimension to Saroja's individuality. This is her sense of herself as an agent or actor. She described herself as doing things and making decisions, and she surmised the outcome of those decisions. She took responsibility for her behavior. Telling her story, Saroja constructed the identity she had made for herself. But Saroja's identity was also defined from the outside, by others. Recall my assistant's whispered asides while I was listening to Saroja to the effect that Saroja was a bad woman. Saroja revealed her clear awareness of this external view and of the interplay between her personal perspective and the views of others. Saroja knew she had a reputation that was based on a view that held her responsible for her behavior. A person is defined socially in part by what she or he does. Saroja accepted this fact, but even in her illness and fear at forty years of age she remained rebellious.

What do we learn about the nature of Tamil individuality—of who a person is—from Saroja's story? Caste, place, gender, age, the balance she strikes between self-interest and her need for others, her struggle to have some control over her life, and her recognition of herself as a responsible agent of her own life—these are dimensions of Saroja's individuality. Of course, manifestations of these dimensions vary for each person; points of view embedded in gender, for example, obviously differ between men and women. It is this variation that produces individuality. Each of the life stories that I collected revealed these dimensions.

But is not this a richer, more complex view of the person than one limited to the "dividual" with its narrow focus on the substance-material nature of who a person is? While a Tamil might agree with the dividualist image if it were explained—for example, that one way of viewing Saroja is as a being whose substance is constantly in flux—this is not the way any of my informants explained themselves. I think, in fact, that Tamils take for granted what Marriott calls their "dividual" qualities. Flux and the transformation of substance is in the nature of things, according to a Tamil world view. Such views frame their lives and affect major areas of behavior: bathing, dining and dietary rules, rules about travel overseas, divisions of labor, and marriage customs. But among my informants, it is issues of caste, gender, age, self-interest, control, agency—the dimensions of self that Saroja's story reveals—that intrigue and concern them, and it is self-interest that has often motivated them to seek social change. In fact, self-interest sometimes runs counter to what a dividualist perspective would lead one to expect: people marry out of caste; sons, daughters-in-law, and wives rebel; some take lovers; members of well-known families convert to Christianity; and caste behavior codes, meant to preserve caste purity, are overthrown. This book has described examples of each of these.

Interestingly, in Marriott's most recent publication (Marriott 1989), he seems to move closer to a multiplex view of person, more in keeping with the one that I have tried to represent in this book. Nonetheless, he still assumes that a Hindu's concept of the person is dividualistic. And his view is still a construction based more on texts than on studies of real persons going about their daily lives. There is something removed and mythical about his conceptual constructions, just as there is in Daniel's semiotic analysis of Tamil persons (Daniel 1984; cf. Appadurai 1986). The reader is left with a sense of having participated in a fascinating mental game, one concerned more with subtexts than with the thoughts that lie on the surface of peoples' day-to-day concerns: the passions, ambitions, possessions, struggles, choices, and mistakes of private lives.

Marriott argues that as long as Hindus are transactors, they are not individuals, meaning by this that they are not unitary beings. But such nonunitary beings can exist only in the mental realm. Look again at the epigraph with which I began this book. In *Malgudi Days*, the south Indian writer R. K. Narayan describes south Indian individuality:

> The material available to a story writer in India is limitless. Within a broad climate of inherited culture there are endless variations: every individual differs from every other individual, not only economically, but in outlook, habits and day-to-day philosophy. . . . Under such conditions the writer has only to look out of the window to pick up a character (and thereby a story).

This observation is as true for the anthropologist as it is for the novelist. Each person has an empirical existence that no one, certainly not Tamils, would deny. Clearly, Tamils see persons as having individuality.

Dumont's rejection of any role for the individual in Indian society is much more extreme than Marriott's. Dumont argues that, except for the empirical fact that each person is physically an individual and for the fact of individualism associated with the religious world-renouncer, there are no social individuals in Indian society. Instead, each person has the holistic collective identity of his or her family and caste. Further, Dumont rejects achievement and the pursuit of wealth, prestige, and power as forces of Indian history because he rejects the presence of the economic marketplace wherein he believes these pursuits are found (Dumont 1970a:105–8). Finally, Dumont outrightly rejects any explanation of Indian history that focuses on the individual. For him, the cause of Indian history is the religious notion of hierarchy that generates the Hindu caste system. Dumont, in other words, disregards Indian self-explanations and allows Indians no causal role as agents of their history. If nothing else, this book should demonstrate the falsity of these views.

Whether explaining their private or public selves, whether describing their families, caste, or social institutions, Tamils express a complex set of ideas about the nature of individuality and individual agency. Recognition of individuality lies at the base of how they govern their lives, judge and value others, and organize their society.

Notes

CHAPTER ONE. INDIVIDUALITY IN SOUTH INDIA

1. After European contact, there are, of course, portraits of Hindus painted in the Western tradition. See *The Raj* (Bayly 1990), a history of British India through portraiture. Less well known is the discovery by Susan Bean, curator of the Peabody Museum at Salem, Massachusetts, of a nineteenth-century tradition of realistic representation of merchants in Bengal (Bean 1990). Bengali merchants engaged in trade with American merchants had life-size representations of themselves made of wicker and plaster and dressed in clothes. These portrait mannequins, which are very realistic and clearly represent named individuals, were shipped to America where they were displayed by their American trading partners. Bean tells me that the idea of the mannequins appears to have originated with the Indian merchants themselves.

One cannot say, therefore, that there are no Indian traditions of portraiture, as Indian Muslim traditions also amply demonstrate. The presence of realistic portraiture as a highly developed tradition among Indian Muslims, and its near absence among Hindus, illustrates how differently the two populations conceptualized the individual. In Mogul India, portraiture was an art form cultivated by the Muslim courts. We can see, for example, how Shah Jahan (1591?–1666), the Mogul emperor, looked in 1631 during his fortieth year. In other portraits, we see him as a younger man and as an older man, knowing from his pictures that we would be able to recognize him in person. When his portraits are set chronologically, he ages before our eyes. And from other sources contemporary to his time, we know quite a bit about Shah Jahan's life, including his great love for his favorite wife, Mumtaz-i-Mahal Banu Begam, in whose memory he built the Taj Mahal, and his imprisonment in old age by one of his sons. By contrast, in the Hindu courts of Rajput kings in Rajasthan, which were contemporary with Shah Jahan and contiguous to his territory, there was no portraiture.

Depictions of persons, even kings, are generic, although considerable attention
is paid to sumptuary detail, and painting styles are clearly influenced by Mogul
ideas. Attention to clothes and surroundings indicates that status was important
to those who commissioned these paintings. The viewer can tell who is king. But
the individuality of persons is not represented in faces. I conclude from this that
India does encompass traditions that stress individuality in a manner familiar
to the West, but these traditions are Muslim, not Hindu (cf. Brown 1988;
Coomaraswamy 1931).

   2. On the one hand, Mauss distinguishes between the existence of the self,
which he considers the universal locus of awareness and emotion, and the concept of person, which he sees as a cultural variable. He sets aside an interest in
the former in order to examine the latter. In his article on the notion of person
and self, Mauss writes (1985:3):

> I shall leave aside everything which relates to the "self" (moi), the conscious per-
> sonality as such. Let me merely say that it is plain, particularly to us, that there has
> never existed a human being who has not been aware, not only of his body, but also
> at the same time of his individuality, both spiritual and physical. . . . My subject is en-
> tirely different, and independent of this . . . ; how has it [the notion of self, not the sense
> of self] slowly evolved. What I wish to show you is the succession of forms that this
> concept has taken on in the life of men in different societies, according to their systems
> of law, religion, custom, social structures and mentality.

In other words, Mauss recognizes the empirical individual, but is uninterested
in it because he thinks self-awareness a universal fact, no different from one
person—or social context—to the next. His interest is in notions of the person, which he sees as "entirely different and independent of this [experiential
self]." It is my view that Mauss's dichotomy is artificial, leading him, and those
who were to follow him, to lose sight of the connection between interpretations of the self and experience. In life, experience and interpretation are
always linked.

   Weber, on the other hand, is enamored with the Hindu penchant for shared
identities. He speaks of Indian collective identities in terms of group charisma,
a trait normally applied to the individual. In India, charisma is "routinized"—
made hereditary—and applied to groups (Weber 1958:49–54). For example, the
charisma of the Hindu individual is always understood as an innate shared quality of his kin or caste group, and should a special individual emerge, his charisma
and achievements are claimed by his group as part of their innate nature. Likewise, when a person who is in line to inherit a position is incapable, he will be
replaced by a successor from within his group because the position and requi-
site abilities will be seen as innate "charismatic" features of the group. Consequently, individual achievement plays little role in the organization of Indian society. Founded in religion, Hindu castes epitomize charismatic groups. A caste
is a hereditary collectivity whose members share its innate (charismatic) characteristics. To me, Weber's understanding of Indian groups reifies them by emphasizing their charismatic cohesiveness and discounting the roles that self-
interest and conflict play as forces of group plasticity and transformation.

   3. But what about Americans who, returning from vacation, say that California (or some other place) has gotten in their blood? Or what of the American

belief that husbands and wives come to look like each other? Are not Americans dividuals, too?

4. Notice how much Dumont's idea of holistic-collectivist identity sounds like the historian Jacob Burckhardt's conceptualization of the person in the context of Western European feudal society. "'In the Middle Ages . . . man was conscious of himself only as a member of a race, people, party, family or corporation—only through some general category'" (Quoted in Davis 1986:332n). See Davis (1986:53–63) for a critique of Burckhardt's view. Davis writes, "Burckhardt describes the discovery of personality as a process of distinguishing oneself from the group."

In that Burckhardt's sense of the medieval person implies that the medieval person lacked a clear notion of being a bounded individual, separate from others, his notion is very much like Marriott's idea of the dividual. This is how Davis (1986:56) describes this medieval sense:

> The line drawn around the self was not firmly closed. One could get inside other people and receive other people within oneself, and not just during sexual intercourse or when a child was in the womb. One could be possessed by someone else's soul; a magician or a sorceress could affect one's thoughts, feelings, and bodily movements, sometimes even without physical contact.

5. Confusion may be a product partly of Trawick's use of a literary style to convey her message. I certainly agree with her when, during her discussion of Lacan, she writes "the true and whole self which knows and owns itself, can never be captured or appropriated" (1990:145). If we are to be true to our subjects, we must necessarily depict them incompletely.

6. Americans might argue that the way Indian matrimonial ads are worded actually negates individuality because they seem to reduce the person to a limited, abstract set of qualifications. But for Indians these qualities (qualifications) do distinguish individuals in important ways one from another. However, no Indian would ever restrict the qualities that distinguish an individual to such a limited set. Indian ads stress those individual qualities that are particularly desired in potential spouses, but ads are also recognized by Indians as incomplete and possibly false portrayals. At later stages in engagement negotiations, the ad's veracity, the candidate's family (an individual's family distinguishes him or her), and other features of individuality, such as disposition, are scrutinized.

7. Recently, Marriott (1989) has outlined what he claims is an Indian ethnosociology of action and motivation. Within this interpretation Marriott includes behavior that is goal-oriented and self-interested. And in an earlier talk, given in 1988, at the University of California, Santa Barbara, he has noted that certain limited categories of what he labels "tight-fisted" persons—those who have limited food and service transactions with others, such as ascetics and merchants—are conceptually more like individuals than the average Indian. This is because in his view merchants and ascetics seem singularly free of these kinds of ritually significant "givings and takings," which Hindus think transform the physical substances of persons, distinguishing them as dividuals. Nonetheless, Marriott clearly sees such persons as representing an extreme. Further, he continues to insist that one can understand Indian ideas of the person only in terms of their own conceptualizations and not through any form of comparison with Western

notions, although his idea of the "dividual" is itself his own conceptual invention and is meant to contrast with his equally extreme notion of the Western individual. I think his "dividual" notion a good one, reflecting as it does the Indian perception that a person's substance both absorbs what it interacts with and is itself in part absorbed in return (consider the example of cooking previously described in the text). But comparison that is allowed for himself is forbidden others, and Marriott insists that because Indians are "dividuals" they cannot be "individuals." For me, this attitude is unnecessarily extreme and tends to distort the true importance Indians place on individuality, expressed as an aggregate of a person's traits that together distinguish him or her from others. In my view, Indians have attributes of both dividuality, explaining some features of their conceptualization of personhood, and individuality, expressing others.

8. In Tamil Nadu, when I ask my Tamil friends what word they would use to express the idea of "individuality," they say, "*tanittuvam*," using here a word that has a literary as opposed to a colloquial feeling. This bookish quality reflects the fact that in day-to-day speech Tamils are less likely to talk about individuality as an abstract reference than they are to talk about the particular qualities that distinguish a person. Tamils have never intellectualized an overarching concept of the indivisible individual in the manner familiar to Americans, wherein all persons are in the same ways individuals, but Tamils do have a highly developed sense of individual uniqueness, that is, of individuality. In one sense, Tamils understand the individuality of each distinct person as that person's manifested self, those qualities that are clear to others. Reflecting shared perspectives among Indians, A. K. Ramanujan, a distinguished scholar of Indian languages and literature, told me that in many Indian languages the modern colloquial term for individual is "*vyakti*," a Sanskrit word meaning "the manifested self." The person who fully manifests his or her selfhood is seen as truly unique.

9. For an exception that proves the rule see Susan S. Wadley, "The 'Village Indira': A Brahman Widow and Political Action in Rural North India" (1992). Although Wadley's widow plays an activist role within the village, she is clearly marginal to the power structure of the village, and her fellow villagers consider her eccentric.

10. The film *Kamala and Raji* is a good illustration of both the restraints imposed on women at the local level and of women as leaders among women. Incidentally, Ela Bhatt, the founder of SEWA, the Self-Employed Woman's Association that this movie is about, is herself what I label an institutional big-woman (see chapter 2).

11. This emphasis on individual responsibility for one's life is also a theme in south Indian literature. Consider the Kanada novel *Samskara: A Rite for a Dead Man* by U. R. Anantha Murthy, A. K. Ramanujan (trans.), Oxford University Press, 1976.

12. Again, the novel *Samskara* (see preceding note) expresses a south Indian sense of how responsibility for action individuates the person.

13. In this regard, what I am proposing as a concept of civic self agrees, I believe, with Ramanujan's (1989) sense of an "Indian" way of thinking as particularistic and contextual. What defines the civic individual are the particulars of who he is, including his relations, and what he does, to whom. "To be moral for

Manu [the author of the Hindu moral code] is to particularize—to ask who did what, to whom and when" (1989:46). Each is unique in the particulars of his relationships, who he is (including his character), and his actions.

14. Although my informants would undoubtedly disapprove of Praneshacharya's desire at this point to return to his village, reenter society by confessing all, and then live with the concubine.

CHAPTER TWO. THE NATURE OF CIVIC INDIVIDUALITY

1. I use the word community as a general term with the aim of conveying several meanings. In Madras City today, a person's community is demarcated by his or her kin, classmates and friends, business or workplace relations, organizational memberships, often the neighborhood and the self-defined set of relationships that frame the neighborhood, and caste group. Community in its several features frames the person's social context, and he or she identifies and is identified closely with its multiple facets.

2. This percentage is according to projected figures for 1990 (*India Today*, international ed., Jan. 31, 1988:62).

3. U.S. crime categories considered were rape, bike theft, auto theft, forced entry, and simple burglaries.

4. This ratio is calculated from figures published in *India Today*, international ed., Jan. 31, 1988:60–6.

5. This is characteristic of certain relationships in U.S. society, as well. Consider the hypothetical case of a married couple. When spouses trust one another, within the limits that the couple mutually set for themselves, each spouse has considerable private discretion over how he or she spends money.

6. This is not the firm's real name.

7. I have elsewhere (Mines 1992) labeled this form of individuality an "individualism of inequality," but because the term "individualism" denotes a Western ideology, it conveys senses that are inappropriate to the Indian context. I prefer "individuality of inequality" or "individuality of eminence."

8. For example, consider how in 1989 the Annadurai Dravida Munnetra Karagam party was split, following the death of its head, the chief minister of Tamil Nadu, M. G. Ramachandran, popularly known as "MGR."

9. This, of course, is a characterization of Western values, not necessarily of reality.

CHAPTER THREE. INSTITUTIONS AND BIG-MEN OF A MADRAS CITY COMMUNITY: GEORGE TOWN TODAY

1. *Kaasu* is the origin of our word "cash," designating a coin of small denomination. *Kaasukaarar* (Cashier) is the name of a subdivision of the Beeri Chettiar caste, some of whom were cashiers in businesses and bankers during the period of British trade. A few still are.

2. The temple is dedicated to the god Kandasami. Kandasami is one of many names Tamils use to refer to Murugan, son of Siva and brother to the elephant god, Ganesh.

3. The traditional occupations of the Smiths are those of goldsmith, black-smith, brass worker, carpenter, and stone carver/mason. Different members of the same family may pursue any one of these occupations, and marriage between families engaged in different occupations is common.

4. This section draws upon Mines and Gourishankar (1990) and Mines (1991) for its description of the institutional big-man.

5. A friend from Andhra tells me the Telugu term for an institutional big-man is *palukubadi*, a man whose individuality is stressed by his importance in a social context because of his association with an institution or society.

6. Hereafter, I use "Muthialpet" to refer to the area of George Town that lies east of Popham's Broadway, including Mannady.

7. A paise is one-hundredth of a rupee.

8. A green leaf lightly rubbed with lime and chewed with betel nut and sometimes tobacco.

9. I follow here Tambiah's (1976) terminology.

10. According to the son of this headman, the current heir of this "*suroo-diriyamtaar*-ship," a *suroodiriyamtaar* has the hereditary right to the head trusteeship of the temple, including rights to manage temple lands and income.

11. According to this man's foster son, this hereditary right was lost by the family in 1925 as a result of lawsuits lodged by competitors that charged malfeasance.

12. Caste leaders believe the *maḍam* (monastery) was shifted to Muthialpet in the eighteenth century.

13. According to my informant, the twelve institutions included the caste *maḍam*, the Kandasami temple, the Tiruvaalangadu shrine, the just mentioned major kingly temples at Tiruvotriyur and Tiruvanmiyuur and the Adhi-pureeswarar temple in Chintadripet, just to the southwest of Park Town. Yet other *taambuuḷam* temples included sites at Hanumanthapuram, eight miles from Chingleput City; Sriperumbatur; Koyambedu, near Amjikarai; Nazarath-pet, near Poonamallee; Tirutani; and a Sengammal temple on the way to Tiru-poruur. These were temples and shrines that were either controlled by Town Beeri Chettiars or in which caste members maintained rights to sponsor one day of the temple's annual festival (*brahmootsavam*).

14. Following Raheja's (1988a,b) analysis, this relationship between Brah-mans and the Beeri Chettiars legitimated the dominant status of the caste's head-men in their role as commanders of ritual, while it subordinated the Brahmans who received their gifts.

15. In 1986, the garden was in reality an urban vacant lot.

16. However, in this instance, to the best of my knowledge, Bala did not later directly assist this man.

CHAPTER FOUR. MAKING THE COMMUNITY:
GEORGE TOWN IN SOCIAL HISTORY

1. This chapter is adapted from my article, "Individuality and Achievement in South Indian Social History," *Modern Asian Studies* 26, no. 1 (1992):129–56. For the first two time periods I rely heavily on British East India Company

records, located at the Tamil Nadu State Archives (TNSA), Madras, and the India Office Library (IOL), London. But my aim is not a Company history of prominent Indian traders. Rather, as an anthropologist, my aim is to decipher from the records what it is that the Indian communities and their leading merchants were saying about themselves.

2. Warren Hastings (1734–1818), governor of Bengal in the service of the British East India Company, replaced "Company merchants" with the "gumasta [clerk] system" in 1771.

3. Dumont's denial of a role for the individual in Indian society is closely associated with his rejection of the economic market as a force integrating "traditional" Indian society. In market societies, Dumont (1970a:105) believes, individuality prevails: "the reference is to the *individual* pursuing his own gain." But traditional India, he feels, lacks the economic market; instead, Indian society is integrated by a distributive economy, which he characterizes by the *jajmani* system, "a sort of co-operative [economy] where the main aim is to ensure the subsistence of everyone in accordance with his social function." In the final analysis traditional Indian society is a *"hierarchical collectivity"* (105) integrated by interdependence derived from a caste-based division of labor that is itself derived from religion (108).

4. For etymology and glosses of this and other Anglo-Indian terms appearing in the records of the British East India Company, I depend on the second edition (William Cooke, ed.) of *Hobson-Jobson: A Glossary of Colloquial Anglo-Indian Words and Phrases, and of Kindred Terms, Etymological, Historical, Geographical and Discursive*, 1986 [1886].

5. Haynes (1987) and Rudner (1989) describe the nature and importance of symbolic markers of public reputation for Indian merchants.

6. J. Talboys Wheeler's ([1861–2] 1990, 2:37–64) analysis of this great dispute differs somewhat from mine. First, Wheeler, characteristic of his times, is more interested in descriptions concerning the dividing of the Town into right-hand and left-hand moieties, in British attempts at quelling the dispute, and in the rivalry that existed between the British governor in council, Thomas Pitt, and the "second of council," Mr. William Fraser (later governor), than he is in Indian perspectives. Second, Wheeler sees the source of the dispute in this personal rivalry between Pitt and Fraser and in Pitt's decision to award the merchandising of British goods, which had come out in Company ships, to the headmen of the left-hand Chettiar caste. Prior to this the Komatis had had the contract to sell these goods. But, clearly, there is more to the dispute than this: in a letter to Governor Pitt, Beeri Chettiar leaders refer to right-hand attempts to prevent production and procurement of Indian textiles for export on Company ships (see chapter 4 discussion).

7. Consider the warning of the head of police in Madras to his colleague in nearby Kanchipuram concerning the instigators of riots by low castes of that locale:

A steady eye should also be kept upon the conduct of the Nautawars or heads of the Moodelly Cast [Mudaliars], the several other Desoys or heads of the Buljawars [Balijas], the heads of the Chitty Caste termed Comtees [Komatis] and the other principal heads of the right-hand. They seldom actually commit riots themselves, but are always those who incite (P.C., 456, June 30, 1818:1892).

8. Interestingly enough, Mahatma Gandhi's (1927:29–30) account of his own outcasting occasioned by travelling to England to study is similar to and contemporary with Ratnavelu's experience. Gandhi also describes a division among his caste, involving those who, as merchants, felt it necessary to observe his expulsion and those nonmerchants who did not.

CHAPTER FIVE. A PORTRAIT OF CHANGE

1. This is a pseudonym.

2. This also is a pseudonym.

3. My informants used the word "dictator." As one informant said, caste headmen were like Marlon Brando in the movie *The Godfather*. Take away the violence, and in fact there were many similarities between the Brando-style Mafia "boss" and the caste headman. A headman's constituents, for example, would always seek their headman's blessing when they arranged a marriage or decided other major family events. By comparison, the contemporary south Indian big-man is generally unable to command this kind of "respect," although Indians also sometimes refer to these men as bosses.

CHAPTER SIX. THE DECLINE OF COMMUNITY AND THE ROLES OF BIG-MEN

1. Madras has adopted a policy dropping caste designations in street names. Achari designates a Brahman Iyer (old spelling, "Aiyer"). The official designation for the street is now Krishnama Road, but the road continues to be known to locals by its old name, Krishnamachari. Politicians have also changed many of Madras City's British street names to Indian names. This has created the curious situation where on maps and signs a street is designated by one name, but many locals still use the old English name in their speech. Anna Salai, for example, is still Mount Road to most Madrasis.

2. Handloom weaver production cooperatives are one example. In the state of Tamil Nadu, locality-based handloom cooperatives are big-man institutions that are integrated by a statewide umbrella organization, Cooptex, itself a big-man organization. The big-men of the Kaikkoolars, a traditional weaver caste, dominated Cooptex until the mid-1970s, while at the local level the cooperatives were controlled by big-men belonging to the dominant weaver caste of a locality. These cooperatives provided local leaders with the largess to attract their constituents and to verify their status as patrons of their communities (see Mines 1984).

3. In George Town, the Malighe Chettiars, also known as the Achirapakatars, are an example. A caste of about five thousand families, each of which registers marriages and births with its caste guru located in Pudupet in Madras (map 8), it is divided into locality subgroups known as *paiykats*, each of which is headed by a council chaired by a *periyadanakaarar*. The Achirapakatars are closely related to the Beeri Chettiars, and many are successful merchants. But as a community, perhaps because they appointed their own separate guru after the nineteenth-century lawsuits, they are barred from voting in Kandasami temple elections. Except for the Achirapakatars, all of the George Town Beeri Chettiars

are theoretically under the aegis of the Dharma Siva Acharya Maḍam. Achira-pakam is a town in Chingleput District, the district that surrounds Madras City, and is the caste's reputed place of origin. In Pondicherry, to the south of Madras, the Achirapakatars are a fully integrated subgroup of the Beeri Chettiars.

4. Madras University was founded in 1865, just to the south of the Town area.

5. Many leading Beeri Chettiars recited similar lists of preeminent former Muthialpet-Park Town Beeri Chettiars. I have not always been able to verify the actual designations and titles of the various positions held by these men and women. I give titles and statuses, therefore, as they were told to me in oral recitals, as titles and accomplishments that underscored the singularity of well-known big-men and women of the first half of the twentieth century.

6. These are respectively the offices of the land revenue officer (*tahsildar*) of the subdistrict (*taluk*) and district.

7. This informant was himself a leading merchant and, in his capacity as head of the Betel Nut Merchants' Association, was sponsor of an important ritual dur-ing the Kandasami temple's Spring Festival, the marriage of the god to Valli.

8. The unofficial name of the South Indian Liberal Federation, the "Justice Party," was an elite non-Brahman pre-Independence political party, founded in 1917 (Hardgrave 1965:15–16).

9. The HRCE Department put this temple under the management of an ex-ecutive officer and appointed board of trustees in 1959.

10. The other petitioners were T. Kesuvan Chetty, C. T. Shanmugan Chetty, and T. T. Kuppasamy Chetty.

11. When elections for the Kandasami temple managing board of trustees were held on September 6, 1987, 2,459 Beeri Chettiars voted to select five trustees from among twenty-four candidates. Bala received 1,548 votes com-pared to 1,117 cast for his ally and runner-up. Kaliraja, Bala's chief opponent, placed a humiliating ninth with 550 votes. During a time when his leadership successes had led rivals to lodge lawsuits challenging his management, Bala's Beeri Chettiar constituency had increased by a third over his 1978 showing.

12. To give a perspective on the Tamil's perception of the value of money, Tamils speak of lakh-aires the way we do millionaires. Of course, inflation has devalued the aura associated with being either.

13. Not that the George Town Beeri Chettiars are a disadvantaged commu-nity, quite the contrary. But in Tamil Nadu, in response to affirmative action ef-forts, most castes have managed to claim a certain number of government ben-efits by having their community declared to one degree or another "backward."

14. If any of the forty members of a chit were to default, say due to death or bankruptcy, then the fund would be potentially jeopardized. The reserve funds of the association are supposed to protect against the consequences of such events.

CHAPTER EIGHT. LOCATING INDIVIDUALITY WITHIN THE COLLECTIVE CONTEXT

1. For a published version of this parable see Koilpillai J. Charles, *The Power of Negative Thinking and Other Parables from India*. Bombay: Orient Long-man, 1973:144–6.

Reflecting the popularity of this story, another published version is reported in the *Illustrated Weekly of India*, March 5, 1972, p. 16, which I quote here:

Heinrick [*sic*] Zimmer narrates a story of Sankara [the great sage] and one of his disciples. The sishya, who was a king, one day decided to put his guru to the test. When Sankara was approaching the palace to give his lecture on the doctrine that the Self alone is real and that all else is illusion, an elephant was let loose at him. The great Acharya [Sankara] fled for his life and took refuge on the top of a palm tree. The king later asked the teacher why he should have fled since he must have been aware that "the elephant was a purely illusory character."

The sage replied: "Indeed, in highest truth, the elephant is non-real. Nevertheless, you and I are as non-real as that elephant. Only your ignorance, clouding the truth with this spectacle of non-real phenomenality, made you see phenomenal me go up a non-real tree."

The source of the *Illustrated Weekly*'s story is Heinrich Zimmer, *Philosophies of India*, 1960:19–20.

2. Although a recent survey reported in *India Today* indicates that a majority of urban Indian couples, where both spouses work, prefer joint-household living to living separately as a couple because of built-in child-care and other advantages.

3. Heller and Wellbery (1986:12) describe a person's self-reflexive multiple perspectives as founded on a dichotomy between awareness of cultural order, which constitutes the social frame within which the individual is free to act, and awareness of the indeterminacy of life, which is given direction through action:

Subjectivity is experienced simultaneously as dependent on a cultural order and as an undetermined, productive instance. The individual is actor when observer and artifact when observed. It is a self in motion that makes use of the discourse of autonomous individuality in conjunction with an ongoing series of displacements of its position in order to reinterpret the history of its own behavior from continuously shifting vantage points. (Heller and Wellbery 1986:12)

Paraphrasing Geertz, at the beginning of adulthood, there are a thousand paths to choose. Looking back in old age, the path we have chosen appears to have been the only one.

CHAPTER NINE. CONCLUSIONS

1. "Every institution is the lengthened shadow of one man" ("Self-Reliance," Emerson).

2. Marriott does say (Santa Barbara Conference, May 1988) that certain Indians—notably merchants and religious world-renouncers—have the appearance of individuals in the Western sense of skin-bounded indivisible beings. This is because merchants and renouncers do not engage in transactions with persons of other castes in ways that involve exchanges of personal substance. Money is not a transmitter of substance and renouncers separate themselves from society. Marriott's sense of the individual presumes a Western definition, of course. I have argued, however, that Tamil notions of individuality are not of this skin-bounded indivisible type but, rather, have their own valued senses of individu-

ality. Further, I believe Marriott's argument gives the impression that Indians are not much interested in personal wealth, prestige, and power, separate from others. Quite the contrary, as Marriott himself argues in earlier writing (Marriott 1969), these are attributes that distinguish individuals and in which Indians are very much interested. For example, they are the sources of individual fame. In Marriott's most recent writing (1989), in which he portrays a complex multidimensional paradigm for upper-caste, rural, Hindu male action, he again seems to recognize individuality and goal-oriented self-interest as features of Hindu motivation, although he still relegates these to a minor place in his scheme of Hindu motivations, in keeping with his spoken remarks in 1988.

3. Daniel (1984) offers an excellent explanation of the concept of *uur*, or place, in his book, *Fluid Signs*.

Bibliography

I. SECONDARY SOURCES

Appadurai, Arjun. 1974. "Right and Left-hand Castes in South India," *Indian Economic and Social History Review* 11 (2–3):216–59.

———. 1981. *Worship and Conflict under Colonial Rule: A South Indian Case.* Cambridge: Cambridge University Press.

———. 1986. "Is Homo Hierarchicus?" *American Ethnologist* 13:745–61.

Arasaratnam, Sinnappah. 1986. *Merchants, Companies and Commerce on the Coromandel Coast, 1650–1740.* Delhi: Oxford University Press.

Baker, Christopher. 1976. *The Politics of South India, 1920–1937.* Cambridge: Cambridge University Press.

Barnett, Steve A. 1976. "Coconuts and Gold: Relational Identity in a South Indian Caste," *Contributions to Indian Sociology* (n.s.) 10:133–56.

Bayly, Susan. 1984. "Hindu Kingship and the Origin of Community: Religion, State and Society in Kerala, 1750–1850," *Modern Asian Studies* 18 (2):177–213.

Bayly, C. A. (ed.). 1990. *The Raj: India and the British, 1600–1947.* London: National Portrait Gallery Publications.

Bean, Susan. 1990. "Calcutta Banians for the American Trade: Portraits of Early Nineteenth Century Bengali Merchants in the Collections of the Peabody Museum, Salem and the Essex Institute," in Pratapacharya Pal (ed.), *Changing Visions, Lasting Images: Calcutta Through Three Hundred Years.* Bombay: Marg Publications.

Bellah, Robert N., Richard Madsen, William M. Sullivan, Ann Swidler, and Steven M. Tipton. 1985. *Habits of the Heart: Individualism and Commitment in American Life.* New York: Harper and Row.

Béteille, André. 1986. "Individualism and Equality," *Current Anthropology* 27 (2):121–134.

————. 1987. "Individualism and the Persistence of Collective Identities," in André Béteille (ed.), *The Idea of Natural Inequality and Other Essays*. Delhi: Oxford University Press.

Brown, Donald E. 1988. *Hierarchy, History, and Human Nature: The Social Origins of Historical Consciousness*. Tucson: University of Arizona Press.

Buchanan, Francis. 1807. *A Journey from Madras through the Countries of Mysore, Canara, and Malabar* (vols. 1–3). London: Bulmer.

Caplan, Patricia. 1985. *Class and Gender in India: Women and Their Organizations in a Southern Indian City*. London: Tavistock Publications.

Charles, Koilpillai J. 1973. "On Seeing God in Everything," *The Power of Negative Thinking and Other Parables from India*, pp. 144–46. Bombay: Orient Longman.

Chaudhuri, K. N. 1985. *Trade and Civilization in the Indian Ocean: An Economic History from the Rise of Islam to 1750*. Cambridge: Cambridge University Press.

Coomaraswamy, Ananda K. 1931. Foreword to *Portrait Sculpture in South India*, by T. G. Aravamuthan. London: India Society.

Cutler, Norman. N.d. "Interpreting Tirukkural: The Role of Commentary in the Creation of a Text," *The Journal of the American Oriental Society*. Forthcoming.

————. 1992. "Constructions of the Person by Tirukkural's Interpreters." Paper presented at the 44th Annual Meeting, Association for Asian Studies, Washington, D.C. Photocopy.

Daniel, E. Valentine. 1984. *Fluid Signs: Being a Person the Tamil Way*. Berkeley: University of California Press.

Davis, Natalie Zemon. 1986. "Boundaries and the Sense of Self in Sixteenth-Century France," in Thomas C. Heller, Morton Sosna, and David E. Wellbery (eds.), *Reconstructing Individualism: Autonomy, Individuality, and the Self in Western Thought*. Stanford: Stanford University Press.

Dickey, Sara. 1993. "The Politics of Adulation: Cinema and the Production of Politicians in South India," *The Journal of Asian Studies* 52 (2):340–72.

Dirks, Nicholas. 1987. *The Hollow Crown: Ethnohistory of an Indian Kingdom*. Cambridge: Cambridge University Press.

Dumont, Louis. 1970a. *Homo Hierarchicus: The Caste System and Its Implications*. Chicago: University of Chicago Press.

————. 1970b. "The Individual as an Impediment to Sociological Comparison and Indian History," in Louis Dumont, *Religion/Politics and History in India: Collected Papers in Indian Sociology*, pp. 133–50. The Hague: Mouton.

————. 1987. "Discussion and Criticism: On Individualism and Equality," *Current Anthropologist* 28:669–72.

Ewing, Katherine P. 1991. "Can Psychoanalytic Theories Explain the Pakistani Woman? Intrapsychic Autonomy and Interpersonal Engagement in the Extended Family," *Ethos* 19 (2):131–60.

Ganguli, B. N. 1975. *Concept of Equality: The Nineteenth Century Indian Debate*. Simla: Indian Institute of Advanced Studies.

Gandhi, M. K. 1927. *An Autobiography: Or the Story of My Experiments with Truth*. Mahadev Desai (trans.). Ahmedabad: Navajivan Publishing House.

Giddens, Anthony. 1991. *Modernity and Self-Identity: Self and Society in the Late Modern Age*. Stanford: Stanford University Press.

Gittinger, Mattibelle. 1982. *Master Dyers to the World*. Washington, D.C.: The Textile Museum.

Hall, Kenneth R. 1980. *Trade and Statecraft in the Age of the Colas*. New Delhi: Abhinav Publications.

Hardgrave, Robert. 1965. *The Dravidian Movement*. Bombay: Popular Prakashan.

Hart, George, III. 1975. *The Poems of Ancient Tamil: Their Milieu and Their Sanskrit Counterparts*. Berkeley: University of California Press.

Haynes, Douglas E. 1987. "From Tribute to Philanthropy: The Politics of Gift Giving in a Western Indian City," *Journal of Asian Studies* 46 (2):339–60.

Heller, Thomas C., and David E. Wellbery. 1986. Introduction, in Thomas C. Heller, Morton Sosna, and David E. Wellbery, eds., *Reconstructing Individualism: Autonomy, Individuality, and the Self in Western Thought*, pp. 1–15. Stanford: Stanford University Press.

Illustrated Weekly of India. 1972. March 5, p. 16.

Inden, Ronald. 1986. "Oriental Constructions of India," *Modern Asian Studies* 20:401–46.

———. 1990. *Imagining India*. Oxford: Basil Blackwell.

India Today. 1988. International ed., January 23, pp. 60–66.

Irschick, Eugene F. 1989. "Order and Disorder in Colonial South India," *Modern Asian Studies* 23 (3):459–92.

———. 1994. *Dialogue and History: Constructing South India, 1795–1895*. Berkeley: University of California Press.

Jaer, Oyvind. 1987. "The Ideological Constitution of the Individual: Some Critical Comments on Louis Dumont's Comparative Anthropology," *Contributions to Indian Sociology* 21 (2):353–62.

Kakar, Sudhir. 1981. *The Inner World: A Psycho-analytic Study of Childhood and Society in India*. 2d ed. Delhi: Oxford University Press.

———. 1982. *Shamans, Mystics and Doctors: A Psychological Inquiry into India and Its Healing Traditions*. Chicago: University of Chicago Press.

———. 1989. *Intimate Relations: Exploring Indian Sexuality*. Chicago: University of Chicago Press.

Lewandowski, Susan J. 1985. "Merchants and Kingship: An Interpretation of Indian Urban History," *Journal of Urban History* 11 (2):151–79.

Love, Henry Davison. 1913. *Vestiges of Old Madras* (vols. 1–3). London: John Murray for Govt of India.

Marriott, McKim. 1968. "Multiple Reference in Indian Caste Systems," in James Silverberg (ed.), *Social Mobility in the Caste System in India: An Interdisciplinary Symposium, Comparative Studies in Society and History*, supp. 3. The Hague: Mouton.

———. 1969. "Review of Homo Hierarchicus: Essai sur le Systeme des Castes by L. Dumont," *American Anthropologist* 71 (6):1166–75.

———. 1976. "Hindu Transactions: Diversity without Dualism," in Bruce Kapferer (ed.), *Transaction and Meaning: Directions in the Anthropology of Exchange and Symbolic Behavior*, pp. 109–42. Philadelphia: Ishi Press.

———. 1989. "Constructing an Indian Ethnosociology," *Contributions to Indian Sociology* (n.s.) 23 (1):1–39.

Marriott, McKim, and Ronald Inden. 1977. "Toward an Ethnosociology of South Asian Caste Systems," in Ken David (ed.), *The New Wind: Changing Identities in South Asia.* The Hague: Mouton.

Mauss, Marcel. 1985. "A Category of the Human Mind: The Notion of Person; the Notion of Self," W. D. Halls (trans.), in Michael Carrithers, Steven Collins, Steven Lukes (eds.), *The Category of Person: Anthropology, Philosophy, History.* Cambridge: Cambridge University Press.

McHugh, Ernestine L. 1989. "Concepts of the Person among the Gurungs of Nepal," *American Ethnologist* 16:75–86.

Mines, Mattison. 1972. *Muslim Merchants: The Economic Behaviour of an Indian Muslim Community.* New Delhi: Shri Ram Centre for Industrial Relations and Human Resources.

———. 1984. *The Warrior Merchants: Textiles, Trade, and Territory in South India.* Cambridge: Cambridge University Press.

———. 1988. "Conceptualizing the Person: Hierarchical Society and Individual Autonomy in India," *American Anthropologist* 71 (6):1166–75.

———. 1992. "Individuality and Achievement in South Indian Social History," *Modern Asian Studies* 26 (1):129–56.

Mines, Mattison, and Vijayalakshmi Gourishankar. 1990. "Leadership and Individuality in South Asia: The Case of the South Indian Big-man," *Journal of Asian Studies* 49 (4):761–86.

Morris, Brian. 1978. "Are There Any Individuals in India? A Critique of Dumont's Theory of the Individual," *The Eastern Anthropologist* 31 (4):365–77.

Murthy, U. R. Anantha. 1978. *Samskara: A Rite for a Dead Man.* A. K. Ramanujan (trans.). New York: Oxford University Press.

Narayan, R. K. 1982. *Malgudi Days.* New York: Viking Press.

———. 1967. *The Vendor of Sweets.* London: Viking Penguin Books.

Neild-Basu, Susan. 1984. "The Dubashes of Madras," *Modern Asian Studies,* 18 (1):1–31.

Obeyesekere, Gananath. 1992. *The Apotheosis of Captain Cook: European Mythmaking in the Pacific.* Princeton: Princeton University Press; Bishop Museum Press.

Pearson, M. N. 1988. "Brokers in Western Indian Port Cities: Their Role in Servicing Foreign Merchants," *Modern Asian Studies,* 22 (3):455–72.

Pope, Rev. G. U. 1980. *The "Sacred" Kurral of Tiruvalluva-Nayanar.* New Delhi: Asian Educational Services.

Presler, F. A. 1987. *Religion under Bureaucracy: Policy and Administration for Hindu Temples in South India.* Cambridge: Cambridge University Press.

Raheja, Gloria G. 1988a. "India: Caste, Kingship, and Dominance Reconsidered," *Annual Review of Anthropology* 17:497–522.

———. 1988b. *The Poison in the Gift: Ritual, Prestation, and the Dominant Caste in a North Indian Village.* Chicago: University of Chicago Press.

Ramanujan, A. K. 1989. "Is There an Indian Way of Thinking? An Informal Essay," *Contributions to Indian Sociology* (n.s.) 23 (1):41–58.

———. 1991. "Toward a Counter-System: Women's Tales," in Arjun Appadurai, Frank J. Korom, and Margaret A. Mills (eds.), *Gender, Genre, and Power in South Asian Expressive Traditions*. Philadelphia: University of Pennsylvania Press.

Rudner, David. 1989. "Banker's Trust and the Culture of Banking among the Nattukottai Chettiars of Colonial South India," *Modern Asian Studies* 23 (3):417–58.

Shweder, Richard A., and E. J. Bourne. 1984. "Does the Concept of Person Vary Cross-culturally?" in R. A. Shweder and R. A. LeVine (eds.), *Culture Theory: Essays on Mind, Self, and Emotion*, pp. 158–99. Cambridge: Cambridge University Press.

Silverberg, James (ed.). 1968. *Social Mobility in the Caste System in India: An Interdisciplinary Symposium, Comparative Studies in Society and History*, supp. 3. The Hague: Mouton.

Simmel, G. 1950. "Individual and Society in Eighteenth and Nineteenth Century Views of Life," in K. Wolff (ed.), *The Sociology of Georg Simmel*. Glencoe: The Free Press.

Srinivas, M. N. 1976. *The Remembered Village*. Berkeley: University of California Press.

Tambiah, Stanley J. 1972. "Review of Homo Hierarchicus: An Essay on the Caste System, by Louis Dumont." *American Anthropologist* 74:832–35.

———. 1976. *World Conqueror and World Renouncer: A Study of Buddhism and Polity in Thailand against a Historical Background*. Cambridge: Cambridge University Press.

Trawick, Margaret. 1990. *Notes on Love in a Tamil Family*. Berkeley: University of California Press.

———. 1991. "Wandering Lost: A Landless Laborer's Sense of Place and Self," in Arjun Appadurai, Frank J. Korom, and Margaret Mills (eds.), *Gender, Genre and Power in South Asian Expressive Traditions*. Philadelphia: University of Pennsylvania Press.

Wadley, Susan S. 1992. "The 'Village Indira': A Brahman Widow and Political Action in Rural North India," in Patricia Lyons Johnson (ed.), *Balancing Acts: Women and the Process of Social Change*. Boulder: Westview Press.

Washbrook, David A. 1988. "Progress and Problems: South Asian Economic and Social History, c.1720–1860," *Modern Asian Studies* 22 (1):57–96.

———. 1990. "South Asia, the World System, and World Capitalism," *Journal of Asian Studies* 49 (3):479–508.

Weber, Max. 1958. *The Religion of India*. Glencoe: The Free Press.

Wheeler, J. Talboys. [1861–2] 1990. *Annals of the Madras Presidency: Being a History of the Presidency from the First Foundation of Fort St. George Compiled from Official Records* (vols. 1–3). Delhi: Low Price Publication.

Wink, André. 1990. *Al-Hind: The Making of the Indo-Islamic World*. Delhi: Oxford University Press.

II. PRIMARY SOURCES

P.C. (Public Consultations) of the Governor's Council of Madras, British East India Company.

July 31, 1707, India Office Library [IOL].

Aug. 9, 1707, IOL.

Aug. 20, 1707, IOL.
Aug. 22, 1707, IOL.
Aug. 25, 1707, IOL.
Aug. 27, 1707, IOL.
Oct. 20, 1707, IOL.
Nov. 6, 1707, IOL.
Dec. 2–6, 1707, IOL.
Jan. 15, 1708, IOL.
391A, Mar. 6, 1812, Tamil Nadu State Archives [TNSA].
456, June 30, 1818, TNSA.
Madras District Records 989, 1815–16, TNSA.

III. LAW RECORDS

ILR (Indian Law Reports). 1887 Madras Series, vol. 10.
O.S. (Original Suit) No. 155 of 1956. In the court of the Subordinate Judge of
    Erode, M. Kumaraswami Pillai, Subordinate Judge, Dec. 24, 1958.
Madras High Court, Civil Miscellaneous Petition [C.M.P.] No. 10345 of 1987
    in Ordinary Side Appeal [O.S.A.] No. 108.

Index

Compositor: BookMasters, Inc.
Text: 10/13 Sabon
Display: Sabon
Printer and Binder: BookCrafters, Inc.